PHOENIX

First published in Great Britain in 2018 by Christopher Bradbury.
Copyright © Christopher Bradbury 2018

The moral right of Christopher Bradbury to be identified as the author of this work has been asserted in accordance with the Copyright Designs and Patents Act of 1988.

All rights reserved. No part of this publication may be reproduced, stored in a retrieval system, or transmitted in any form or by any means, electronic, mechanical, photocopying, recording, or otherwise, without the prior permission of both the copyright owner and the above publisher of this book.

Every effort has been made to trace all copyright holders. The publisher will be pleased to make good any omissions or rectify any mistakes brought to their attention at the earliest opportunity.

Cover: © Christopher Bradbury 2018

www.christopherbradbury.co.uk
www.facebook.com/christopher.bradbury.779

ISBN - 978-1721545599

For
Bobby Harper
and
Bob Jackson

and
For
Sally, George, Ellie and Frankie
and
Norma

Contents

The Flight of the Phoenix 9

Part One: THE DISTANT HORIZON 11

The Butterfly Effect 13

Everything Affects Everybody. 21

    Woodrow Wilson's 14 Points 22

    The Treaty of Versailles 34

    The League of Nations 40

    The Economic and Social Consequences of the War and the Versailles Treaty. 43

    The Dawes Plan, 1924 54

    The Depression of 1929 58

The Rise of Adolf Hitler 63

    Hitler Joins German Workers' Party and Forms the Nazi Party 65

    The Beer Hall Putsch 74

    The Golden Years 78

    The Wall Street Crash and the Rise of the Nazis 81

        The Stormtroopers 83

        Article 48 83

        Kurt von Schleicher 85

        The Reichstag Fire 87

        The Enabling Act 87

        The Night of the Long Knives - June 29th – June 30th 1934 89

- Kristallnacht and the 'Jewish Problem' 92
- Hitler's Economic Miracle 100
- Rearmament 104
- Appeasement 107

Part Two: INTO SERVICE 115

The Phoney War? 117

The State of Military Readiness in Britain in 1939 119

- The Army 120
  - The Combat Arms – The Teeth 121
  - The British Expeditionary Force and Dunkirk 127
  - The Services – The Tail 132
- The Royal Navy 135
  - The Fleet Air Arm 147
- The Royal Air Force 148
- Women at War 167
  - The Auxiliary Territorial Service (ATS) 172
  - Special Operations Executive (SOE) 178
  - First Aid Nursing Yeomanry (FANY) 188
  - The Women's Auxiliary Air Force (WAAF) 200
  - The Women's Royal Naval Service (WRNS) 210

Part 3: HOME 219

- Conscription 221
- The Conscientious Objectors 225

Rationing 231

- Food 231
- What Else Was Rationed? 245
  - Petrol 245
  - Clothes 247
  - The Blackout 257
  - Crime During the War 262
  - The Blitz 272
  - Evacuation 289
- In Search of the Phoenix 296
- Sources 299

The Flight of the Phoenix

Sunlight fell through the windowed arches and dropped in pools of gold upon the grey platform. From above, the same summer glow fell through the skylights, drenched the tops of trains, the dark suits and khaki uniforms of those who came and went in stuttered droves or marched with determined eyes towards a distant point. It fell in gilt layers upon the rails and against the paintwork of the whispering giants.

The station was hot, the air thick with particles of soot and dust that fell through the golden shafts like black snow and drifted down, down towards the ground in the airless glass cavern. It was full of people, people in a hurry, on their own, in pairs or in hunched and hurried groups, a world away in their minds, though their feet scampered across the same earth as the hundreds around them, as they scurried towards their carriages, their only concern that the train would pull thoughtlessly away as they reached for the warm brass handle upon the heavy door.

Myriad noises echoed across the concrete; the hiss of trains as they sighed to rest and the grinding of wheels; the quick, staccato chatter of passers-by and guards and drivers and baggage men. There was the echo of footsteps, the rhythmic click of high heels and the regimental tap of quarter-irons and somewhere the laughter of children and the bark of an unseen dog.

There was the smell of coal, that unique railway smell that sat strong and solid through the decades and brought back memories of far away; the sadness of departure, the joy of return, the confusion of the crowd, the certainty and the mystery of the destination and the excitement of the rickety flight along the two thin rails towards a world unknown.

That morning, that early summer morning in June 1944, Bobby Harper, three years old and dressed in a coat for which he had no need, overlarge suitcase and gas-mask case to hand, eyes wide with trepidation and anticipation, walked in a crocodile towards a distant carriage located somewhere along the curved shoreline of platform as the surf of steam hissed from the depths to evaporate beneath the sun-soaked dome. With him were others who were to make the journey to another land across the distant metal and concrete sea.

He was to leave Islington behind. Six hundred and seventy-four bombs had been dropped between 1940 and 1941 and now the V1s were here; soon the V2s would come; it was no longer safe to be there.

Bobby had no idea why he was here and no idea where he was going and when he stepped onto the train and into the stuffy carriage with strangers upon a journey to another land, he had no idea when he would return.

As the train pulled away, he saw the golden eye of the station recede into the shadows and felt the hot sun pour through the carriage window.

Somewhere, far away, other strangers fought across fields and between hedges and over bridges, shot at men they had never met because the men they had never met were shooting at them.

They aimed for one thing, a small, distant pinpoint of darkness that had slowly strangled the light of Europe with twisted words and barbarous acts and spread spectre-like across the continent. A small pinpoint of darkness that had put the lights out in London, Glasgow, Sheffield, Birmingham, Manchester and all places in between. A small pinpoint of darkness that had stolen Bobby Harper from all he knew and thrown him as a stranger into a strange land, with strange people who spoke in a strange tongue.

The train juddered across the points and turned its back on London, its eyes turned north.

Part One
THE DISTANT HORIZON

The Butterfly Effect

'How horrible, fantastic, incredible, it is that we should be digging trenches and trying on gas masks here because of a quarrel in a far away country between people of whom we know nothing.'

Neville Chamberlain, British Prime Minister, 27 September 1938

The Butterfly Effect, a term first suggested by the meteorologist and chaos theory scientist Edward Lorenz, suggests that, in theory, a butterfly flapping its wings in New Mexico could cause a hurricane in China.

It was hyperbole used to express a genuine concept (originally it was a gull flapping its wings, but a butterfly was deemed more poetic), applied to weather models, to show that even the tiniest variable could have an unexpected effect upon events elsewhere. It became a metaphor for the effect of events, either in time or in physical distance, having an effect upon something apparently unrelated far away. The Urban Dictionary describes it as: 'The scientific theory that a single occurrence, no matter how small, can change the course of the universe forever'. That sums it up perfectly.

This is the fascinating thing about history. I would not be in front of this keyboard at this moment had someone, fifty, five hundred or five thousand years ago, decided to go left instead of right.

Here's a story to highlight the point.

Alois Schicklgruber was born on June 7, 1837, in a small place called Strones, in North-West Austria. He was illegitimate, the result of the conjoining of a peasant girl, Maria Schicklgruber and a passing fancy known, at the time, only to Maria.

The butterfly had probably flapped its wings a couple of centuries prior to this event, but this was the point at which the high winds, caused by the inconsequential first flutters of those wings, began to gather the clouds, to turn them grey with the heaviness of the oncoming deluge and charge them with the restless particles of the storm to come.

When Alois was five years old, Maria married Johann Georg Heidler. He at last had a father figure. Johann would have an impact on the young man but, one could surmise, not necessarily in the right way, whatever his intentions.

When Maria died five years later Alois, at the age of ten, was sent away from his home to live with his step-father's brother, Johann Nepomuk Heidler, a well-off farmer in a place quite nearby, called Spital. It is not really known why Johann Nepomuk took Alois under his wing. The two theories postulated are fairly obvious: one, which said that he was really Alois' father and two, that he did it out of the kindness of his heart. Johann Nepomuk was married to a woman fifteen years older than him, Eva Maria Decker, might not have wanted the scandal and could not therefore publicly acknowledge his paternity. To take him in quietly to help out his bereaved brother was possibly a good way to get his son into his custody. This, however is speculation and in all probability, the eventual outcome to this tale of insects and hurricanes, is that the final suggestion is more than likely the correct one. We shall see.

Whether this was a successful move on the part of the two Johanns and young Alois is uncertain. What is certain is that at the age of thirteen, Alois left the farm for Vienna to become and apprentice cobbler. This was a drastic move, even allowing for the fact that they were different times and independence at an early age was to be encouraged. Vienna was about sixty-seven miles away, some considerable distance in what was, pre-war, a quite isolated area without the benefits of today's highways and transport. The chances are that it was simply to give him a trade; apprenticeships were commonplace in most of Europe and would not have been seen as out-of-the-ordinary. He stuck at this for five years or so until he grew tired of it and then, as the Austrian government drove forward a campaign to recruit people from rural areas to become civil servants, joined the customs service in a semi-military capacity. In 1871 he wound up at Braunau am Inn, near the German border. This was in 1855. Alois was eighteen. Now he was on the social ladder as well as the career ladder. He eventually rose, in 1875, to become an inspector of customs, but could go no further due to a lack of education.

In between times, Alois became adept at doing what men do, namely drinking and copulating. He was what we nowadays would call a 'serial philander' or, more simply, a randy womaniser.

Now, I make no excuses for him. A man lives by the sword and he dies by the sword. Every action has a consequence, but there are certain aspects of Alois' life that, with the benefit of hindsight and today's willingness to accept the psychology of environment, might explain Alois' behaviour. He was illegitimate. This was frowned upon in the mid-nineteenth century and his birth certificate was marked with the dreaded word 'illegitimate' scrawled across it and a blank chasm where the name of the father should have been. His mother died when he was ten, a mother about whom he might well have had mixed feelings due to her 'waywardness' and his resulting bastardy, the fact that she was his mother, that there was a bond and that this bond, this unique love, had been taken away. On top of this, his step-father rejected him and sent him away. We don't know what went on in Johann Georg's mind; he might have sent Alois away with the best of intentions or for the worst, most selfish reasons; he didn't want a kid hanging onto his coat-tails. He might also, as has been said, have been sending him back to his rightful father.

These circumstances can have a great impact on a young mind. For Alois, it seems that there was a residue of rejection glowing within him and that he was searching constantly for a stability that would never really come to him. It is easy to dismiss philandering as simply the wanderings of uncontrolled lust, but sometimes it is a search for love.

Alois' searchings began in the 1860s and was quickly fruitful. In 1869 he had an affair with Thekla Penz. On October 31, 1869, Thekla gave birth to a girl, Theresia Penz. Thekla later married Johan Ramer and went on to have at least six children with him. It's not known why she and Alois failed to stay together, but I suspect that, knowing what Alois got up to in later years, she made the wise choice.

In 1873, he married Anna Glasl-Hörer. Anna was fourteen years older than him (he was 36, she was 50) and, as John Simkin said in 1997:

> 'It is unlikely to have been a love-match. The marriage to a woman fourteen years older than himself had almost certainly a material motive, since Anna was relatively well off, and in addition had connections within the civil service.'

Was this all a part of his social mobility and his new-found status? Or the excitement of sex with a wealthy woman? The fact that she was the daughter of a customs official might have strengthened his social standing and suggests that perhaps this was a marriage of convenience rather than love, at least on his part. The woman was in poor health and might well have been disabled by illness at this stage or soon after the marriage. No doubt it was heady, combustible mixture of all these things that attracted Alois.

> 'In a small town like Braunau am Inn, his position was a prestigious one. A customs Inspector's wages were equivalent to the principal of the local school, with a generous pension provided upon retirement. With his military-like uniform, cocked hat embroidered with gold braid, and a sweeping mustache, Alois made quite an impression. Although one colleague called him rigid, others said he was a warmhearted, earthy man with a wry sense of humor and a gift for friendship.'

Hitler: 1889-1933 - Donna Faulkner

It wasn't long, however before Alois was back at his old ways. He began an affair with 19-year-old Franziska 'Fanni' Matzelsberger, a waitress at a local inn. She was one of numerous affairs, but she was probably the one that broke the camel's back as Anna and Alois separated in 1880.

In 1876, 16-year-old Klara Polzl left her family farm and went to live with Alois and Anna as a household servant. Klara was the daughter of Johann Baptist Polzl and Johanna Heidler; the niece of Johann George Heidler, Alois' stepfather. This meant that she was a second cousin to Alois, at least on paper, but without Alois' certain paternity, it was at this stage not possible to say.

Then, in 1877, Alois changed his name from Alois Schicklgruber to Alois Hitler.

Hitler was an alternative spelling to Heidler, as was Hüttle and Huettler. It means 'smallholding' in German, but the name Heidler comes from 'one who lives near a subterranean river' – a heidl. Quite why this particular spelling, 'Hitler', was chosen, is unknown. What is known is Alois' reason for changing his name. Johann George, on his deathbed, had left Alois both money and his name, along with an admission of his paternity. Johann Georg died in 1857, so this took a while to seep into Alois' brain, but it was a name to be added to his birth certificate and might well therefore, in his eyes at least, have given those around him one less reason to look down upon him. It could be because he wanted to find his own identity, to give himself some solid, legitimate roots and perhaps, with a touch of foresight, ensure that his future children had a 'name'. Perhaps it was just for the money left to him by Johann Georg. Who knows?

On 13 January 1882, Fanni gave birth to Alois' illegitimate son, whom they also called Alois. On 6 April 1883 Anna Glasl-Hörer died. This left Alois free to marry Fanni and, on 22 May that year, the ceremony took place. His son was then legitimised. On 28 July, Alois Jr got a sister, Angela.

Prior to their marriage, no doubt in a quite reasonable fit of jealousy, Fanni had demanded that Klara Polzl be removed from Alois' presence and by doing so remove any temptation he might have had.

In 1884 Fanni became ill with a lung disorder (probably tuberculosis) and was moved to Ranshofen, a small village nearby, either to promote recovery or to protect others. At this point, Klara took the opportunity to return to Alois' home (or might have been there already to care for Fanni and the children, depending upon the source taken) and an affair commenced.

> 'As to Alois Hitler's feelings, there is no escaping the fact that he married Klara Polzl partly out of convenience. Barring a miracle he knew full well that Fanni would not recover from her illness, and knowing that in the meantime he needed someone to mother his children, Alois Hitler obviously traveled to Spital to bring Klara back to the family home in Braunau. Moreover, because we know that Alois Hitler was a man devoted to logic and duty above all else, it is safe to speculate that while visiting the Polzl family home he arranged with Klara's parents for a future marriage... Johann and Johanna Polzl were certainly in favor of the union... Alois Hitler was an extremely good catch for a rural peasant girl.'
>
> *Adolf Hitler's Family Tree – The Untold Story of the Hitler Family* – Alfred Konder

At any rate, Klara returned to the Hitler household in Braunau am Inn where she had a close friendship with both Fanni and her mother, Maria Matzelberger (Maria Matzelberger would later serve as a godparent for two of Klara's children). Thereafter she frequently visited the dying Fanni in Ranshofen, which was just outside of Braunau, and spent considerable time helping nurse her. Fanni died, aged just 23, on 10 August 1884. Klara Polzl remained as Alois' housekeeper. On 7 January 1885, Alois slid into his third marriage, to Klara and their first child, Gustav, was born on 15 May 1885 (for those of you, like me, with limited maths ability, 15th May minus 9 months does not equal 7 January). The marriage, because of the risk of consanguinity and the confirmation of Alois' parentage, had to be appealed to the church for a humanitarian waiver. The waiver was given and the wedding went ahead in a small ceremony, after which Alois went to work.

Gustav died of diphtheria in December 1887. Before that, in 1886, Klara presented her husband with a girl, Ida. Ida also died of diphtheria in 1888. In 1887, Klara gave birth to another son, Otto, but he died only a few days later.

Then, in 1889, on 20 April, Adolphus Hitler, to become known as Adolf, was born.

In 1892, the family moved to Passau and then in 1894 (according to Alfred Konder; 1883 according to Anna Rosmus in *Hitler's Nibelungen*) to Linz, both work-related moves.

In March 1894, Klara gave birth to Edmund, but he died at the age of only 6 in 1900, probably of measles. Their final child, Paula, was born on 21 January 1896.

It was not necessarily a happy family. Alois was prone to the effects of alcohol and:

> 'Robert G. L. Waite noted, "Even one of his closest friends admitted that Alois was 'awfully rough' with his wife [Klara] and 'hardly ever spoke a word to her at home.'" If Hitler was in a bad mood, he picked on the older children or Klara herself, in front of the rest.'

Hitler: A Biography – Ileen Beer

At the age of 58, Alois retired and bought a farm in Hafeld. As a farm, it was unsuccessful and he lost money. On 3 January 1903, as he was having a glass of wine at a local *gasthaus*, he died, probably from either a stroke or a heart attack, but it has also been noted as a 'lung haemorrhage' or 'pleural haemorrhage', a fairly broad term that can be due to various primary causes.

Klara died of breast cancer on 27 December 1907. Adolf was 'devastated by her death'. According to Dr Eduard Block, who had treated Klara's condition, Adolf was devastated by her death.

He had been, like his father before him, deserted by his mother. He was left with a bullying, drinking father, had lost numerous siblings to disease and had as skewed a vision of what was normal as anyone of his young years should have had, which was to be reinforced by the waste and humiliation of the Great War yet to come. Every significant other around him had, in some way, faded away. That virgin paper of childhood, upon which the world etched its message to the formative child, was blotted and scored beyond redemption. Instead of turning the pain and anger in upon himself, instead of finding a way to contain the explosive emotions, Adolf Hitler erupted outwardly and, in the shockwave, caused devastation to every generation outside of and including his own in an attempt to right the perceived wrongs of his life.

What is astounding, out of all of this, is that Bobby Harper, a young boy, from Islington, London, along with millions of others, who had never met or heard of Alois, Klara or Adolf Hitler, had their lives turned inside out and, in many cases, curtailed.

The total number of deaths caused by World War Two was between 50 million and 85 million. 5,700,000 people or 8.23%[1] of the German population as of 1939 died as compared to 450,000 or 0.94% of the 1939 population from the United Kingdom and its colonies and 419,000 or 0.32% of the 1939 population from the USA[2]. I use these figures solely as something for us in those countries to relate to, not to make the rest of the world's losses any less significant. This does not include the military wounded which increases the figures of those affected massively, especially when disability and the effects upon families and communities are taken into account.

This was caused by one man who, by the merest chance of nature and timing, in the beat of a butterfly's wings, changed the world forever.

The sky was darkening across Europe and yet no one was

---

[1] Wirtschaft und Statistik October 1956, Journal published by Statistisches Bundesamt Deutschland. (German government Statistical Office)

[2] Clodfelder, Michael (2002). Warfare and Armed Conflicts – A Statistical Reference to Casualty and Other Figures, 1500–2000 and Commonwealth War Graves Commission Annual Report 2013-2014 & 2014-2015

aware of the storm flickering upon the distant horizon.

Everything Affects Everybody.

It is all but impossible to separate the Treaty of Versailles from the German economic depression of the early 1920s and the rise of extremist politics. The period from 1914 to 1939 was described by none other than Winston Churchill, in the first volume of his memoirs of the Second World War, as 'another Thirty-Years War', while Marshal Foch, the leader of the Allied armies in France in the Great War, described the Treaty of Versailles as 'an armistice for twenty years'.

The Treaty of Versailles was signed on 28 June, 1919. From it was sought not just peace, but revenge and humiliation, particularly by the French towards the Germans.

It is understandable that the French should react in the way they had; most of the fighting during the Great War took place on French soil and the French suffered some 1.5 million military deaths, with 4,200,000 wounded. Their country had been the stagnant pond in which, hour by hour, day by day and year by long year, the two main antagonists had dug themselves in and peered across the body-strewn wastes of No-Man's Land. Of course, other areas in in the world - Poland, Greece, Turkey, Russia, Japan, China - were affected, deeply so, but France gave not only lives to the cause, but the soil itself, churned as if tilled by a fifth apocalyptic horseman driving a murderous plough; the scars, the crevices and mounds can still be easily identified today, over one hundred years later. For France and Belgium though, the Treaty was not about going forward in peace, but in striding towards vengeance and the oppression, forever if necessary, of their enemy.

Before the Treaty of Versailles though, came President Woodrow Wilson's 14 points and the League of Nations, both of which contributed enormously to the formation of and final wording of, the Treaty of Versailles and yet, ironically, came to represent the futility, the vacuousness and maybe even naivety of such lists and elite boys' clubs.

Woodrow Wilson's 14 Points

It is worth looking at the Fourteen Points, proposed on 8 January 1918, as written:

> We entered this war because violations of right had occurred which touched us to the quick and made the life of our own people impossible unless they were corrected and the world secure once for all against their recurrence. What we demand in this war, therefore, is nothing peculiar to ourselves. It is that the world be made fit and safe to live in; and particularly that it be made safe for every peace-loving nation which, like our own, wishes to live its own life, determine its own institutions, be assured of justice and fair dealing by the other peoples of the world as against force and selfish aggression. All the peoples of the world are in effect partners in this interest, and for our own part we see very clearly that unless justice be done to others it will not be done to us. The programme of the world's peace, therefore, is our programme; and that programme, the only possible programme, as we see it, is this:
>
> I. **Open covenants of peace**, openly arrived at, after which there shall be **no private international understandings** of any kind but **diplomacy** shall proceed always frankly and **in the public view**.
>
> II. **Absolute freedom of navigation upon the seas**, outside territorial waters, alike in peace and in war, except as the seas may be closed in whole or in part by international action for the enforcement of international covenants.

III. **The removal**, so far as possible, **of all economic barriers and the establishment of an equality of trade conditions among all the nations consenting to the peace** and associating themselves for its maintenance.

IV. **Adequate guarantees** given and taken **that national armaments will be reduced to the lowest point consistent with domestic safety**.

V. **A free, open-minded, and absolutely impartial adjustment of all colonial claims**, based upon a strict observance of the principle that in **determining all such questions of sovereignty the interests of the populations concerned must have equal weight with the equitable claims of the government whose title is to be determined**.

VI. **The evacuation of all Russian territory** and such a settlement of all questions affecting Russia as will secure the best and freest cooperation of the other nations of the world in obtaining for her an unhampered and unembarrassed opportunity for the independent determination of her own political development and national policy and assure her of a sincere welcome into the society of free nations under institutions of her own choosing; and, more than a welcome, assistance also of every kind that she may need and may herself desire. The treatment accorded Russia by her sister nations in the months to come will be the acid test of their good will, of their comprehension of her needs as distinguished from their own interests, and of their intelligent and unselfish sympathy.

VII. Belgium, the whole world will agree, must be evacuated and restored, without any attempt to limit the sovereignty which she enjoys in common with all other free nations. No other single act will serve as this will serve to restore confidence among the nations in the laws which they have themselves set and determined for the government of their relations with one another. Without this healing act the whole structure and validity of international law is forever impaired.

VIII. **All French territory should be freed and the invaded portions restored, and the wrong done to France by Prussia in 1871 in the matter of Alsace-Lorraine**, which has unsettled the peace of the world for nearly fifty years, should be righted, in order that peace may once more be made secure in the interest of all.

IX. A readjustment of the frontiers of Italy should be effected along clearly recognizable lines of nationality.

X. The peoples of Austria-Hungary, whose place among the nations we wish to see safeguarded and assured, should be accorded the freest opportunity to autonomous development.

XI. Rumania, Serbia, and Montenegro should be evacuated; occupied territories restored; Serbia accorded free and secure access to the sea; and the relations of the several Balkan states to one another determined by friendly counsel along historically established lines of allegiance and nationality; and international guarantees of the political and economic independence and territorial integrity of the several Balkan states should be entered into.

XII. The Turkish portion of the present Ottoman Empire should be assured a secure sovereignty, but the **other nationalities which are now under Turkish rule should be assured an undoubted security of life and an absolutely unmolested opportunity of autonomous development**, and the Dardanelles should be permanently opened as a free passage to the ships and commerce of all nations under international guarantees.

XIII. **An independent Polish state should be erected which should include the territories inhabited by indisputably Polish populations, which should be assured a free and secure access to the sea, and whose political and economic independence and territorial integrity should be guaranteed by international covenant.**

XIV. **A general association of nations must be formed under specific covenants for the purpose of affording mutual guarantees of political independence and territorial integrity to great and small states alike.**

In regard to these essential rectifications of wrong and assertions of right **we feel ourselves to be intimate partners of all the governments and peoples associated together against the Imperialists**. We cannot be separated in interest or divided in purpose. We stand together until the end.

On the surface, the Fourteen Points look like a prescription for Utopia. Together they represent the most ideal of worlds, an open and honest world where there are no secrets between nations, where financial equality provides a meeting of all needs and where the status quo of the pre-war years is re-established and held together by the sugary glue of sweet dreams.

It is an idealistic, perhaps even naïve, piece of writing and that it should come from a President of the United States sharpens the juxtaposition between the real world and its fantasy counterpart. There is nothing wrong with thinking like this – just don't do it aloud.

The bolded sections, my highlights, no one else's, of the various points show several points about the USA which still stand true today. It thought of itself as a moral compass and, with the economic power that it had in 1918, believed that it had the right to lecture the world about how it should behave. The contrast is sharper because, with the semi-isolationist policy (AKA 'neutral') that the US was taking at this time and the tardy reluctance with which it joined the Great War, it was the equivalent of someone shouting the odds from the shadows beneath the balcony at the back of the hall.

> President Woodrow Wilson encouraged the U.S. as a whole to avoid becoming emotionally or ideologically involved in the conflict. Americans were more than happy to stay out of the war, and Wilson won a second Presidential term in 1916 by running on a platform of non-interference.
>
> *Isolationism and U.S. Foreign Policy After World War 1*
> - www.graduate.norwich.edu

The Fourteen Points might also have been no more than a political expedient. America was made to pay both emotionally and financially and, even though only 2% of the total allied military personnel lost were American, this still amounted to 400,000 men. Europe lost. It was nothing compared to Russia's 30% contribution, France's 25% or the British Empires 16%, but it nonetheless left the Americans nervous of any future involvement in what it saw as other people's problems.

It is also entirely possible that Wilson was genuinely horrified by the slaughter of the war and once the Germans resumed indiscriminate attacks against shipping – the sinking of the Lusitania was still fresh in people's minds - he felt that he had little choice but to ask Congress for a declaration of war.

In March 1916, Germans resumed unrestricted submarine warfare, sinking the Sussex and killing dozens. The Germans, of course, promised never to do this again, then continued to attack merchant shipping. When, in January 1917, they decided to break their half-hearted promise, America cut diplomatic ties with Germany. As the Germans continued unabated with attacks on US merchant ships, Congress and the president were left with little room to manoeuvre, little choice but to declare war and on 6 April 1917, they did so.

The US was also, against the will of the President and the people, being manipulated into war by the machinations of a Germany with one eye on the future.

The British were of course glad to have the US in the war; having the Americans on board might just be enough to tip the balance in the Allies' favour and when, on 1 March, they had intercepted a coded message from the German Foreign Minister Arthur Zimmerman to the German minister in Mexico, Heinrich von Eckhart, the British had few qualms about spilling the beans to the Americans. In what became known as the Zimmerman telegram, an alliance between Germany and Mexico was proposed by the Germans should the Americans join the war on the Allies' side. The Germans offered the Mexicans the tasty bait of a return of the territory lost in the Mexican-American war of 1846-48; this would amount to Texas, New Mexico and Arizona. Germany also wanted Mexico to stir the pot with Japan and get them to swap sides.

The telegram really couldn't have come at a better time for the British; along with the resumption of submarine attacks, it was further proof of the Germans' duplicitousness.

Remember, at this point, the war would continue for some time and many more were yet to die. To a well-educated and humanitarian man such a Woodrow Wilson, the sense of disillusionment and betrayal must have been enormous. This combined with his need to survive politically, for the man who had been re-elected in 1916 with the slogans 'He Kept Us Out of War' and 'America First' (while he was at the time making preparations for war), must have been dreadfully conflicted.

This inner conflict might go some way to explain the rather candy-floss feel to the Fourteen points, but then so would political nous. *The Encyclopedia of the New American* points out:

> The president's international commitment in this area...was not matched by any personal dedication to ensure that African Americans be allowed to participate in the domestic political process, nor did his push for self-determination extend to the victims of European colonialism in Africa, India, or East Asia...Wilson was both eloquent and passionate on the theoretical rights of peoples, and he had problems reconciling his rhetoric with his practices...Wilson pursued a domestic program...that segregated the federal service, one of the few places where African Americans could enjoy some semblance of equal employment opportunities. Regionally, Wilson acted with what had become customary American arrogance when he dispatched marines to Haiti in 1915, denying Haitians the right to determine their own political system...Wilson intervened with military force more times in Central America and the Caribbean than any other president. He also spurned the inclusion of a racial equality clause at the Versailles Conference in 1919 when the matter was raised by the Japanese delegation. Better for the Japanese to be given territory in China against Chinese wishes than have any language referring to racial equality make its way into the final text.

It is easy to be flippant and judgmental towards someone

in his position. The chances are that he was trying to do right by everyone, himself included and, under those conditions, no man or woman ever won. The point of the Fourteen Points was probably to make clear the idea that peace was a possibility, that somebody had the guts to come to the table with something that would break the muddy stalemate in Europe. Certainly, once the German people caught a whiff of the concept, they agitated for a negotiated peace.

Without doubt, the leaders of the major allied powers – France, Britain and Italy – were 'highly sceptical of the practicality of Wilson's points':

> But because at this point in the First World War those nations were highly dependent upon the United States, not just for soldiers and convoy escorts, but for food, fuel, munitions, and money, these political leaders reluctantly signed off on the Fourteen Points.
>
> *Recalling the Failure of Wilson's "Fourteen Points"* - Bruce Walker

The very idea of Point I, '**there shall be no private international understandings of any kind but diplomacy shall proceed always frankly and in the public view**', was an incredibly naïve and unrealistic stand to take. There had always been and would always be 'private understandings' and most of them would most certainly not be in public view. He was here fighting human nature and this would not work. Clandestine politics was a part of politics. It got things done, probably because it was whispered in dark hallways. It was likely that very little would be achieved by honest and open means.

Likewise, '**absolute freedom of navigation upon the seas**' presented problems of its own. Edward Mandell House, advisor to Wilson, wondered what the rights of neutral shipping would be in the event of 'a limited war' which required the enforcement of international agreements, when the League of

Nations had no intention of enforcing anything. Neither would the British government, driven by the forceful David Lloyd George, concede to anything that impeded its use or freedom of the Royal Navy. The use of blockades was too valuable and too efficient to risk any curtailment of naval activities. The Americans were not too happy with the idea either. Was the freedom of the seas to be administered solely by the League of Nations, as a collection of nations with a common goal? Without dominance i.e the strong leadership of one or two nations, the Americans feared some sort of oceanic anarchy that would affect not only military shipping but, ultimately, and possibly more importantly, the freedom of merchant shipping around the world.

Given the fairly simple equation that money equals power and that each nation wanted to jealously guard its trade policy, '**the removal**, so far as possible, **of all economic barriers and the establishment of an equality of trade conditions among all the nations consenting to the peace**' (Point III), was an unrealistic hope. Nobody wants financial or social equality, not really and, as has been proved by the utter failure of Social Democracy, Fascism and Communism to become anything other than dictatorships, it is simply not a practical concept in light of human nature and psychology. Combined with Point IV, '**adequate guarantees...that national armaments will be reduced to the lowest point consistent with domestic safety**', where armaments were a major part of GNP and employment and that dealings in those arms with other countries was (and remains) a major source of income, it was unlikely that any arms-producing country would give up such a lucrative business by encouraging others to cut back on their military hardware.

It would always boil down to human nature, the need to be the alpha or, at the very least, to not let the other guy be the alpha, and the maintenance of peace through power. In later years, during the Cold War, it was the balance of power that stopped the worldwide descent into Communism or Fascism or the use of nuclear arms to gain the upper hand. To reduce national arms to the lowest point consistent with domestic safety simply did not allow for the desire of others to impose their belief on weaker nations, the need for countries to expand as they became overpopulated and low on resources and use the resources of other countries for their own gain.

This, as will be shown later, was the essence of *Lebensraum*, the drive by Hitler and the Nazis to possess other lands, with a view to creating more land for their expanding population and to use the resources of those conquered lands. It is easy to think of this as the one-off behaviour of a lunatic, but it simply isn't, it has always been so (look at the British Empire) and continues to be so (look at the tussle for oil and gas and the clamour for diminishing resources that continue to this day).

Point V, '**a free, open-minded, and absolutely impartial adjustment of all colonial claims...determining all such questions of sovereignty the interests of the populations concerned must have equal weight with the equitable claims of the government whose title is to be determined**' is at the very least hypocritical. It has already been established that Woodrow Wilson gave very little regard to oppressed minorities (it had not been so long since the ethnic cleansing of the Native American race in pursuit of land and resources; Americas own *Lebensraum*) that he did not allow equal rights to black Americans, that he turned a blind eye towards segregation and that he had little interest in the well-being of the dominant powers' colonies. Given America's colonial interests in the Philippines, Cuba, Honduras, Panama, Mexico, Nicaragua, Haiti et al, it was probably not in their interests to look too closely at the rights of others to determine their own present and future. Empires brought in money, they brought in resources, they imported business and exported business and they cemented military alliances. Without the Empire and its resources, would Britain ever have dared to enter World War Two? I'm sure it helped sway the decision.

When the Russians had withdrawn from the Great War after the revolution of 1917, it had by then sustained casualties at an estimated 1.8 million killed, 2.8 million wounded and 2.4 million taken prisoner. **The evacuation of all Russian territory** (Point VI), demanded the return of all Russian territories taken by Germany. Although the Fourteen Points predated Russia's withdrawal from the war (and followed the revolution), Russia's losses were reinforced by the severity of the Brest-Litovsk Treaty signed a couple of months later in March, 1918, which in turn coloured the Treaty of Versailles. These territories were returned via the Treaty of Versailles. The Russians, so desperate were they to get out of the conflict and dissociate themselves from the remaining imperialist states, had been coerced by the threat of greater land loss and violence into signing the Brest-Litovsk Treaty by Germany. This recognised the independence of Urkraine, Georgia and Finland and surrendered Poland and the Baltic states of Lithuania, Latvia and Estonia to Germany and Austria-Hungary. They also gave up Kars, Ardahan and Batum to Turkey. Overall, they lost one million square miles, one third of their population and about thirty-five million people. On top of this, it lost about 50% of its industry along with most of its coal, iron and oil stores. To rub salt in the wound, the Germans then charged the Russians 3000 million roubles in reparations for their troubles.

It was not the magnanimity of a good winner. It was also a foreshadowing of things to come – what we today might call karma.

Was the US sympathetic towards the new-found Bolshevik ideal? Far from it. There had been some inclination towards the interim government of Kerensky, who rose from the February Revolution, but he was never in a strong position. The October Revolution toppled him and the Bolsheviks came to power. Wilson was far more condemnatory of the new Communist regime than of the old Imperialist leadership, and he hadn't held the old regime in too high esteem. Yet his attitude towards the Bolsheviks has been described as 'ambiguous'[3], possibly because of the myriad opposing opinions that came his way. He described Communism as 'government by terror, government by force, not government by vote'. Maybe by maintaining such 'ambiguity', Wilson was trying to ensure that there remained the possibility of a future alliance between the two

---

[3] *Woodrow Wilson's diplomatic policies in the Russian Civil War* - Donald Wayson: The University of Toledo

nations. He could well have been afraid of losing an ally; the war was not yet over, and he perhaps held the hope that Russia would re-enter the war. It was also one further way to tighten the screw on Germany. Woodrow Wilson was shocked by the destruction, the human and financial costs, of the war; if he could remove the German appetite for it, or anybody else's for that matter, all the better. Germany was to return Russian territories.

America's hypocrisy though could only go so far and in August 1920 it became official US policy to not recognise the Russian government. The Republican view of 'left wing bad, right wing useful when it was a benefit to the physical and financial welfare of the country' took a hold and has dictated US foreign policy ever since.

The return of French territory in Point VII, **all French territory should be freed and the invaded portions restored, and the wrong done to France by Prussia in 1871 in the matter of Alsace-Lorraine,** did little more than stick pins in old wounds and served in 'perpetuating the discontent between the German-speaking people of Alsace and French-speaking people of Lorraine'[4].

On the same basis, India et al should have been taken away from the British (as should Scotland, Wales and Ireland). Morocco, Algeria and the Ivory Coast, Cambodia, Vietnam et al should have been taken from France, along with all the other territories devoured by the military might of other nations. But then, Britain and France hadn't lost the war, had they.

The Polish State of Point XIII was 'inhabited by other peoples — Ukrainians, Germans, Mausrians, Lithuanians, Ruthenians, and others'[5]. What did those people of many tongues and no doubt of many cultures have to say? They and their descendants would pay dearly in the years to come for being a part of the chequerboard.

The final point, Point XIV, is perhaps the most interesting. It gave impetus, a platform, to the Paris Peace

---

[4] *Recalling the Failure of Wilson's "Fourteen Points"* - Bruce Walker
[5] As above

Conference which started in January 1919, to the Treaty of Versailles, signed on 28 June 1919 which, in Part I, created the Covenant of the League of Nations.

The Treaty of Versailles

Each nation that took part in the Paris Peace Conference and helped to draw up the Treaty of Versailles had its own agenda. Their measures, their *demands*, were punitive. The only nation that was there with no more to offer than the integrity of its leader's ideals, was the USA. Woodrow Wilson wanted 'a peace without victory'. He was not out for revenge, but a 'lasting peace'. He had reluctantly brought America late into the war and had no desire for the USA take part in another war. The President was only too aware that some form of punishment had to be meted out to the Germans but he was also mindful of the fact that too punitive a punishment would foster resentment and a desire for revenge among the German people. This slightly holier-than-thou approach was an irritant to those with more extreme desires, especially the French.

Georges Clemenceau, the French Prime Minister, wanted revenge, reparations and a weakened Germany. This was completely understandable. As a politician, he had to get something back for the people, to sustain them and his government.

> Clemenceau, according to Keynes[6]...was a foremost believer in the view of German psychology that the German understands and can understand nothing but intimidation, that he is without generosity or remorse in negotiation, that there is no advantage he will not take of you...that he is without honour pride or mercy...
>
> *1918: The Last Act* – Barrie Pitt

---

[6] John Maynard Keynes, British economist

As a human being, it must have broken his heart to see the devastation that had been wreaked upon battleground France. Whole villages had been eradicated, divested of both buildings and of people. There was not enough food to go around. 1,697,800 people or 4.29% of the population had died[7]. By the time of the Paris Peace Conference, with the help of the USA, things had improved considerably for the French, but it would not remove the deep-seated need for revenge, for the living and the dead.

The Franco-Prussian War of 1870-71 had gained Germany most of Alsace and a large part of Lorraine, from which was created Alsace-Lorraine and this still galled the French. The Great War had been fought largely on French soil and the damage was enormous. The financial cost was estimated at $24,265,583,000[8] (at 1918 values). The country's debts were enormous: France owed $3,030,000,000 to Britain and $3,991,000,000 to the USA. They were owed $3,463,000,000[9] by Russia, Italy and others, money they weren't guaranteed to ever see again. Clemenceau did not want Germany to ever again have the capacity to make war upon them. The Treaty of Versailles was the perfect opportunity to claim that pound of flesh, blood and all.

David Lloyd George, the British Prime Minister, came at the situation from a slightly different angle. He had an empire to protect, land to hold onto, resources to protect. 994,138 people or 2.19% of the population had died; 885,138 of these were military deaths, 109,000 civilian. If the whole Empire was taken into account, there were 1,225,914 deaths.

There were holes in all layers of society. The whole structure of society teetered on monumental change, not least the fires fed to the suffrage movement of the value of women as not just placeholders in the absence of men, but as instigators and

---

[7] *World War I casualties* - www.centre-robert-schuman.org

[8] *Financial Cost of the First World War* - John Simkin

[9] *The Origins of the Second World War in Europe* - PMH Bell

leaders in their own right.

> The war...opened up a wider range of occupations to female workers and hastened the collapse of traditional women's employment, particularly domestic service.
>
> *Women on the Home Front in World War One* - Professor Joanna Bourke

Those who might have traditionally gone into service no longer did. Unions became more active and stronger. Wages rose and the traditional barriers to class became blurred.

> The war-time 'emancipation of women' is a commonplace...more controversial is the question of the effects of the war on the working classes. Their gains, in fact, were threefold: because of their strengthened role in the market, their wages and living standards rose; because of their increased participation in activities and decisions that were, and were seen to be, important, their political and industrial organization was toughened; because the government needed them, it gave them, mainly through the processes of legislation, enhanced recognition and status. The average income of all working-class families between 1914 and 1920 rose by 10 per cent, which slightly more than cancelled out the rise in the cost of living...it is apparent that the taste of affluence, afforded to some workers during the war, greatly accelerated that quest for a higher standard of living which in itself has proved so potent an agent of continuing social change.
>
> *The Impact of the First World War on British Society* - Arthur Marwick: *Journal of Contemporary History, Vol. 3, No. 1 (Jan., 1968)*

Lloyd George was prepared to play it canny and come into the negotiations with a more moderate approach than the French and a more hard-edged approach than the USA. There was little doubt that he wanted Germany to pay for the damage it had caused – the slogan 'Make Germany Pay' was prominent during his 1918 election campaign - but he would not simply blindly agree to the Fourteen Points – for one, he was perturbed by the idea of self-determination; he had an empire to hold together and all that it represented. To this end, he was in favour of Germany losing its navy and its overseas possessions, but neither did he want to dismantle Germany as France did; Germany was an important peacetime trading partner and he did not want to give Germany any excuse for a later war of revenge. He played Britain as America's friend in the League of Nations negotiations and took an avuncular stance with France in the reparations debate. When negotiations ground to a halt in March, because the US could not accept the French's fervent need to dismember Germany or the enormous sum France requested for reparations, it was Lloyd George who broke the deadlock by playing the mediator.

When asked by journalists how he thought he had done at the negotiations, Lloyd George replied: 'Not bad, considering I was seated between Jesus Christ and Napoleon'.

The document was formally signed in the Hall of Mirrors at the Palace of Versailles on June 28th 1919. The Germans were at no stage invited to take part in the formation of the document – it was, according to the Germans, a 'diktat', an order, a command. They had been excluded from the proceedings until May and, even then, their attendance was only required so that they could listen to the punishments inflicted upon them. It must have all seemed a little 'public school' as they sat in an enraged and humiliated silence while they were lectured about their wrongdoings. The greatest humiliation, to which they were obliged to agree, was Article 231, the Guilt Clause:

> 'The Allied and Associated Governments affirm and Germany accepts the responsibility of

Germany and her allies for causing all the loss and damage to which the Allied and Associated Governments and their nationals have been subjected as a consequence of the war imposed upon them by the aggression of Germany and her allies.'

Treaty of Peace with Germany (Treaty of Versailles) - Treaty and protocol signed at Versailles June 28, 1919

Represented in the treaty were the United States, Great Britain, Canada, Australia, South Africa, New Zealand, India, France, Italy, Japan, Belgium, Bolivia, Brazil, China, Cuba, Ecuador, Greece, Guatemala, Haiti, The Hedjaz (Modern Day Saudi Arabia), Honduras, Liberia, Nicaragua, Panama, Peru, Poland, Portugal, Rumania, Serbia, Croatia, Slovenia, Siam (Modern Day Thailand), Czechoslovakia, Uruguay and Germany. The treaty was constructed of 15 parts and 440 articles. It consisted mainly of the return of lands to whoever the conference deemed were the rightful owners.

> Germany lost thirteen per cent of its land; six million Germans found themselves citizens of other nations. Fifteen per cent of German agricultural land and ten per cent of its industry was surrendered, mainly to the French. Most of Germany's merchant fleet was seized by Britain; she...lost all of her colonial possessions. Alsace and Lorraine were returned to France, the Rhineland was demilitarised and occupied, while Northern Schleswig was given to Denmark. Germany was forbidden from political or economic unification with Austria. Posen and West Prussia were ceded to Poland, cutting off East Prussia from the rest of Germany. The German army was reduced to 100,000 men and forbidden from having tanks,

> warplanes or heavy artillery; its navy was restricted to 15,000 personnel, six battleships and no submarines. Germany was also indefinitely excluded from membership of the newly formed League of Nations.

The Treaty of Versailles - Jennifer Llewellyn, Jim Southey and Steve Thompson[10].

The treaty was unsatisfactory to nearly everybody who took part in it. The French thought it not harsh enough, the British and the Americans thought it too harsh. The French thought the USA was not empathetic enough; how could it be when the war did not touch its soil and they were only there for a quarter of the time? The USA had simply not suffered enough. They thought the British too soft. The British thought the French too hard and the Americans too idealistic. The Americans sat between the two of them and tried to find the middle ground.

The Germans were aghast.

> The final telegraphed communication from the German National Assembly to the Allies in Versailles stated, "The government of the German Republic in no wise abandons its conviction that these conditions of peace represent injustice without example."

The Elusiveness of Peace in a Suspect Global System - Tatah Mentan

Reparations were enormous; land loss was enormous; the quashing of the military was humiliating. 'The treaty of Versailles

---

[10] J. Llewellyn et al, "The Treaty of Versailles" at Alpha History, http://alphahistory.com/worldwar1/treaty-of-versailles/, 2014

did indeed emasculate and infuriate Germany'[11].

> This, so the victors argued, 'would render possible the initiation of a general limitation of the armaments of all nations'. It did not, and its failure to do so was to be used by the Germans when they denounced those restrictions and began rearming fifteen years later.

The First World War: A Very Short Introduction – Michael Howard

The League of Nations

PART I

THE COVENANT OF THE LEAGUE OF NATIONS

THE HIGH CONTRACTING PARTIES,
In order to promote international co-operation and to achieve international peace and security

by the acceptance of obligations not to resort to war,
by the prescription of open, just and honourable relations between nations,
by the firm establishment of the understandings of international law as the actual rule of conduct among Governments, and
by the maintenance of justice and a scrupulous respect for all treaty obligations
in the dealings of organised peoples with one another,

---

[11] *Why the Germans Lose at War: The Myth of German Military Superiority* – Kenneth Macksey

Agree to this Covenant of the League of Nations.

Treaty of Peace with Germany (Treaty of Versailles)

The Covenant of the League of Nations was drawn up with the intention of preventing war. Aggression was the last resort. It sought to bring about equality, fairness, impartiality and understanding. Its objectives were honourable but, as a wise Roman fellow[12] once wrote: 'Si vis pacem, para bellum'. If you want peace, prepare for war. The only problem with this was that, if you were prepared for war, there was always someone else who was prepared for war. Empty bluffs rarely suffice. Escalation on such grounds was inevitable. There was always a pup willing to challenge the alpha dog and there would always come a day when the alpha dog's heart just wasn't in it any more.

The fact that it was the American President's dream and that the Americans boycotted it did not help. It was rejected by the senate. Why? Because America did not want to do anything that might drag them into another war, and that included helping to maintain the peace. They did not want to have any more deaths on their hands in the cause of others and they did not want to risk their economy by pumping more money into distant events which may or may not have any effect on them.

It was the beginning of America's isolationism.

It was an unrealistic ideal in the climate of a growing world economy and financial interdependence. They needed to trade with the rest of the world; they had to export and they had to import. They had to have bigger guns than their cousins, just in case those cousins decided to hedge-hop. They had to maintain employment. They had to keep their place in the world or their voluntary isolation would become isolation full stop, out of their control.

So, what was the world to think of a club that even its founder refused to join? Well, the French tromped into the Ruhr

---

[12] Publius Flavius Vegetius, a writer from the later Roman Empire

without a problem. Japan smacked up China without a second glance at the League. When the League objected, Japan picked up its bat and ball and walked out. Italy invaded Abyssinia without a parental finger of disappointment being raised. Germany, initially banned from joining the League of Nations, they joined at their own request, and after initial rejections, in 1926. They resigned in 1933. If that wasn't a sign of things to come...

Italy left the league in 1937.

What started out as a well-intentioned yellow-brick-road to everlasting peace, actually turned out to be built by the council and was full of potholes within a short time of being laid.

The idea was for the League of Nations to prevent wars through disarmament, collective security and negotiation. World War Two rendered it null and void.

The League of Nations did eventually morph into the UN, which has done untold good in the war-ravaged parts of the modern world but, it has to be said, it's often only when the sound of the horse's hooves can be heard receding over the distant hills.

There was a certain inevitability to World War Two. The Versailles Treaty was a stimulus to war instead of a deterrent. In 1928, The Kellogg-Briand Pact was signed. What did it say? It said that everyone must live peacefully, must not fight each other and, if anyone was naughty enough to break the pact, nothing would happen. It was naïve, self-congratulatory, back-slapping puff that completely ignored the realities of Europe – the widening gap between rich and poor, the need for land, for resources, the hate engendered by the war and the Treaty of Versailles. It was signed initially by France, the United States, the United Kingdom, Ireland, Canada, Australia, New Zealand, South Africa, India, Belgium, Poland, Czechoslovakia, Germany, Italy and Japan. Later, an additional forty-seven nations followed suit, so the pact was eventually signed by most of the established nations in the world[13].

The thing that worries me is that someone somewhere felt that such a pact *needed* to exist. Did the co-signees really think that

---

[13] *The Kellogg-Briand Pact, 1928* – www.history.state.gov

their mark on a piece of paper would negate human nature? Did they think that someone like Adolf Hitler would give any credibility to such childish scribblings? Did they think that the pain of the Treaty of Versailles and all its consequences would be evaporated by a bit dry ink on expensive paper? Of course not. Even the most Disneyfied among them must have realised that they were in a tornado trying to keep a grip on the final roof tile. If a treaty like this needed to exist, then the problem was already there. It might have taken a few years for the house to leave the ground, but there was nothing anyone could do to divert the great wind. The storm had begun long ago and left its path of devastation in its wake; already the long dark tail was snaking across the European plains in search of more to nourish itself.

The Economic and Social Consequences of the War and the Versailles Treaty.

The eminent British economist John Maynard Keynes, who had 'resigned as the principal representative of the British Treasury and stormed out of the conference to protest the high reparations demanded of Germany'[14], was scathing in his assessment of the treaty:

> The treaty includes no provisions for the economic rehabilitation of Europe...no arrangement was reached at Paris for restoring the disordered finances of France and Italy, or to adjust the systems of the old world and the new. The Council of Four [Britain, France, Italy and the US] paid no attention to these issues. It is an extraordinary fact that the fundamental economic problem of a Europe starving and disintegrating before their eyes was the one question in which it was impossible to arouse the interest of the four. Reparation was their

---

[14] *Winning the War in Europe* - Scott Minerd, Guggenheim Partners LLC: www.advisoranalyst.com

main excursion into the economic field, and they settled it from every point of view except that of the economic future of the states whose destiny they were handling...In a very short time...Germany will not be in a position to give bread and work to her numerous millions of inhabitants..."We do not know, and indeed we doubt," the [German Economic Commission] report concludes, "whether the delegates of the allied and associated powers realise the inevitable consequences that will take place if Germany, an industrial state, very thickly populated, closely bound up with the economic system of the world, and under the necessity of importing enormous quantities of raw material and foodstuffs, suddenly finds herself pushed back to the phase of her development that corresponds to her economic condition and the numbers of her population as they were half a century ago. Those who sign this treaty will sign the death sentence of many millions of German men, women and children." I know of no adequate answer to these words...

After Versailles: a warning from John Maynard Keynes – The Guardian. September 2009.

He continued, in *The Economic Consequences of the Peace* in 1919, to say:

...even if we put on one side the burden of the internal debt, which amounts to 210 milliards[15] of marks, as being a question of internal distribution rather than of productivity, we must still allow for the foreign debt incurred by Germany during the

---

[15] A milliard is 1000,000,000. I had no idea...Sadly, the Americans call this one billion. What is the matter with them?

war, the exhaustion of her stock of raw materials, the depletion of her livestock, the impaired productivity of her soil from lack of manures and of labour, and the diminution in her wealth from the failure to keep up many repairs.

Written within six months of the treaty, this is an astute, prescient indictment of the treaty. Keynes saw the future, a future seemingly invisible to all but him and the German Economic Commission whose report he quotes.

CREDITORS (MILLIONS OF DOLLARS)[16]				
DEBTORS	US	UK	FRANCE	TOTAL
UK	3,696			3,696
FRANCE	1,970	1,683		3,653
RUSSIA	188	2,472	955	3,615
ITALY	1,031	1,855	75	2,961
BELGIUM	172	434	535	1,141
OTHERS	21	570	672	1,263
TOTAL	7,078	7,014	2,237	16,329

The economic sanctions and the confiscation of land from Germany had dire, far-reaching consequences, its pervasive corrosion eventually eating like rust into the fragile framework of Europe.

The debts stored up by all concerned were frightening. As previously stated, the cost to France alone was estimated at

---

[16]Inter-Allied Government Debts at Time of Armistice. From: *The First World War 1914-1918* - G. Hardach & World War I Economic Causes and Burdens - Lecture by Robert M. Coen, Professor Emeritus of Economics, Northwestern University, 2015 From: *The First World War 1914-1918* - G. Hardach & *World War I Economic Causes and Burdens* - Lecture by Robert M. Coen, Professor Emeritus of Economics, Northwestern University, 2015

$24,265,583,000.

On 24 March 1926, the MP Philip Snowdon announced in the House of Commons that Britain was owed £800,000,000 by Russia, £700,000,000 by France, £600,000,000 by Italy and £100,000,000 by other European countries. Britain paying £34,000,000 a year back to the US, which was to increase to £38,000,000. Had Britain asked its debtors to pay it back at the same rate as it was paying the Americans back, it would have been receiving £84,000,000 a year, instead of the £38,000,000 it was receiving. That would have given Britain a positive balance of £46,000,000 a year.

These were mind-boggling numbers for the allied nations. This was on top of the psychological damage, the structural damage, the lost businesses, the lost lives, the homeless, the unemployed, the upset to the long-established social system, the stateless, the unwillingly repatriated and the simmering anger. How are these things valued? Someone had to do it. And someone did. Every single loss, from pensions to people, from military machines to money, from railways to roads, was taken into account. Germany was audited minutely, every mattress turned and every safe prised open. This was done by the Reparations Commission in accordance with Articles 231–235 of the Treaty of Versailles, and the 'fine' was set at 132 billion gold marks or $33 billion (equivalent to $451,281,452,514 in 2017).

> Germany will perform in the manner laid down in the schedule her obligations to pay the total fixed in accordance with Articles 231, 232 and 233 of the Treaty of Versailles, 132,000,000,000 gold marks, less; (a) the amount already paid on account of reparations; b) sums which may, from time to time, be credited to Germany in respect of state properties in ceded territory, etc.: (c) any sums received from other enemy or former enemy Powers, in respect to which the commission may decide credits should be given to Germany, plus the amount of the Belgian debt to the Allies, the

amounts of these reductions to be determined later by the commission.

German Reparations - Amos S. Hershey - *The American Journal of International Law Vol. 15, No. 3 (Jul., 1921), pp. 411-418*[17]

Its debt was not paid off until 2010, with a final payment of $60 million, ninety-two years after the Great War had ended.

Of course, there were some who disagreed:

> However, this analysis does not allow sufficiently for the prospect that payments could be progressively raised as the German economy expanded, or for the extreme reluctance of Germans to accept even a modest increase in taxation to meet what was universally regarded as an unjustified and oppressive imposition by hostile adversaries. Thus even if the economic aspects of the problem were not as crippling as had been assumed in the 1920s, the exaction of reparations was still of deep political and psychological significance for Germany. The payments were a paramount cause of instability and a barrier to international economic co-operation.
>
> *Banking, Currency, and Finance in Europe Between the Wars* - Charles H. Feinstein

Sally Marks in The Myth of Reparations, argues that inflation in Germany actually 'mushroomed' between 1921 and 1922, when Germany was paying very little in reparations. In fact, she goes so far as to suggest that this was a deliberate ploy by the Germans to postpone tax-reform and currency stabilisation measures in the hope of acquiring substantial reductions in

---

[17] From www.jstor.org

repayments.

> In the end, the victors paid the bills. It is evident that the net effect of World War I and the peace settlement was the effective enhancement of Germany's relative strength in Europe, particularly in regard to her immediate neighbors. As Gerhard Weinberg has remarked, "The shifting of the burden of reparations from her shoulders to those of her enemies served to accentuate this disparity." In addition to reinforcing German economic superiority, the history of reparations generated...much bitterness, endless propaganda...and just over 20 billion gold marks or $5 billion, which was predominantly financed by foreign loans...It is evident that Germany could have paid a good deal more if she had chosen to do so...But Germany saw no reason to pay and from start to finish deemed reparations a gratuitous insult. Whether it was wise to seek reparations from Germany is arguable...Certainly it was unwise to inflict the insult without rigorous enforcement.
>
> *The Myths of Reparations* - Sally Marks. *Central European History* Vol. 11, No. 3

It wasn't just Germany that had to suffer - Austria-Hungary, Ottoman Turkey and Bulgaria all lost substantial lands and suffered financially under various treaties agreed between 1919 and 1920.

Under the Treaty of Trianon, Hungary's army was limited to 35,000 volunteers and three patrol boats. It had to pay 200,000,000 gold crowns in reparations and the Austro-Hungarian Empire was torn in two. The Treaty of Saint-Germain-en-Laye established the Republic of Austria. From the debris of both countries were born Poland, Czechoslovakia, Yugoslavia and

Rumania. Hungary lost at least two-thirds of its territory and its people. Czechoslovakia gained Slovakia among other places while Austria gained Western Hungary. Croatia and Slovenia were given to the newly formed and very grand-sounding Kingdom of Serbs, Croats and Slovenes (later Yugoslavia). Romania did pretty well by getting Banat and Transylvania. Italy got Fiume, eleven square miles of ruralness between itself and Croatia.

Under the Treaty of Neuilly, Bulgaria was restricted to an army of 20,000 volunteers, four torpedo boats and no air force. Reparations were set at 2.25 billion francs, equivalent to £90,000,000 (or about £2,615,193,000 in today's money) and land was given to Yugoslavia, Rumania and Greece. It lost about 300,000 of its population. The Aegean territories gained in the Balkan Wars to the Allies, were turned over to Greece at the Conference of San Remo in 1920.

In the Treaty of Sèvres, Turkey's army was limited to 50,000, its flotilla limited to seven sailboats and six torpedo boats and they lost land to Greece and to Italy. Kurdistan, Armenia and Hejaz (today an area of western Saudi Arabia) were created and Iraq and Palestine became British mandates, a mandate simply being a permission granted by the League of Nations to a member nation to administer a former German or Turkish colony. Syria became a French mandate.

The people of Turkey fell into revolution and refused to accept the treaty.

> Popular resentment at this diktat brought to power a new regime under Mustapha Kemal Ataturk, which drove the Greeks out of Anatolia and threatened to do the same to the British forces occupying the Straits.
>
> *The First World War: A Very Short Introduction* – Michael Howard.

It was ratified in 1923 as the Treaty of Lausanne, in which dropped demands for autonomy for Turkish Kurdistan and the loss of Turkish land to Armenia. Controls over the Turks' military were also abandoned.

It's seems surprising that other nations who had had their wings clipped did not similarly revolt, but of course, Germany's reaction was a little delayed and rather more impactful.

Inevitably, the hardships imposed upon the German people by the Treaty of Versailles and all that followed took their toll and thus began a slide into the financial and social chaos predicted by Keynes and the German Economic Commission.

In 1919 Germany became known as the Weimar Republic. The country had descended into such a state of civil unrest after the abdication of the Kaiser, when the left-wing Social Democratic Party took over power, that the first meeting of the National Assembly could not, for safety reasons, be held in Berlin. It was held in Weimar, just over 138 miles to the west of Berlin. The Weimar Republic was a genuine attempt at democracy but, as is often the case in these situations, it was impossible to please all the people for almost any of the time. Those who had agreed to the Treaty of Versailles were the leaders of the Social Democratic Party. Although they won 38% of the vote at the 1919 election, they were heavily criticised for their part in accepting the treaty, despite the fact that the army generals encouraged them to accept it (the same generals that denied them thrice when he cock of revolution crowed). They were condemned by the right wing as the 'November Criminals', who had stabbed Germany in the back and left the country susceptible to the whim of the world about them.

Prior to this, in 1916, two activists, Rosa Luxemburg and Karl Liebknecht formed the Spartacists, an anti-war left-wing party named after the leader of the slaves' revolt against the Romans, Spartacus. They were essentially communist in ideal and, after the war, disillusioned by the ineffectiveness, as they saw it, of the Social Democratic Party. At the end of 1918 (and a spell in jail for their activities in 1915), they formed the Communist Party of Germany, which was led by Luxemburg and Liebknecht. An uprising, aimed at creating a German Bolshevik state, quickly followed against the Social Democratic Party and its leader,

Friedrich Ebert. At this point, the Ebert government fled to Weimar.

> Luxemburg initially opposed it, but joined in after it began and it was supported by the Red Flag. The Berlin police chief, a radical sympathiser who had just been dismissed, supplied weapons to protesters who erected barricades in the streets and seized the offices of an anti-Spartacist socialist newspaper. Calls for a general strike brought thousands of demonstrators into the centre of the city, but the Revolution Committee, which was supposed to be leading the uprising, could not agree what to do next. Some wanted to continue with the armed insurgency, others started discussions with Ebert. Attempts to get army regiments in Berlin to join the revolt failed.
>
> *The Spartacist Uprising in Berlin* - Richard Cavendish: *History Today Volume 59 Issue 1 January 2009*

They were crushed by the army and Luxemburg and Liebknecht were murdered by members of the Freikorps, 'consisting largely of World War I veterans who were raised as right-wing paramilitary militias, ostensibly to fight on behalf of the government'.[18]

> On January 15th (1919), meanwhile, a Frei-korps unit had seized Liebknecht and Luxemburg in a house where friends were hiding them. They were taken to the Hotel Eden, where Luxemburg's skull was smashed in with a rifle butt. She was subsequently shot and her body was thrown into the Landwehr Canal. 'The old slut is swimming now,' one soldier said. Liebknecht was also shot

---

[18] *Defying Hitler* - Sebastian Haffner

and his corpse was taken to a morgue. The official version of their deaths had Liebknecht shot while trying to escape and 'Red Rosa' attacked by a mob...A Freikorps soldier named Otto Runge was sentenced in May to two years in jail for killing Luxemburg. He was afterwards awarded compensation by the Nazis.

The Spartacist Uprising in Berlin - Richard Cavendish: *History Today Volume 59 Issue 1 January 2009*

They were never going to win. The real enemy was now 'the Red Peril', the Communists, from the east. Hundreds of protesters were shot, murdered, even while trying to surrender. Now the left was split and through the tear in the political fabric, the right wing would emerge.

In the meantime, it was the German people, through the tatters of the German economy, who began to feel the hunger and cold of the winds of Versailles.

Germany was simply unable to keep up with the payments. This was interpreted by France as a refusal to pay. It was the excuse they needed. In 1923, the French and Belgian governments sent troops into the Ruhr, the centre of Germany's coal, steel and iron production. One way or another, they were going to get their money back. The fact that it broke the very rules that the League of Nations was there to enforce, meant nothing, certainly not to the League of Nations.

The German government supported a policy of peaceful non-cooperation by the workers. The invaders brought their own workers in. The German strikers were arrested. Violence ensued. The French killed 100 workers and 10,000 were expelled from the region for protesting. Without this vital part of their resources, the German economy went into freefall. Because Germany was unable to produce anything (though their government kept paying the wages of the Ruhr workers), they had nothing to export and the very fires of industry could only smoulder; they had no money coming in. To cover the cost of all this, to keep the country running, the German government simply printed more money.

This indicated to other nations that Germany was in financial trouble; that made Germany a bad investment and overseas money was quickly withdrawn and investments in Germany halted. Because there was more money printed and therefore more money in circulation, prices increased, therefore inflation increased. Wages increased to keep up with inflation. To combat this, the government printed even more money. As more money was printed to compensate for inflation, so the value of that money became diluted further. This led to hyperinflation. Those on fixed incomes or who worked for people who simply could not afford to keep up with wages, had to go without food, warmth and in some cases, their homes. As small businesses were swallowed up by larger businesses or simply became unable to trade, unemployment increased. People's savings dissolved. The mark-dollar exchange rate rose from 4.2 to one in 1914 to a peak of around 4.2 trillion marks to the dollar by November 1923[19]. An often-used example of the excessiveness of inflation was the price of bread. A loaf of bread which had cost 250 marks in January 1923 had risen to 200,000 million marks in November 1923. In 1913, there had been 4.2 marks to the dollar. Now, in 1923, it was 4,200,000,000,000[20] marks to the dollar. The Mark had become worthless.

> In 1922, a loaf of bread cost 163 marks. By September 1923, this figure had reached 1,500,000 marks and at the peak of hyperinflation, November 1923, a loaf of bread cost 200,000,000,000 marks...People were paid by the hour and rushed to pass money to loved ones so that it could be spent before its value meant it was worthless. People had to shop with wheel barrows full of money. Bartering became common – exchanging something for something else but not accepting

---

[19] *Germany's hyperinflation-phobia* - www.economist.com
[20] Gordon Martel - *A Companion to Europe 1900–1945*

> money for it...Pensioners on fixed incomes suffered as pensions became worthless. Restaurants did not print menus as by the time food arrived...the price had gone up! The poor became even poorer...The very rich suffered least because they had sufficient contacts to get food etc. Most of the very rich were land owners and could produce food on their own estates. The group that suffered a great deal...was the middle class. Their hard earned savings disappeared overnight.
>
> *Hyperinflation and Weimar Germany* - C N Trueman[21]

The Weimar government was blamed because it had agreed to the Treaty of Versailles.

The world watched on as Germany fell into a spiral of financial and social despair, some elements, no doubt, with satisfaction. They could not be blamed for their feelings, but those feelings were short-sighted. It built up resentment of the treaty in Germany, of those countries who had implemented it. In extreme situations, people will act in extreme ways and extremists will always take advantage of this.

In September 1923, the new German Chancellor, Gustav Stresemann, called off the passive resistance and ordered the strikers in the Ruhr to go back to work. The mark, the deadest of flogged horses, slaughtered by hyperinflation, was replaced with the Rentenmark, backed by American gold.

Then, in 1924, the Dawes Plan came to fruition.

The Dawes Plan, 1924

> The United States was alert to the impact such events might have in Europe. If Germany could

---

[21] C N Trueman - *Hyperinflation And Weimar Germany*. historylearningsite.co.uk. The History Learning Site, 22 May 2015. 24 Mar 2018.

not meet her reparations obligations, the French would respond and possibly instigate another war. The Americans also had their own interests in mind. The US was itself owed large sums by Paris and London; the repayment of these loans hinged on the French and British taking receipt of German reparations. In 1924 the Americans organised a ten-man international committee to examine the situation in Germany and consider the problem of reparations.

American Assistance to Weimar Germany - J. Llewellyn et al, *American assistance to Weimar Germany*, www.alphahistory.com

It wasn't just reparations that led to hyperinflation. It was, as ever, a combination of things; bad financial management, the massive national debt from war bonds, which people had bought in the sincere belief that they would quite easily win the war and were shocked when they lost, so effective was the German control of news and propaganda - the national debt shot up from 5 to 156 billion marks[22] - and the government's almost ostrich-like belief in the financial printing press. Things evened out a little with the coming of brave Stresemann as Chancellor, but it was not enough.

The Dawes Plan was named after the American banker, Charles Dawes, who had also been a soldier, diplomat and was to become the Vice-President of the US from 1925-29 under the presidency of Calvin Coolidge. He received the Nobel Peace Prize for his work on the Dawes Plan.

Dawes was asked by the Allied Reparations Committee to take a look at the problem of Germany's reparations repayments, which they were still finding to be a burden. A committee of ten was set up, two each from the USA, UK, Italy, Belgium and France. The final report of the committee was issued in 1924. The idea was to give Germany longer to pay the reparations. The

---

[22] *Germany in the Era of Hyperinflation* - Alexander Jung: www.spiegel.de

recommendations made were that there should be a reduction in repayments, starting at one billion marks a year with a steady rise over four years to two and a half billion marks, therefore allowing time for the economy to build and Germany to cope with the payments. There was also the requirement for the Reichsbank to come under Allied supervision. Despite the invasiveness of this idea, the Germans (the significant ones at the time) did not object. They knew that they were in trouble and had to find enough humility within themselves to get them out of it. There was also a two-year freeze on the payment of reparations – anyone who has had a mortgage break will understand the breathing space that this gives. The French 'agreed' to remove their troops from the Ruhr. Finally, America agreed to huge loans to Germany.

It was a great deal for the Germans and initially successful. Inflation was brought under control. The loans from the US were used to invest in the country and by building new factories and, as business picked, so unemployment was reduced. Germany, with the Ruhr back and an increased labour force, was back in the export market and able to stimulate its internal economy. Germany was also, much to the pleasure of the French and the British, able to meet its reparations obligations. As individuals too, the Germans were better off with a stable, if not raised, standard of living.

There were however, a couple of problems.

One was that there was now a cycle to the payments that almost bordered on the absurd. It went something like this:

> America loaned a very large amount of money to Germany.
>
> ↓
>
> $2.5 billion in loans
>
> ↓
>
> Germany used that money to pay their debts to France, Britain et al.

↓

$2 billion in reparations

↓

France, Britain et al used those repayments
to repay their loans to America.

↓

$2.6 billion in war debts
(from here you just pop back to the start and collect $2.5 billion
for passing Go)

America might as well simply have written itself a big fat cheque and left out the middle-man. It wanted isolation and was actually doing a very good job of achieving the opposite.

As a result of the loans, the standard of living of many Germans began to increase. New houses were constructed and German cities were improved. Her world trade increased and by that fatal year of 1929 her exports were up by 34% on 1913.

The Dawes plan was not universally popular. The communists in Germany disliked it and condemned it as economic imperialism, as if the country had sold its soul at the crossroads of life and would eventually pay the Devil's dues, the Devil, of course, being the USA. The NSDAP dismissed the plan as a stunt. Hitler said that Germany should refuse to make reparations payments, describing the Dawes plan and the influx and impact of American money as the work of self-serving Jewish bankers.

From a German perspective, it could perhaps be understood. The loss of land and loss of dignity that came with the punitive Treaty of Versailles and now the debt required to get them out of the hole that, to be honest, they had dug themselves, took some swallowing. It was fertile ground in which Hitler could grow the nation's indignity.

When, in 1929, after a comparatively good and productive time in Germany, its 'golden years', repayment problems cropped up again and the Americans were dragged back into Europe's troubles. The Dawes Plan was superseded by the Young Plan, which reduced the amount of reparations, to be paid over 59 years, until 1988.

After the Treaty of Versailles, Germany was paying back, as a percentage of its GDP, 295%[23]. That was, whether you had any sympathy for the Germans or not, an absurdity and it's clear why it brought the reaction that it did from JM Keynes.

It was the equivalent of you or I borrowing a tenner from the bank and being asked to pay back £29.50 by tomorrow. Now imagine that as £1000 – that would be £2950 by tomorrow. If you go for the cool million? Now we have to pay £2,950,000 by tomorrow. Yes, it's a payday loan as advertised on TV. And if you don't pay it back, your neighbours, Mr and Mrs France, who own shares in the company that loaned you the money, will get annoyed and invade your back garden and maybe take all the tools from your shed. That's not so bad if you work in an office, but if you earn your living as a gardener...

It simply did not make sense, either business-wise or morally.

The Dawes Plan brought it down to 123%. The Young Plan then brought it down to 80%. Later, at the Lausanne Conference in 1932, that percentage would be down to 19%[24], but before then, something even bigger would happen.

The Depression of 1929

Few people expected the American bubble to burst and those that did hoped no one would notice. They were too busy making money. Ironically, it was the good times that were the cause of the bad times.

It was, as ever, a combination of things that made the Americans' world turn inside out.

The stock market was on a high. People were lending and

---

[23] *Winning the War in Europe* - Scott Minerd, Guggenheim Partners LLC: www.advisoranalyst.com
[24] As above

borrowing money without consequence, 'on the margin', as it was called. They paid 10% of the money required to buy the stock and the banks, who had no reason to believe that they would not get their money back, lent them the other 90%; these were same small banks that had helped bail out Europe with money for the Dawes Plan. By 1929, 2 out of every 5 dollars a bank loaned were used to purchase stocks. In some cases, the borrowers were charged 20% interest on their loans, but dismissed the high levels with a shrug, so great was their confidence in the markets. Stock-market millionaires were created overnight. Banks got their money back and then some. Surprisingly, only a very small percentage of Americans actually invested in the stock market, only four million in all. The richest Americans owned over one third of all American assets, whereas 42% of all Americans were living below the poverty line. 60% of American families earned less than the amount necessary to support their basic needs.

The problem was that, despite the fact that wages were rising, the distribution of income was unequal. The top 1% of the population had incomes which were 650 times greater that the 11% of Americans at the bottom of the pile. Because so much of the American wealth was in so few hands, it meant that the economy, especially the luxury economy, was dependent upon the investment of those few who had the financial means. However, the fact that something so large as the American economy was dependent upon the financial well-being of the few, it made it very fragile and susceptible to even the slightest fluctuations. People would always buy food and drink and bread, these were the pillars of spending, but those expensive luxury goods dependent on the few would soon be put aside once those few began to feel the cold winds of a winter economy begin to bite.

The problem with such a small number of people having such a large proportion of the wealth was that, if they got the jitters, then the country jittered with them.

The agricultural industry was actually struggling after the supply demands of the war. Demand had dropped, output had dropped, prices had dropped, the cost of running a farm had increased so, to some extent, there was already a mini-depression in agriculture. Gross farm income in 1919 amounted to $17.7 billion. By 1921, exports to Europe had plummeted and farm income fell to $10.5 billion.

Grain prices were low because of a global glut. Adversely, American farmers, who were trapped by their trade, had to keep planting what were vast acreages of land in the hope that they would be able to pay off their debts. Wheat prices remained low and level during the Twenties; some farmers were able to scrape by, others did not. Those that didn't had to sell their land and become tenant farmers on what was once their own land or find jobs in town, when all they had ever known was the land.

However, because people were generally on a better income and because the country as a whole was in such a positive state, people began to borrow more. They began to buy things on hire purchase, which resulted in the production of luxury goods such as cars and fridges and televisions increasing to meet the demand. It also resulted in greater, longer-term debt. Production techniques had improved (the production line etc) and technology had advanced, all making production and selling easier and increasing the temptation to the individual to become a part of the heady rush into the future.

In 1919 the Fordney - McCumber Tariff had been introduced. This was an attempt by the US to once again distance itself from Europe and to become, quietly, an autarky - a self-sufficient state. It was a protectionist move intended to safeguard the already nose-diving agricultural industry. It raised taxes on imported goods. This meant that those countries with whom the US traded had to pay more tax to export to the USA. To be able to afford that, they would have to raise their prices and, if they raised their prices, it was quite natural for the American people to go for the cheap, home-grown, option.

The trading partners' response to this was to introduce their own tariffs. In the space of just four years, twenty-six European nations made over thirty changes to their tariffs. The countries of Latin America made seventeen. Australia, Canada and New Zealand all changed their tariffs in 1928. The French targeted the American car industry by increasing duties from 45% to 100%, although they were willing to negotiate should the US be willing to allow certain specific concessions. The Spanish acted in the same vein by increasing their duties on US exports to 40%. Italy and Germany hit America where it really hurt by imposing high tariffs on American wheat. Like America, they all said that they had done this as a protectionist measure; they were only looking after their own.

It was short-sighted of the US to say the least. These people, of whom they were now raising the tariffs, were their debtors. They were their debtors because they were in financial difficulties. If the tariffs were raised by the US, how were they to successfully export, make money, and repay their debts?

Then the small banks, who had been loaning out money left, right and centre for pretty much anything, but especially for the stock-markets, but had also been investing their clients' money in the stock-market and into building projects, did not have enough money to cover the amount of withdrawals being made.

Between 1920 and 1929, when the stock market crashed, 15% of banks went under. Once the banks fell into crisis, so did the small business owners because they could no longer get loans or lost money on the stock market, money that was probably invested by the banks without their knowledge. Spending went down because income went down. Because spending went down, industrial output was forced to decrease and because production decreased, there was no work and people were laid off. It was a house of cards. Unemployment lines grew longer. Trade tariffs, the cost of trade between countries, increased because of American protectionism of its own agricultural and other industries, which also affected industrial output. Other countries had raised their own tariffs in response, so there was a merry-go-round of increases that affected all.

The financial stomach began to rumble.

In 1929 some businessmen, a part of that wealthy elite who owned one third of the nation's wealth, decided to bail out while the going was good. This caused a chain reaction among other investors.

Over a period of a few months, the economy experienced

a few wobbles, such as a 'mini- crash' in March; On September 5, economist Roger Babson gave a warning 'Sooner or later, a crash is coming, and it may be terrific' and then on October 23, the stock prices began to plummet. Panic set in. The next day, Black Thursday, saw further price drops. Some losses were reportedly as high as high as $5billion. On October 28, Black Monday, despite the desperate attempts of some to pour money back into the system (to the tune of $250,000,000), the market fell like a brick.

Unemployment slowly ground the economy down. No one could spend, no one could save. The New York Stock Exchange fell from its 1929 value of $87 billion to $15 billion in 1932, just over 17% of its original worth, while unemployment rose from 1.5 million to 12 million in the same period, an 800% increase.

And, as they say, when America sneezes, the world catches a cold.

The Rise of Adolf Hitler

> The man who is born to be a dictator is not compelled: he wills it.

Adolf Hitler at his trial, 1924

> When your mother has grown old
> And with her so have you,
> When that which once came easy
> Has at last become a burden,
> When her loving, true eyes
> No longer see life as once they did
> When her weary feet
> No longer want to wear her as she stands,
> Then reach an arm to her shoulder,
> Escort her gently, with happiness and passion
> The hour will come, when you, crying,
> Must take her on her final walk.
> And if she asks you, then give her an answer
> And if she asks you again, listen!
> And if she asks you again, take in her words
> Not impetuously, but gently and in peace!
> And if she cannot quite understand you,
> Explain all to her gladly
> For the hour will come, the bitter hour
> When her mouth will ask for nothing more.

Denk' es! (Be Reminded!) 1923, first published in *Sonntag-Morgenpost*, 14 May 1933.

It is easy to blame Adolf Hitler for World War Two. There is the argument that, without him, it would never have happened. This is probably untrue. Without him, it would undoubtedly have happened *differently*. Europe was fragile. Hitler had nothing to do with the Treaty of Versailles, he was just another consequence of it.

That he was part of a country screaming out for help, for dignity, for food, for revenge, is true. That he was an opportunist is undoubtedly true. That he had severe mental health problems is probably true. That he was a sociopathic manipulator of people, a murderer, a racist, an ethnicist and an extremist are also valid points.

It is also true to say that he was a very complicated man who was a product of his environment. He didn't just appear one day as the ranting, raging, hyperbolic, hypnotic, frenzied demagogue that we see now. He was *created*. He was the Frankenstein's Monster of Austria, of his father and his mother, of his down and out days in Vienna, of his political indoctrination, of his personal alienation, the First World War and the Treaty of Versailles. Without each of these and many other things laid layer upon layer, he would not have been what he became.

The same man who wrote the ridiculously touching, maybe cloying, manipulative but also impactful poem above, also wrote this, in *Mein Kampf* a couple of years later:

> At the beginning of the War, or even during the War, if twelve or fifteen thousand of these Jews who were corrupting the nation had been forced to submit to poison-gas, just as hundreds of thousands of our best German workers from every social stratum and from every trade and calling had to face it in the field, then the millions of sacrifices made at the front would not have been in vain. On the contrary: If twelve thousand of these malefactors had been eliminated in proper time probably the lives of a million decent men, who would be of value to Germany in the future, might have been saved.

Is it possible to reconcile the two, almost schizophrenic personalities, that wrote both the love and the vitriol? Of course it is. Most people love their mother and most people have dark thoughts. There is a Darth Vader in every one of us. I'm sure your neighbour loves his Mum, but does he or she also vote for the right-wing, the left-wing, the death penalty? Would they harangue someone else for their less immoderate beliefs, perhaps even harm them? If you take, what in normal society are just traits of personality and stretch them to their limits, then you have extremism: Fascism, Communism, dictatorships, oppression; Idi Amin, Robert Mugabe, Kim Jong-Il, Stalin, Vladimir Lenin, Ho Chi Minh, Mao Tse Tung, Adolf Hitler et al.

In the same way that the beginnings of humanity were formed in the primeval soup, so does extremism rise from the broth of an extreme society.

Hitler loved dogs, he was a Christian, he had a strict moral code, but he was also a murderer of six million Jews and his actions, stemming from the electricity that pulsed through the world around him and finally though him, more than likely played a part in his contribution to the deaths of between fifty and eighty million people during World War Two. It is remarkable to consider that there was not one person on earth who was not affected in some small way by his actions. It is even more incredible to think that we are, today, still responding to what he did.

So how did we take that fatal step from the armistice to the Second World War? What part did Adolf Hitler play in this?

Actually, through sheer willpower, through determination, through scheming and terror, with his skills as a manipulator and demagogue and his own personal wall of hate, he played a massive part.

Hitler Joins German Workers' Party and Forms the Nazi Party

The German Workers' Party was born from the ashes of the Pan-German Fatherland Party, a nationalist, anti-Semitic party that, importantly, advocated territorial expansion, later to become known as *Lebensraum*, a major policy and motivation for the Nazi party. The party, which had no ambition for power, only for agitation, was dissolved in 1918. On January 5, 1919, Anton Drexler, Gottfried Feder and Dietrich Eckart formed the *Deutsche Arbeiterpartei*, the German Workers Party, the GPW, in Munich.

Ironically, Hitler was actually sent by the army as an infiltrator to spy on them. There were fears that the extreme political leanings of the GPW, and a fear of Marxism in Germany in general, were a threat to stable government. Hitler joined the GPW on 24 September 1919, he claimed, as member number 7. They didn't issue any membership cards at this point and when they did, Hitler was member number 55. This number was changed to 550, because, in order to make it look as if they had more members than they actually did, they started the membership count at 500.

Prior to joining, Hitler went to his first meeting on September 12th:

> On September 12th, dressed in civilian clothes, Hitler went to a meeting of the German Workers' Party in the back room of a Munich beer hall, with about twenty five people. He listened to a speech on economics by Gottfried Feder entitled, "How and by what means is capitalism to be eliminated?" After the speech, Hitler began to leave when a man rose up and spoke in favor of the German state of Bavaria breaking away from Germany and forming a new South German nation with Austria.
>
> This enraged Hitler and he spoke out forcefully against the man for the next fifteen minutes uninterrupted, to the astonishment of everyone. One of the founders of the German Workers' Party, Anton Drexler, reportedly whispered: "He's got the gift of the gab. We could use him." After Hitler's outburst ended, Drexler hurried over to Hitler and gave him a forty-page pamphlet entitled: "My Political Awakening." He urged Hitler to read it and also invited Hitler to come back again.

The Rise of Adolf Hitler - www.historyplace.com

The German Workers' Party held its first public meeting on February 24th 1920, in a Munich beer hall. This was an important moment. The spy within Hitler died and with his death was born the future Führer.

> It was at this meeting that Hitler stated that the party had to adopt his '25 Points', which later became known as the 'Twenty Five Points Programme'. **In April 1920, the name of the party was changed to National Socialist German Workers' Party (NSDAP).**
>
> "The program of the German Workers' Party is limited as to period. The leaders have no intention, once the aims announced in it have been achieved, of setting up fresh ones, merely in order to increase the discontent of the masses artificially, and so ensure the continued existence of the party.
>
> 1. We demand the union of all Germans to form a Great Germany on the basis of the right of self-determination enjoyed by nations.
>
> 2. We demand equality of rights for the German people in its dealings with other nations, and **abolition of the peace treaties of Versailles** and **Saint-Germain**[25].
>
> 3. We **demand land and territory (colonies)** for the nourishment of our people and for settling our

---

[25] Which officially recognised the dissolution of the Habsburg Empire and, from it, the creation of new states. Austria was also forbidden to unite with Germany.

excess population.

4. None but members of the nation may be citizens of the state. **None but those of German blood, whatever their creed, may be members of the nation. No Jew, therefore, may be a member of the nation.**

5. **Anyone who is not a citizen of the state may live in Germany only as a guest** and must be regarded as being subject to foreign laws.

6. The right of voting on the leadership and legislation is to be enjoyed by the state alone. We demand therefore that all official appointments, of whatever kind, whether in the Reich, in the country, or in the small localities, shall be granted to citizens of the state alone. **We oppose the corrupting custom of Parliament of filling posts merely with a view to party considerations, and without reference to character or capacity.**

7. We demand that the state shall make it its first duty to promote the industry and livelihood of citizens of the state. **If it is not possible to nourish the entire population of the state, foreign nationals (non-citizens of the state) must be excluded from the Reich.**

8. **All non-German immigration must be prevented.**

9. **All citizens of the state shall be equal as regards to rights and duties.**

10. It must be **the duty of each citizen of the state to work with his mind and his body. The**

activities of the individual may not clash with the interests of the whole, but must proceed within the frame of the community and be for the general good. We demand therefore:

11. **Abolition of incomes unearned by work.**

12. In view of the enormous sacrifice of life and property demanded of a nation by war, **personal enrichment due to a war must be regarded as a crime against the nation. We demand therefore ruthless confiscation of all war gains.**

13. We demand **nationalisation of all businesses.**

14. We demand that the **profits from wholesale trade shall be shared.**

15. We demand extensive **development of provision for old age**.

16. We demand **creation and maintenance of a healthy middle class, immediate communalisation of wholesale business premises**, and their lease at a cheap rate to small traders, and that extreme consideration shall be shown to all small purveyors to the state, district authorities, and smaller localities.

17. We **demand land reform suitable to our national requirements**.

18. We demand **ruthless prosecution of those whose activities are injurious to the common interest. Sordid criminals against the nation, usurers, profiteers, etc. must be punished with**

death, whatever their creed or race.

19. We demand that the **Roman Law**, which serves the materialistic world order, **shall be replaced by a legal system for all Germany.**

20. **With the aim of opening to every capable and industrious German the possibility of higher education and of thus obtaining advancement, the state must consider a thorough reconstruction of our national system of education.**

21. **The state must see to raising the standards of health in the nation by protecting mothers and infants, prohibiting child labour, increasing bodily efficiency by obligatory gymnastics and sports laid down by law,** and by extensive support of clubs engaged in the bodily development of the young.

22. We demand **abolition of a paid army and formation of the national army.**

23. **We demand legal warfare against conscious political lying and its dissemination in the press.** In order to facilitate creation of a national press we demand: a) that all editors of newspapers and their assistants, employing the German language, must be members of the nation b) that special permission from the state shall be necessary before non-German newspapers may appear. These are not necessarily printed in the German language c) that non-Germans shall be prohibited by law from participation financially in or influencing German newspapers. It must be forbidden to publish papers which do not conduce

to the national welfare. We demand legal prosecution of all tendencies in art and literature of a kind likely to disintegrate our life as a nation, and the suppression of institutions which militate against the requirements above-mentioned.

24. We demand liberty for all religious denominations in the state, so far as they are not a danger to it and do not militate against the moral feelings of the German race. **The party as such stands for Positive Christianity, but does not bind itself in the matter of creed to any particular confession. It combats the Jewish-materialistic spirit within us and without us.**

25. That all the foregoing may be realised we **demand the creation of a strong central power of the state; unquestioned authority of the politically centralised Parliament over the entire Reich and its organisations**; and formation of chambers for classes and occupations for the purpose of carrying out the general laws promulgated by the Reich in various states of the confederation.

The leaders of the party swear to go straight forward – if necessary to sacrifice their lives – in securing fulfilment of the foregoing points."

The German Workers Party - C N Trueman.

The bold is, of course, mine.
This is a truly astonishing document. It is fascistic, communist, socialist, harbours the roots of dictatorship, offers health and education and social equality but subjugates the needs of the individual to the needs of the state by the threat of death and the substitution of traditional, accepted law.

Point three, the demand for land and territory, was the root of *Lebensraum*. *Lebensraum* could be translated as 'living space'; the expansion of Germany to cope with the burgeoning population, the amassing of foreign territory for living and agricultural purposes and the opportunity to gain natural resources. It was also possible, via the concept of *Lebensraum*, to carry out what today would be called 'ethnic cleansing'.

> The drive to clear the East of inferior populations in preparation for German colonization led to intensive planning for the mass starvation of over 30 million people there. Policy guidelines issued before the invasion of the Soviet Union stated unequivocally that "many tens of millions of people in this territory will become superfluous and will have to die or migrate to Siberia…Known as the Generalplan Ost, this set of economic and demographic plans placed the necessity for Lebensraum and the colonization of the East at the center of the invasion. By blaming Jews and Bolshevists for the "backwardness" of the region, the plans also reinforced other forms of Nazi antisemitism demanding the removal of Jews from the territory and eventually their physical destruction.

Lebensraum - www.ushmm.org

The idea of the extermination of 'weaker' and 'inferior' races was not a new to Germany. The German geographer and ethnographer Fredrich Ratzel had written about this in his work *Lebensraum* in 1901, but prior to that,

> Oscar Peschel, Ratzel's predecessor at the chair of geography in Leipzig, began promoting Darwinian ideas immediately after Origin of Species appeared, most noticeably in a review in the journal for which

he was the editor at the time, Das Ausland. Here Peschel develops the term Lebensraum in order to translate Darwin's hypothesis into geographical terms. For Peschel the notion of Lebensraum drew attention to the fact that, according to him, natural selection was always already a telluric[26] selection (Peschel, 1860).

On the Genealogy of Lebensraum - C. Abrahamsson

In theory, the idea of the survival of the fittest, as postulated in Darwin's work, was translated into the geographical struggle for resources.

The call for the death sentence against 'sordid criminals against the nation, usurers, profiteers, etc' is excessive to say the least, but also very vague. What exactly is a 'sordid criminal'? Is it simply whatever the state says it is? At the same time as the party demands equality for all – 'all citizens of the state shall be equal as regards to rights and duties' – it excludes the rights of the individual as subordinate to the needs of the state. It evokes 'positive Christianity' and in the next breath denigrates the Jews.

It is indeed a confused piece of writing – dogmatic, perverse, contradictory, politically meandering – and the wanderings of a man who cannot quite get a grasp upon his hatred, so spreads it thickly in the hope of covering all.

The terrible thing is, he spoke for so many. This incandescence lay nascent in the souls of so many good people, people who had been brought low by war and the consequences of being the loser of that war. These words, these 875 words, these twenty-five points, struck at people like arrows and awakened within them those suppressed desires for, if not justice and retribution, then the righting of what they saw as wrongs.

On 29 July, 1921, after some arch-manipulation on Hitler's part, in which he sulkily threatened to take his bat and ball and resign from the party after he was accused of being dictatorial

---

[26] of or relating to the earth; terrestrial.

and overbearing by some of the original members (which, in fairness, he probably was), he was named as Führer of the Nazi Party.

The Beer Hall Putsch

The Weimar Republic stumbled on. Reparations, after the occupation of the Ruhr, recommenced, accompanied by the recriminations of the people who could no longer afford such luxuries as the repayments of debts or food.

It was fuel to the Nazi fire.

Hitler, along with others in the party, decided to kidnap the leaders of the Bavarian government and force them to accept Adolf Hitler as their leader. Bavaria, the *Free State* of Bavaria as it was known, was seen as a state distinct of Germany by those that lived there, even though it was a part of the Weimar Republic. The 'kidnapping' was to take place on 8 November, 1923 as the leading Bavarian politicians were meeting in the Buergerbraeukeller Beer Hall, in Munich. They were supported by General Ludendorff, whom they intended to install as president. Ludendorff was a proponent of the 'stab-in-the-back' myth which stated that the country had lost the war due, not to the generals, but to a lack of resources.

> Immediately after the end of the war, a huge variety of "stab-in-the-back" legends...appeared, but there was still no consensus about who was to blame. Generals accused the parliament, politicians, and the government. The protestant clergy, which had been extremely nationalist during the war, lamented the general moral decline and accused socialism, communism, trade unions, and sometimes the Jews for their betrayal. For the conservative and nationalistic Deutsch-Nationale Volkspartei (the German National People's Party or DNVP) the legend fit perfectly well into the political strategy for mass mobilisation against the republic. In 1918

the leadership of the Pan-German League decided to spearhead radical anti-Semitism and to place the full blame for defeat on the Jews. All these different interpretations of the causes for defeat played to two deep-rooted traditions in German political culture: anti-socialism and anti-Semitism.

Stab-in-the-back Myth - Boris Barth. International Encyclopedia of the First World War.

From this place of power, they intended to take over the Weimar Republic.

Hitler, along with a detachment of six hundred of the SA, the *Sturmabteilung*, the paramilitary wing of the party, stormed the meeting and threated those present with violence. The leaders of the police and the army were locked in a back room and forced to publicly announce their support for the Nazis.

Hitler was forced to leave the hall to attend the violence outside between the army and the insurgents.

It was not long after this that Eric Ludendorff, the leader of the German army at the end of the Great War, arrived. He liked the idea presented by Hitler that it had not been the army that had lost the war but the insidious influence of the Jews, socialists, communists and the then German government. He was a strong supporter of the Nazi Party and agreed to become the head of the German army in Hitler's government.

Meantime, Ernst Röhm and the SA had seized the War Ministry while Rudolf Hess arrested Jews and left-wing politicians in Bavaria.

At this point, Ludendorff released the prisoners, who back-tracked on their public support for the party. Hitler and Ludendorff were arrested as they and three thousand supporters marched on Munich the next morning. In the violence that followed, four state police officers and sixteen Nazis were killed. Hitler and Göring (ex-WW1 fighter pilot ace and early Nazi party member) were both injured.

> For Munich's Jewish community, the Putsch would indeed be a night of terror. Nazi street fighting units and Stormtroopers prowled the downtown Munich area looking for Jews to rob or attack, while others smashed Jewish owned stores and dragged away Jews they found on their rampage. There were gangs of hooligans just roaming the streets, going through telephone books and names on door bells that sounded Jewish for people they could attack...So a lot of Jews were beat up the night of the Putsch. The police records document about 50 or 60 Jews being seized from their homes. But the trial [only] covered Hitler's high treason...And so crimes like attacking the Jews, or storming the [Jewish] printing press just didn't get coverage in the trial... The [final] speech in the trial helped define Hitler from this buffoon to an international [figure]...It was Hitler's biggest audience hitherto, his moment in the spotlight and arguably one of the most important talks of his career.

> *The 1924 Trial of Adolf Hitler That Made the Nazi Party A Household Name* - JP O' Malley. www.timesofisrael.com. Interview with US historian and author David King.

Although found guilty and sentenced to five years in prison (Ludendorff was found not guilty; Röhm was found guilty), Hitler used the trial as a chance to promote his agenda.

> It may seem strange that a man who, as a soldier, was for six years accustomed to blind obedience, should suddenly come into conflict with the State and its Constitution. The reasons for this stem from the days of my youth. When I was seventeen I came to Vienna, and there I learned to study and

observe three important problems: the social question, the race problem, and, finally, the Marxist movement. I left Vienna a confirmed anti-Semite, a deadly foe of the whole Marxist world outlook, and pan-German in my political principles. And since I knew that the German destiny of German-Austria would not be fought out in the Austrian Army alone, but in the German and Austrian Army, I enlisted in the German Army...We wanted to create in Germany the precondition which alone will make it possible for the iron grip of our enemies to be removed from us. We wanted to create order in the state, throw out the drones, take up the fight against international stock exchange slavery, against our whole economy being cornered by trusts, against the politicizing of the trade unions, and above all, for the highest honorable duty which we, as Germans, know should be once more introduced—the duty of bearing arms, military service. And now I ask you: Is what we wanted high treason? The army which we have formed grows from day to day; it grows more rapidly from hour to hour. Even now I have the proud hope that one day the hour will come when these untrained [wild] bands will grow to battalions, the battalions to regiments and the regiments to divisions, when the old cockade will be raised from the mire, when the old banners will once again wave before us: and the reconciliation will come in that eternal last Court of Judgment, the Court of God, before which we are ready to take our stand. Then from our bones, from our graves, will sound the voice of that tribunal which alone has the right to sit in judgment upon us. For, gentlemen, it is not you who pronounce judgment upon us, it is the external Court of History which will make its pronouncement upon the charge which is brought against us. The verdict that you will pass I know. But that Court will not ask of us, 'Did you commit high treason or did you not?' That Court will judge us as Germans who wanted the best for their people and their fatherland, who wished to fight and to die. You may pronounce us guilty a thousand times, but the Goddess who presides over the Eternal Court of History will with a smile tear in pieces the charge of the Public Prosecutor and the verdict of this court. For she acquits us.[27]

It was a great piece of rhetoric. It appealed to the sense of epic, the sense of injustice, the sense of betrayal, the underlying sense of an independent destiny that lay in both Germany and in this man, who was fated to become their leader, and to the gods themselves. It was *perfectly* Teutonic.

The court, being in Bavaria and sympathetic to his beliefs - Bavaria was a hotbed of nationalist fervour - was happy to allow his tirade and to eventually give him a lighter sentence than would normally have been justified in such cases of insurrection. He was out in nine months, having used the time to write *Mein Kampf.*

The putsch, a violent, short-lived and poorly thought-out moment of insurgency, although a failure, was ultimately one of Hitler's greatest successes. It presented him with publicity that could not have been bought. It made him a martyr to his own cause. It brought the Nazi party into the limelight and it gave him time to condense his thoughts, to purify his vitriol and make some sort of crazy logic of it in the self-indulgent, relentless yet very enlightening ramblings of *Mein Kampf.*

The Golden Years

After the Dawes Plan had been implemented, Germany

---

[27] Nazism 1919-1945, Vol. 1, The Rise to Power 1919-1934. Jeremy Noakes and Geoffrey Pridham, eds Exeter: University of Exeter Press, 1998, pp. 34-35

calmed. The Nazi Party grew slowly to about 17,000 in 1926. As a part of his sentence for the putsch, Hitler was not allowed to speak publicly until 1927 and remained on parole. If he broke the conditions of that parole, he could be sent back to Austria.

Hitler didn't however allow the time to be spent twiddling his thumbs. He knew that beneath the patina of content, there was still a considerable gap between rich and poor and that, as the lower-middle and working classes were more likely to vote for communist or socialist candidates, the middle-class and well-off would vote for anyone who could keep the threat of Communism in abeyance. Such seething discontent and fear was food for the hungry monster that Nazism required to grow.

Hitler, despite his own social discomfort and awkwardness, consorted with the wealthy and used them for funding and support. He was happy to play upon their fears and insecurities. Despite the better times in Germany, people were wary and knew, almost instinctively, that there were clouds upon the horizon.

Electorally, the Nazis weren't quite dynamite. They lost the May '24 election, only receiving 6.5% of the vote, which gave them a fairly insignificant 32 seats out of a total of 472. There was another election in December of that year in which they received only 3% of the vote and just 14 seats out of 493. On both occasions they stood as the National Socialist Freedom Movement (Nationalsozialistische Freiheitsbewegung or NSFB), the party formed after Hitler's trial and imprisonment to carry on the work of the Nazi party, which had been banned after the putsch of 1923. It was the Nazis in all but acronym.

However, in April 1926, Hitler found the man who would, possibly more than any other, create the myth from the man: Joseph Goebbels.

Goebbels is a book on his own, but his significance demands attention, especially the fact that, as someone who was disabled and really had nothing against the Jews (so very unNazi), and was on the verge of turning away from supporting Hitler in 1926 for fear that Hitler's anti-Semitism highlighted him as little more than an opportunist, a reactionary, he became a massive supporter of Hitler. With this whole-hearted support, - 'Hitler is great. He gives us all a warm handshake...I love him...He has thought through everything...Such a sparkling mind can be my leader. I bow to the greater one, the political genius'[28], he wrote in his diary - Goebbels's conversion was complete. Ironically, this highly educated, disabled man, a club-footed intellectual with a PhD in Literature from Heidelberg, was probably exactly the kind of person the party did not want - the disabled, the intellectuals, the artists, would soon feel the Nazi's wrath - but Hitler recognised his genius quickly.

Goebbels was made the Gauleiter[29] for Berlin in October 1926. He immediately went into propaganda overdrive where he launched a campaign against Bernard Weiss, the Jewish Chief of Police.

With Goebbels' input, especially as Europe began once again to descend into financial chaos due to the payment of reparations and armed with the 1929 Stock Market Crash to spur on any extremist diatribe, the Nazi share of the vote climbed and climbed. In May 1928, they gained 2.6% of the votes, in 1930 they gained 18.7% of the votes and in 1932 37.3% of the votes. They went from 12 seats in parliament to 230, although in the second 1932 election they took fewer votes and had 190 seats. It was still a remarkable rise.

> The voter support for Hitler's Nazi Party grew from 810,127 in the 1928 election...to 13,765,781 in July, 1932 and reached its zenith of 17,277,180 in March 1933.
>
> *Explaining the Nazi Vote: The Findings and Limits of Ecological Analysis* - Dee R. Wernette, Kean College of New Jersey, July 1976

Not that Goebbels was the only stimulus. Hitler worked

---

[28] *Hitler 1889-1936: Hubris* - Ian Kershaw
[29] a political official governing a district under Nazi rule

tirelessly to promote himself and, in a series of simultaneously remarkable, frightening and laughable photographs taken by Heinrich Hoffmann in 1925, he was snapped in various extraordinary poses animatedly rehearsing his speeches before a mirror, as was his practice. Hitler didn't like the photos and refused to allow them to be published, stating that they were 'beneath his dignity'. It might well have been more of a Wizard of Oz moment – no one should see behind the curtain. He was a clever advocate of self-promotion; Goebbels enhanced what Hitler had already started. They were a perfect team, made in Hell.

Hitler worked at his own image. He was a self-made man in the purest sense. There was very little coincidental about him.

Goebbels noted that Hitler would write and rewrite his speeches, constantly editing them. He would not allow anyone else to write them for him; he was micromanagement, a control-freak, as would be shown later in the war when no one would make a decision without his express permission, much to the detriment of the German cause, but he understood the importance of image, of first impressions, of lasting impressions, the importance of every word and every twist of his raised hand and in these first stages he really was very good at what he did, backed up by a very able and determined crew of self-serving cronies.

The Wall Street Crash and the Rise of the Nazis

If anything proves that it's all about the timing, this is it. The Nazi Party could not have wished for the world to fall into financial chaos at a better time. If the allusions by Sally Marks earlier to a deliberate policy of non-payment by the Germans are true, then the collapse of the world economy gave Germany the chance to stop repayments and the chance to slip into autarky, the state of self-sufficiency that would justify *Lebensraum* and, by extension, the ethnic cleansing of Europe.

Unemployment jumped from 1,862,000 in 1920 to 6,042,000 in 1932. In 1929 it was 2,850,000 and was due to more than double. Because of Germany's dependence upon American loans, it was made to suffer. Businesses were lost, unemployment soared, wages fell, hours were cut and incomes fell and, as Germany turned to Europe to repay its loans, the whole of the continent began to fall apart under the weight of its interdependent debts. The US gave Germany ninety days to repay its debts.

Or what? the Germans must have thought. What could the US possibly do to an already broken country? The same or similar demands were made of the French and the British, but what the US asked was impossible to attain. Nobody had anything to give.

The German population, rich and poor, looked desperately for alternatives. Hitler's dalliances with the big men of industry and the upper-middle classes paid off. Afraid of losing what they had in the crash or to the communists who might still be voted in, they turned for their financial lives to the Nazis. The ordinary man-in-the-street turned to the Nazis because everything that had come before had failed. They had no jobs, no income, no prospects. They needed hope. They needed his whispers of socialist ideals and firm-handedness. They wanted his equality. Hitler's 'fence-sitting', where he was on the one hand the capitalist's friend and on the other the condemner of capitalism, instead of driving people away for his eclectic thinking, united people, if not as classes, then as idealists.

However, it was not, for the population, some sort of Road to Damascus moment where there was a sudden surge in support for the Nazis. The numbers of the electorate voting for them, as we have seen, rose quite slowly and did not reach their peak until 1932 and after. So how did Hitler get into power?

It's easy really. He was invited.

In the July election of 1932, the Nazis had gained 230 seats in parliament and had taken more votes than any other party. The 37.3% that they did get does not seem much, it is clearly way less than half, but there were thirty parties involved in the election. It was still not enough to take power, but it was good enough to put Hitler in a good bargaining position. Before Hitler was able to take his first step towards ultimate power, there was still a certain amount of manipulation and intimidation to be carried out.

The Stormtroopers

The *Sturmabteilung*, SA or Brownshirts as all the textbooks would call them when I was at school, were the paramilitary wing of the Nazi Party. They grew from an official attachment of the army in 1915 as a sort Special Services, an early SAS or Delta Force.

Headed by Ernst Röhm post-war, they acted outside the law and were used by Hitler to intimidate and ultimately remove, one way or another, any opposition. By 1932 it had 400,000 members. That is the equivalent of the town of Leicester going rampant across Britain. In April 2017, there were 78,407 fully-trained troops in Britain; that is 5 times fewer than there were SA members and the SA had access to weapons and were not as tethered to the rulebook as the British army is today. It is almost impossible to imagine a scenario where an entire city or an entire army can have free rein to run rampant in the name of a single man and his ideals, and yet this is exactly what happened.

Article 48

This is one of those times where someone thought that they had come up with a great idea and then, some years later, looked over their shoulder and thought, 'We shouldn't have done that'.

Article 48 was written into the Weimar constitution to help the government in times of crisis. It was essentially a *carte blanche* for whoever happened to be in power at the time to issue edicts that, by the power of Article 48, became law.

The article stated:

> If a state fails to perform the duties imposed upon it by the federal constitution or by federal law, the President…may enforce performance with the aid of the armed forces. If public order and security

are seriously disturbed or endangered within the Federation, the President...may take all necessary steps for their restoration, intervening, if need be, with the aid of the armed forces. For the said purpose he may suspend for the time being, either wholly or in part, the fundamental rights described in Articles 114, 115, 117, 118, 123, 124, and 153...The President...has to inform the Reichstag without delay of any steps taken in virtue of the first and second paragraphs of this article. The measures to be taken are to be withdrawn upon the demand of the Reichstag. Where delay is dangerous a state government may take provisional measures of the kind described in paragraph 2 for its own territory. Such measures are to be withdrawn upon the demand of the President...or of the Reichstag...

This was a very dangerous clause to any constitution (which pretty much exists in every country today; they just don't tell us that) which suspended all rights of the individual, suspended *Habeas Corpus*, so anybody could be detained without cause or trial at any time, and was open to the very abuses for which it was later used.

It was frequently used from 1923 onwards. Between 1923-24, the President, Fredrich Ebert, used the article sixty-three times to deal with financial crises. Hindenburg used Article 48 almost as a matter of routine and as a way to circumvent any of the alternate thinking that annoyingly coincided with the running of a democracy. In 1932 alone, he invoked Article 48 sixty times. The casual implementation of the article weakened the whole concept of parliament, in this case the Reichstag, and led to a lack of faith in the government by the people.

The problem with using a power such as this is that it becomes too easy. It is far easier to invoke than to negotiate. It is far easier to turn one's back on democracy for short-term gain. It made for lazy government and excluded democracy in favour of ruling by decree.

To tackle the previously mentioned Brownshirts, in 1932, the then Chancellor, Heinrich Bruening, invoked Article 48 of the constitution and issued a decree banning the SA and SS all across Germany. It caused outrage among the Nazi and SA supporters, but, canny as ever and very aware of the slow death rattle of the Republic, Hitler simply agreed. He was an opportunist and knew well enough to bide his time.

It also led to Hitler's Enabling Act, more of which a bit later.

Kurt von Schleicher

Kurt von Schleicher had the dubious honour to be the last Chancellor of the Weimar Republic. He was, by all accounts, bit of a slippery customer, a social-climber and not opposed to double-dealing. He is significant because, through his self-serving machinations, he is the one person who inadvertently held the door open for Adolf Hitler.

His hope ultimately was to become Chancellor. While Germany was under the Chancellorship of Heinrich Brüning, von Schleicher was offered the post as aide to the Minister of Defence, William Groener. While in this position, von Schleicher sidled up to the President, Paul von Hindenburg. Neither Brüning nor Groener liked this relationship – it was a threat to their own positions in the eyes of the President. Eventually, by the careful intrigue of von Schleicher, they were both removed from their positions. Von Schleicher then persuaded Hindenburg to select Franz von Papen as new Chancellor while he took on the role of Minister of Defence.

Inevitably, he and von Papen had a falling out, von Papen resigned and von Schleicher slipped neatly into his shoes as Chancellor.

At this point, it is abundantly clear that von Schleicher simply could not help himself. Schleicher's intention had been to create a coalition that was able to maintain a majority in the Reichstag. The plan was to get as many of the opposed and bickering groups to unify. This included the Christian and social democrat labour unions and a section of the Nazi Party. This was not a section of the party led by Hitler, but a left-wing faction led by Gregor Strasser, who was in favour of compromise with other nationalist groups. This was not an idea which appealed to the control-freak Hitler, who wanted undisputed leadership of the party.

Von Schleicher had been too clever by half. In the background, von Papen continued to scheme.

Papen had become closer to Hindenburg, but the president was concerned about Schleicher's plan which involved the Social Democrats, whom Hindenburg disliked intensely. Papen constantly pushed Hindenburg to make Hitler Chancellor, if necessary in coalition with the German National People's Party, the DNVP. Papen believed that he and the DNVP could rein in the potential excesses of the Nazi Party. Von Papen schemed behind Schleicher's back in a series of secret meetings with Hitler and Hindenburg.

The tide turned when Schleicher asked Hindenburg to give him emergency powers. He was refused; not only was he refused, he was, on 30 January 1933, removed from office.

And there you have it. On the same day as Schleicher was removed, Hitler was named as the new Chancellor of Germany. Hitler was in.

Goebbels came into his element. In a triumphal procession through the Brandenburg Gate, Hitler was cheered by thousands as he was driven along the Wilhelmstrasse to the presidential palace.

> A sea of hand held burning torches cast flickering light on red and gold Nazi banners amid the slow beating of drums in anticipation of seeing the Führer. Men, women and children along with the SA and SS waited. He kept them waiting, letting the tension rise. All over Germany, people listened to this on the radio, waiting, and hearing the throngs calling for their Führer. When he appeared in the beam of a spotlight, Hitler was greeted with an

outpouring of worshipful adulation unlike anything ever seen before in Germany. "Heil! Sieg Heil!," (Hail! Hail Victory!) went the chorus of those who believed the hour of deliverance had come in the form of this man now gazing down at them.

The Life and Times of Adolf Hitler – Mahesh Sharma

The Reichstag Fire

The Reichstag (parliament building) fire of February 27th, 1933 was a wonderful, timely event for Hitler. It once again evolved from the mistakes of others, as all of Hitler's opportunities seem to have done.

A young man, Marinus van der Lubbe, was found in the Reichstag as it burned. He was a Dutch Communist and claimed to have set fire to the Reichstag as a protest on behalf of the German people against fascist rule. He was tried, found guilty and executed for his crime.

But it was a perfect moment for Hitler to remove his most serious political rivals, the Communists. The head of the German Communist Party and three Bulgarian members of the Comintern (an international communist organisation that advocated world communism) were also arrested. They were eventually found not guilty, but by then Hitler had managed to firmly place the blame for the fire upon the Communists and, by doing so, Hindenburg was induced to declare that the country was under threat and enact Article 48, no doubt with a bit of encouragement from Hitler.

The Enabling Act

As an extension of Article 48, the Enabling Act passed the power to suspend the constitution from the President (as in Article 48) to the Chancellor i.e. Hitler. How did Hitler manage to sneak this past the parliament? Well, he needed a two-thirds majority in parliament to pass the act. Having silenced and bullied his critics by the use of Article 48 and the Brownshirts, he got his majority. The only dissenters were the Socialist Democrats, but the vote was 441 votes to 84 in Hitler's favour.

He now had absolute power. He had constructed his totalitarian dream. It didn't take long for the freedom of the individual to be curbed. With the Gestapo, taken over by the sinister Himmler from the political weasel Göring, the secret police that came under the wing of the SS thanks to Himmler's involvement, reinforcing the voice and desires of the state, arrests were made of undesirables who were sent to Dachau, which was the first concentration camp to be opened, and did so within weeks of the Nazis coming to power. The press was turned into a puppet through which the state could spread its philosophy and gagged from any expression of opposition. All other political parties were declared illegal.

Hitler had become a dictator.

From this point, the Fuhrer made Germany his own. Trade unions were banned, possibly in reaction to the strikes that had been held in 1917, when Hitler had been, if not on the frontline, then certainly in danger as a *meldegänger*, a runner, in the Great War.

> Then came the munitions strike at home, the most incredible bit of treachery and knavery the world has ever known. The German army was knifed in the back. The lives of hundreds and thousands of our men yet to be slaughtered were to lie at the doors of those who fomented and engineered this monstrous treason...the consequences on our morale were deadly. Everyone was asking what was the good of our carrying on out here if the people at home had thrown up the sponge?

Private Hitler's War - Bob Carruthers

Never one to miss out on the chance for propaganda,

Joseph Goebbels arranged for the burning of 25,000 'unGerman' books. All political parties were banned, therefore ensuring no opposition and, in October, Germany, portentously, withdrew from the League of Nations, which it had been permitted to join in 1926.

The Night of the Long Knives - June 29th – June 30th 1934

If we remember anything from history lessons in school, it is this phrase. Its fearful poetry holds all the terror and violence of the event itself.

Hitler, concerned by the power of the SA/Brownshirts and wishing once and for all to deal with opposition past and present, sent out (allegedly) the SS[30] to murder those he felt were likely to present a challenge to his dictatorship. It makes for a grisly list, a list incidentally drawn up by Heinrich Himmler, Reinhard Heydrich (one of the main architects of the holocaust and chief of the Gestapo), Hermann Göring and Theodor Eicke (commandant of Dachau concentration camp). It was known as the Reich List of Unwanted Persons. Among them were:

- **Ernst Röhm** – Leader of the SA. Shot to death.
- **Gregor Strasser** – Leader of the left-wing faction of the Nazi Party who had been approached as a possible coalition partner by von Schleicher, the last president of the Weimar Republic. Shot to death.
- **Gustav von Kahr** – party responsible for failure of Beer Hall Putsch. Tortured and shot to death.

---

[30] The *Schutzstaffeln (pl)* – protection squads. Originally a group formed in 1922 and called the Adolf Hitler Shock Troops. Under Henrich Himmler, they became an elite instrument of terror, an extension of the German state, independent of the army, which oversaw concentration camps and the murder of those opposed to the Nazis. The Gestapo, the secret police, also came under Himmler's control.

- **Engelbert Dollfuss** – The Austrian Chancellor. Shot to death in attempted coup d'état by Austrian Nazis. Hitler said, so sorry, nothing to do with me. Nothing else happened. Ironically, it was the Italians, who later became involved in Abyssinia much to the displeasure of the League of Nations, who took to the Austrian border and threatened Germany with invasion of Austria if the Germans pursued any further intervention of Austria. Germany backed down.
- **Ferdinand von Bredow** – associate of von Schleicher. Shot to death.
- **Georg von Detten** – previous SA leader associated with Ernst Röhm. Shot to death.
- **Karl Ernst** - SA *Gruppenführer*. Shot to death.
- **Hans Hayn** - SA leader. Shot to death.
- **Edmund Heines** – Röhm's deputy in the SA. Shot to death. His brother, also an SA member, was also shot after he had handed himself in.
- **Peter von Heydebreck** – SA leader. Shot to death.
- **Julius Uhl** – SA *Gruppenführer*. Arrested 30 June 1934. Sent to Dachau. Shot to death 2 July 1934.
- **Kuno Kamphausen** – Architect and civil servant. Murdered because he refused building permission to the brother of SS-Standartenführer Förster. Really. Shot to death.
- **Willi Schmid** – German music critic. I really want to quote this from Wikipedia because it is so dreadful:

He was killed by the Nazi SS during the Night of the Long Knives because he had a similar name to one of the intended targets, apparently either an SA leader named Willi Schmidt,[3][4] or an associate of Otto Strasser (brother of Georg Strasser and left-wing member of Nazi Party. He fled the country) named Ludwig Schmitt.[5][31]. William Shirer's account in The Rise and Fall of the Third Reich mentions that Schmid was playing the cello in his study, while his wife was preparing supper and his three children were playing in the adjacent room, when Nazi agents knocked on the door and took him away. His body was sent to his widow in a casket four days later, with written instructions from the SS not to open it under any circumstances. Rudolf Hess visited the family a few days later to express condolences for the mistake and offer his widow a pension.[4]

- **Kurt von Schleicher** – Last Chancellor of Weimar Germany. Shot to death at his front door. When his wife came to help, she too was murdered.

four inmates of Dachau

- **Julius Adler** – Jewish lawyer. He had originally been arrested in early June supposedly for non-compliance with fire and building regulations.
- **Erich Gans** – Jewish Communist. Shot to death.
- **Walter Häbich** – Communist. Shot to death.
- **Adam Hereth** – Originally arrested for wearing an 'Iron Front' anti-Fascist badge. Shot to death.

The affair, also known as the Röhm Putsch and Operation Hummingbird, was given the name The Night of the

---

[31] [3][4] [5] - Gunther, John (1940). Inside Europe. New York: Harper & Brothers. p. 51. Matthew Hughes and Chris Mann (2002). Inside Hitler's Germany: Life Under the Third Reich. Brassey's. p. 98. ISBN 1-57488-503-0. Ian Kershaw (2000). Hitler: 1889-1936: Hubris. W. W. Norton & Co. p. 515. ISBN 0-393-04671-0.

Long Knives by Hitler himself (from a popular Nazi song). He claimed that 61 had been executed while 13 had been shot resisting arrest and three had committed suicide. Others have argued that as many as 400 people were killed during the purge.

On 2 August, 1934, the final barrier to absolute power, President von Hindenburg, died. Hitler combined the roles of President and Chancellor and created an unassailable power base.

All these extraordinary people and extraordinary events came together, conspired even, either by accident or manipulation, to enable Hitler to create his totalitarian state. He had absolute power. His ideals, hardened by his childhood, his time spent in Vienna in which his intolerance of the Jews and the melting pot of society was hardened, his time in the trenches, his stubbornness and yes, his talents, came to life.

Kristallnacht and the 'Jewish Problem'

> Once I really am in power, my first and foremost task will be the annihilation of the Jews. As soon as I have the power to do so, I will have gallows built in rows—at the Marienplatz in Munich, for example—as many as traffic allows. Then the Jews will be hanged indiscriminately, and they will remain hanging until they stink; they will hang there as long as the principles of hygiene permit. As soon as they have been untied, the next batch will be strung up, and so on down the line, until the last Jew in Munich has been exterminated. Other cities will follow suit, precisely in this fashion, until all Germany has been completely cleansed of Jews.
>
> Statement to Josef Heil, 1922 quoted in *Hitler and the Final Solution* - Gerald Fleming

There are people who deny the Holocaust. There are people in *Britain, today*, who deny that the event took place or declare that it was grossly exaggerated.

The facts however, backed by physical evidence and witness testimony, are undeniable.

The Jewish population in Europe pre-war (including the USSR) was 9,916,840. The numbers murdered amounted to approximately 5,728,051 (including the USSR). Nineteen concentration camps were found by allied and Russian forces at the end of the war. At its peak, Auschwitz-Birkenau was killing 6000 Jews a day. Altogether about 1,100,000 Jews were murdered at this camp alone.

The Germans weren't the first to discriminate against the Jews. Both King Richard and King Edward I were complicit in expelling, robbing, victimising and murdering Jews, while at the same time raising loans, both enforced and voluntary, from them. The Americans were rampantly anti-Semitic at the beginning of the 20th century. Henry Ford ended up in court for his anti-Semitic views, even that American *wunderkind*, Charles Lindbergh was complicit in the persistence of American anti-Semitism. Even that most celebrated of Americans, Charles Lindbergh, toured Germany and was given a medal by Herman Göring no less. He was all for America First and refused to return the medal given to him by Göring even after the dreadful Kristallnacht.

But the concentrated, targeted victimisation and extermination of Jews, simply for being Jewish, was perfected by the Nazi regime under Adolf Hitler. There was never any possibility of a denial by Hitler or on his behalf that this was never his intention. *Mein Kampf* is littered with anti-Semitic clauses and, as far back as 1919, Hitler expressed his intentions in a letter to Adolf Gemlich, a soldier in the Reichswehr, simply now known notoriously as the 'Gemlich Letter'. It is a despicable and stomach-churning letter full of ranting vitriol; I do not say this as one of the 'politically correct', I say it from a sense of detached decency. It was not long before his feelings towards the Jews were amplified and were vented, with the help of Heinrich Himmler, Herman Goring and Reinhart Heydrich, into an extermination of the non-Arian vulnerable.

The formal acceptance of genocide as Nazi policy

did not happen until early in 1941, and was then directly linked in Himmler's mind with the coming invasion of Russia. But by that time his racial prejudice had found outlets which prepared both him and his agents for the supreme test with which they would be faced in 1941. In October 1939 he was required by Hitler to assist in a nation-wide euthanasia programme for the insane, which by 1941 had led to the 'mercy-killing' of some 60,000 German patients in mental institutions.8 Though the idea was Hitler's, originating in a scribbled note to Philip Bouhler, the head of the Führer's Chancellery, the S.S. was responsible for supplying doctors to carry out the task, while Viktor Brack, a friend of the Himmler family and Bouhler's liaison officer with the Department of Health, was put in charge of the administration. The relatives of the people selected for destruction knew nothing of what was happening, and the notification of the cause of death was falsified. Extermination centres were set up under strict guard, and the S.S. doctors and their nursing and ambulance staff underwent their initial experience of selecting, transporting, gassing and cremating large numbers of helpless people.

Heinrich Himmler: The Sinister Life of the Head of the SS and the Gestapo – Heinrich Frankel and Roger Manvell

The Jews were, as consistently promised by Hitler, directly targeted by Nazi policy. At this point I borrow heavily, with thanks, from the Holocaust Encyclopedia to illustrate the legislation brought in against the Jews between 1933 and 1939.

> The following list shows 29 of the more than 400 legal restrictions imposed upon Jews and other

groups during the first six years of the Nazi regime.[32]

1933

March 31 - Decree of the Berlin City Commissioner for Health suspends Jewish doctors from the city's social welfare services.

April 7 - The Law for the Restoration of the Professional Civil Service removes Jews from government service.

April 7 - The Law on the Admission to the Legal Profession forbids the admission of Jews to the bar.

April 25 - The Law against Overcrowding in Schools and Universities limits the number of Jewish students in public schools.

July 14 - The Denaturalization Law revokes the citizenship of naturalized Jews and "undesirables."

October 4 - The Law on Editors bans Jews from editorial posts.

1935

May 21 - The Army Law expels Jewish officers from the army.

September 15 - The Nuremberg Race Laws exclude German Jews from Reich citizenship and prohibit them from marrying or having sexual relations with persons of "German or German-related blood."

---

[32] Antisemitic Legislation 1933–1939 - www.ushmm.org

1936

January 11 - The Executive Order on the Reich Tax Law forbids Jews to serve as tax consultants.

April 3 - The Reich Veterinarians Law expels Jews from the profession.

October 15 - The Reich Ministry of Education bans Jewish teachers from public schools.

1937

April 9 - The Mayor of Berlin orders public schools not to admit Jewish children until further notice.

1938

January 5 - The Law on the Alteration of Family and Personal Names forbids Jews from changing their names.

February 5 - The Law on the Profession of Auctioneer excludes Jews from the profession.

March 18 - The Gun Law bans Jewish gun merchants.

April 22 - The Decree against the Camouflage of Jewish Firms forbids changing the names of Jewish-owned businesses.

April 26 - The Order for the Disclosure of Jewish Assets requires Jews to report all property in excess of 5,000 Reichsmarks.

July 11 - The Reich Ministry of the Interior bans Jews from health spas.

August 17 - The Executive Order on the Law on the Alteration of Family and Personal Names requires Jews bearing first names of "non-Jewish" origin to adopt an additional name: "Israel" for men and "Sara" for women.

October 3 - The Decree on the Confiscation of Jewish Property regulates the transfer of assets from Jews to non-Jews in Germany.

October 5 - The Reich Ministry of the Interior invalidates all German passports held by Jews. Jews must surrender their old passports, which will become valid only after the letter "J" has been stamped on them.

November 12 - The Decree on the Exclusion of Jews from German Economic Life closes all Jewish-owned businesses.

November 15 - The Reich Ministry of Education expels all Jewish children from public schools.

November 28 - The Reich Ministry of the Interior restricts the freedom of movement of Jews.

November 29 - The Reich Ministry of the Interior forbids Jews to keep carrier pigeons.

December 14 - The Executive Order on the Law on the Organization of National Work cancels all state contracts held with Jewish-owned firms.

December 21 - The Law on Midwives bans all Jews

from the profession.

1939

February 21 - The Decree concerning the Surrender of Precious Metals and Stones in Jewish Ownership requires Jews to turn in gold, silver, diamonds, and other valuables to the state without compensation.

August 1 - The President of the German Lottery forbids the sale of lottery tickets to Jews.

Because Jews were no longer officially German, they were no longer included in the unemployment statistics. Those that fled in fear from Germany were also taken out of the unemployment figures and their jobs filled. I'm sure the Führer would have seen this as a pleasing 'double-whammy'.
Then in 1938 came the most overt expression of the Nazi Policy towards the Jews: Kristallnacht.
On November 9 and 10, 1938, Nazis ran rampant throughout Germany, Austria and the Sudetenland and, without inhibition, attacked Jews, regardless of where they were. Over one thousand synagogues were burned down, homes were invaded, people dragged out into the streets and beaten, sometimes to death, sometimes hanged from lamp posts. Between seven and eight thousand Jewish business were destroyed, at least 96 Jews murdered and 30,000 arrested and sent to concentration camps.

> The Kristallnacht on 9 November was not spontaneous: it was the culmination of a series of provocations. The immediate occasion for the outburst of violence was a decree issued at the end of October ordering the expulsion from the Reich of Jews of Polish citizenship, many of whom had lived there for generations. On 7 November a young Polish emigrant killed a senior officer of the

German embassy in Paris as a protest against the deportation of his parents from the Reich[33]. Hundreds of synagogues were set on fire, thousands of shops and offices belonging to the Jews were destroyed, houses were torched, many Jews were attacked and a few dozen were killed. Thousands were arrested and deported to concentration camps. But it was not a spontaneous reaction of the German population, united against an international Jewish plot to overthrow Germany, as Nazi propaganda held it to be. It was one of the mass campaigns promoted and manoeuvred by Goebbels, who was in charge of education and propaganda and who, in fact, authorised the NSDAP and the SA to unleash the pogrom.

Hitler and Nazism – Enzo Collotti

On top of this, the Germans managed to invert and distort the truth by blaming the Jews for Kristallnacht.

Indeed Hermann Goering went out of his way to ensure that the Jews were given the credit for the Reichstag fire. A fine of billions marks was levied against the Jews for the murder of Ernst vom Rath. Six million marks were paid out to the Jewish owners of businesses and places of worship by insurance companies. The German government took that money.

Many people consider this to be the beginning of the Holocaust. It is certainly the moment when the Nazis, in however twisted a fashion they did it, made it clear that anti-Semitism was now a part of their policy, a part of *Lebensraum* and a part of Hitler's personal agenda. It was the most overt piece of anti-Semitic

---

[33] Herschel Grynszpan had shot a German diplomat, Ernst vom Rath, in the German embassy in Paris on 7 November, 1938 five times in revenge for the thousands of Jewish refugees, including members of his own family, who had been expelled from Germany.

behaviour that they had committed and, from then on, they no longer really made any attempt to hide it, but the available evidence makes it clear that the Holocaust was born many years previously in Hitler's mind in the trenches of the Great War.

Hitler's Economic Miracle

It is impossible to separate Hitler's desires for Germany from the economic and social consequences. There are three branches to consider:

1) Autarky - as previously stated, this was the desire for self-sufficiency
2) Lebensraum - Living space. To achieve autarky Germany needed more space for its population and more resources. Lebensraum also fitted in with the 'ethnic cleansing' policy of the Nazi regime and the idea that other races were subordinate to the Aryan elite.
3) Rearmament - It had always been Hitler's intention to rearm. In order to do this, he needed resources. To obtain coal and other natural resources, to build factories, he needed land.

The principles of autarky and rearmament must be viewed as interdependent and inseparable. To reach autarky capital had to be directed toward the building of a wartime economy in the short-term, and the acquisition of Lebensraum would be required in the long-term. The process by which autarky was pursued came to define the economic agenda of the NSDAP after 1934...The long-term solution for autarky would have to be the acquisition of *Lebensraum* through military action...Essentially, autarky depended on...*Lebensraum*, which in turn relied on the success of rearmament.

The Nazi Economy (1933-1939): Unemployment, Autarky and the Working-Class – Rijk Eric Mollema

It was a continuous circle, no part of which could be removed.

Unemployment in Germany had been extraordinarily high since the Stock Market collapse of 1929 and crept to a peak in 1932, with 30% of the population unemployed.

If we look at the figures below, where unemployment was reduced from nearly 10% in 1933 to just 0.43% within 6 years, this was indeed, on the face of it, an economic miracle.

You have to bear in mind that the population figures represent *total* population and not *working* population i.e. those of working age. If we take the figure in January, 1933 of 33% unemployed, that would imply the number of those of working age to be 18,181,818, which would clearly be a grossly exaggerated figure. The drop in figures is still though, on the face of it, impressive.

Unemployment in Germany	Total (millions)	Population	% of population
January 1933	6	66,027,000	9.08%
January 1934	3.3	66,409,000	4.96%
January 1936	2.5	67,349,000	3.71%
January 1937	1.8	67,831,000	2.65%
January 1938	1.0	68,424,000	1.46%
January 1939	302,000	69,314,000	0.43%

However, as was Hitler's way, the figures were really not as straightforward as they at first appeared.

No Jews, women or members of the National Labour Service were included in the figures of unemployed.

The National Labour Service - the RAD or Reichsarbeitsdienst – was introduced in 1935 when the Labour Service Act was passed. This forced every man between the ages of 18 and 25 to complete six months training at the RAD. The training involved staying away from home at an allocated camp (isolation and indoctrination), the wearing of military uniforms and daily military and physical exercises. They were paid no wages, only 'pocket-money'. As they were otherwise occupied, they were removed from the unemployment statistics.

On top of this was the simple expedient of fear. If you weren't working and were considered by the state to be 'work-shy', you could be sent to a concentration camp. Others were put onto public work schemes such as the building of the autobahn or hospitals and houses. These were also removed from the list of unemployed.

Finally, in 1936, as part of the newly introduced Four Year Plan, where 'autarky became the predominant focus of the economic agenda'[34], Germany was put onto a war-footing.

A large amount of government spending was on rearmament – the table below shows the percentage of GDP that was spent on the military between 1935 and 1939. The German spending outstrips UK spending by some way until 1939, when there is almost parity. After this, during the war years, the UK's spending as part of GDP is actually far higher than Germany's, possibly because they had to catch up with Germany, partly perhaps because they had a vast empire to support and were fighting on so many fronts.

> (these figures were) historically unprecedented in a peacetime capitalist state. On the eve of the First World War in 1914, by contrast, the military spending of all the major European powers had hovered between 3 and 4 per cent of GDP.

---

[34] *The Nazi Economy (1933-1939): Unemployment, Autarky and the Working-Class* – Rijk Eric Mollema

The Economics of the War with Nazi Germany - Adam Tooze and James R. Martin

Year	Germany	UK
1935	8%	2%
1936	13%	5%
1937	13%	7%
1938	17%	8%
1939	23%	22%

Spending as a Percentage of GDP in the UK and Germany 1935 - 1939

The problem with the Four-Year Plan is that it would not have been sustainable beyond those four years. It was dependent upon *Lebensraum*, which was dependent upon military conquest, which was dependent upon rearmament, which was dependent upon money, and the only way Germany was going to get money was by taking it, one way or another, from the people, or printing it itself. Either way would lead to massive debt and take them back to the cold, hungry days of inflation. The success of the whole thing was dependent upon a war taking place and, from that war, an unassailable victory. But the people would come second to the country's needs. The public works programs such as the building of the autobahn and buildings, the Strength Through Joy movement, where the workers were provided with state-funded leisure opportunities and the rip-off scheme to sell Volkswagens to the people[35], were all given second billing to rearmament.

---

[35] To purchase a Volkswagen, customers were required to make a weekly deposit of at least 5 Reichsmarks into a DAF account on which they received no interest. Once the account balance had reached 750 Reichsmarks, the customer was entitled to delivery of a VW. The DAF meanwhile achieved an interest saving of 130 Reichsmarks per car. In addition, purchasers of the VW were required to take out a two-year insurance contract priced at 200 Reichsmarks. The VW savings contract was non-transferable, except in case of death, and withdrawal from the

Rearmament

> To what purpose could the Treaty of Versailles have been exploited? In the hands of a willing Government, how could this instrument of unlimited blackmail and shameful humiliation have been applied for the purpose of arousing national sentiment to its highest pitch? How could a well-directed system of propaganda have utilized the sadist cruelty of that treaty so as to change the indifference of the people to a feeling of indignation and transform that indignation into a spirit of dauntless resistance? Each point of that Treaty could have been engraved on the minds and hearts of the German people and burned into them until sixty million men and women would find their souls aflame with a feeling of rage and shame; and a torrent of fire would burst forth as from a furnace, and one common will would be forged from it, like a sword of steel. Then the people would join in the common cry: "To arms again!"

Mein Kampf – Adolf Hitler

> For the generals remained incorrigible war-mongers and the advent of the war-loving Adolf Hitler as Chancellor was a godsend to many among them, as well as to many of the people.

---

contract normally meant the forfeit of the entire sum deposited...270,000 people signed up to these contracts by the end of 1939...by the end of the war...340,000...the DAF netted 275 million Reichsmarks in deposits. But not a single Volkswagen was ever delivered to a civilian customer in the Third Reich. - *The Wages of Destruction: The Making and Breaking of the Nazi Economy* - Adam Tooze.

Why the Germans Lose at War – Kenneth Macksey

There was never any intention on Hitler's part to let sleeping dogs lie. He had been through too much in the Great War; he had won the Iron Cross First and Second Class for his bravery[36], but he had seen too much waste, too many killed and too much capitulation in the Treaty of Versailles to permit him to let it go.

> In 1933, Hitler ordered his army generals to prepare to treble the size of the army to 300,000 men...the Air Ministry to plan to build 1,000 war planes. Military buildings such as barracks were built. He withdrew from the Geneva Disarmament Conference when the French refused to accept his plan that the French should disarm to the level of the Germans or that the Germans should re-arm to the level of the French. Either way, the two main powers of Europe would be balanced. Hitler knew that the French would not accept his plan and therefore when he withdrew from the conference, he was seen by some as the politician who had a more realistic approach to foreign policy and the French were seen as the nation that had caused Nazi Germany to withdraw.

Germany And Rearmament - C N Trueman

Open rearmament commenced in 1935. The League of Nations was very annoyed and jolly well told him so.

> On 16 March 1935, Hitler publicly denounced the Treaty of Versailles and the German disarmament that came as a consequence of the treaty. The

---

[36] *Private Hitler's War* - Bob Carruthers

Fuehrer took advantage of the occasion to promulgate a new defense law that provided for an increase in the size of the peacetime Army to 12 corps and 36 divisions and reinstituted conscription. A subsequent law, of 21 May 1935, brought the Air Force into the open and established it as a separate service. The law of 21 May also set the period of training for conscripts at one year.

The German Campaign in Poland (1939) - Robert M. Kennedy

Also in violation of the Treaty of Versailles, Hitler publicly announced that the German Army was to be expanded. Conscription was introduced. By April 1936, the army numbers were at 530,000.

The navy had increased from 15,000 to 34,000 personnel while the actual tonnage of shipping, under the Anglo-German Naval Agreement of June, 1935 was permitted to go to 35% of whatever the British tonnage was and 45% of submarine tonnage. According to the *Sydney Herald* of February 1936, Germany's naval tonnage was still within the Versailles limits, consisting of 3 armoured cruisers of 10,000 tons, six cruisers at 6,000 tons each, 13 torpedo boats at 800 tons each, bringing the total to 75,600 tons. There were also 106,600 tons in construction, including two heavy cruisers at 10,000 tons each, the maximum weight permitted under the treaty. The whole tonnage, when completed would equal 181,100 tons or 66 vessels. It was thought that this would bring the submersible tonnage to higher than the permitted limits.

By 1939, Germany had 95 warships, 8,250 airplanes and an army of nearly 1,000,000 men. It also had 9 panzer divisions. Each one had 328 tanks, 8 support battalions and 6 artillery batteries. They had used the Spanish Civil War as a testing ground, both politically and mechanically.

It is probably safe to assume that by 1936 any thoughts that Germany might have had about sticking to the Treaty of

Versailles had gone out of the window. This was confirmed when, on 7 March, 1936, Germany invaded the Rhineland. This was the demilitarised area between France and Germany, as stated in the Locarno Treaty of 1925[37]. It was valuable for its coal, iron and steel resources and for this reason, along with its proximity to France, Belgium, Holland and Luxembourg, clearly came within Germany's *Lebensraum* remit. The League of Nations, once again, did nothing. When, in 1938, Germany declared *Anschluss* with Austria, it seemed that all the world could and would do was stand and watch. On 30 September 1938, not only did Britain stand and watch as Germany marched into the Sudetenland, it actually gave them permission to do so via the Munich Conference - without any reference to Czechoslovakia.

Appeasement

Was it appeasement by Chamberlain that allowed the march of Germany into the Sudetenland? And was it this appeasement that eventually led to the full invasion of Czechoslovakia (contrary to the Munich agreement) in March 1939, of Poland in September 1939 and the commencement of the Second World War in September 1939?

Chamberlain has had a rough ride over the years. He is always shown with the piece of paper in his hand, with the allusion to its being a yellow stripe down his back, but this is unfair. I would defy anyone to have come away from the Munich Conference with peace in any other way.

It is important to bear in mind that at this point Britain was not ready for another war. The people weren't ready, the

---

[37] While the Locarno Treaties (1925) reaffirmed the Versailles settlement's demarcation of borders in Western Europe, they left unanswered the question of Eastern European borders, heightening fears in Eastern European capitals that Germany's eastward expansion was tacitly approved by the western powers - *When states appease: British appeasement in the 1930s* - Trubowitz, Peter and Harris, Peter (2015). Review of International Studies, 41 (02).

government was split and the economy was fragile. Britain was by nature a negotiating nation, despite implications to the contrary in the acquisition of its empire and the trend in modern times to empire-bash. Prior to the 'piece of paper', appeasement had meant peace-making, was considered a positive policy and did not have the connotations applied to it post-1938. Chamberlain as Prime Minister had to take a Very British View in that he had to consider a whole empire of British interests, the brittleness of the economy, the voters and the voters not just as voters but as people, people who had been through the ghastliness of war only twenty years previously.

> To sum up, there were always such motives, moral, economic, strategic and domestic, operating in the public consciousness and prompting British governments from the mid-nineteenth century onwards to favour a foreign policy which was, with rare exceptions...pragmatic, conciliatory and reasonable. It was a policy predicated upon the assumption that, provided national interests were not too deleteriously affected, the peaceful settlement of disputes was much more to Britain's advantage than recourse to war. It was not merely in the 1930s, therefore, that "Peace as National Interest" is a valid description of Britain's overall strategy.
>
> *The Tradition of Appeasement in British Foreign Policy 1865-1939* – Paul M Kennedy. British Journal of International Studies 2 (1976). www.jstor.org

A similar approach had been taken in South Africa, Afghanistan, India and Ireland by Gladstone - 'a deliberate attempt to return to what he believed was the traditional moral and pragmatic basis of British policy...a particularly British form of diplomacy since the middle of the nineteenth century'[38]. Was King Alfred's payment of Danegeld not appeasement? Could you not say that King Stephen's agreement with Matilda in 1153, to allow her son Henry to take the throne (as Henry II) upon his death, thereby ending the 12th century Anarchy, was appeasement?

There were many reasons why Chamberlain chose appeasement over aggression. One was that the British people probably would not have tolerated it. The Great War was not forgotten, along with the social hardship that came with it, the social upheaval, the financial costs and, above all, the deaths.

To many of the world's leaders, including those in Europe, the Treaty of Versailles was too harsh and too humiliating. Yes, Germany had to be punished for the war, they had, to some extent, be made to pay and they had to be prevented from ever being the cause of another war. The Treaty of Versailles, however, was probably not the solution. It was too punitive, too degrading and gave Germany little chance of rebuilding itself with dignity. This is not said to excuse the Germans; they had been building up to a European war for many years, but their exclusion from post-war Europe made them view the peace as outsiders, as losers, emasculated them and, instead of giving them to become a part of the team, urged them on as self-serving agitators bent on revenge. Chamberlain genuinely wanted peace and knew that the way things had been handled were not inclusive or inducive to peace. He was left with little alternative but to offer more and more, probably in the knowledge that Germany would take and take until there was no more slack to take up.

Britain also needed Germany economically. Chamberlain was well aware of what an economic powerhouse Germany was and how much it could contribute to Europe. More importantly, it could contribute to the continued financial well-being of Britain with trade deals, not just in Europe, but world-wide.

Neither was Britain ready for war. Chamberlain and those

---

[38] *The Tradition of Appeasement in British Foreign Policy 1865-1939* – Paul M Kennedy. British Journal of International Studies 2 (1976). www.jstor.org

around him were not stupid; living in hope does not necessarily concede naivety, weakness or a lack of common sense. The fact was, as has been seen from the figures above, that Britain was behind Germany in the rearmament battle. The fact that spending had increased towards 1939 showed that Britain was prepar*ing*; not that it was prepared. Negotiation meant delay; delay meant time to prepare. Yes, in hindsight, we can see exactly what Germany was up to many years before the onset of the Second World War, and perhaps Britain, the USA and France should have been more aware and more united in putting a stop to the Nazi's progress, but even outside of the German build-up, the world was in chaos. Each of those countries had their own internal problems that much of the time had to be treated as a priority over things happening so far away.

There was also concern about Russia. It was now a fully-fledged dictatorship which had recently been through the murderous Great Purge. The communist threat was perhaps seen as an even greater threat than the fascist. Certainly, Germany gave no indication of any love for the Communists in any shape or form, but the German/Soviet non-aggression pact of 1939 was disturbing to both the British and the French as both Germany and Russia invaded Poland through September 1939.

The two countries had agreed not to attack each other, either alone or as part of an agreement with another country, or to lend any support to a third party who might attack either of them. On top of this, the pact secretly agreed the division of Eastern Europe into German and Russian sections and established a new German/Polish border. Was this a foreshadowing of things to come?

In the end, Chamberlain was left with little choice but to handle it the way he did. It was very easy for people to say 'told you so' after the event, but 20/20 vision is not a luxury many wartime politicians have. Had he gone to war in 1938, he would have been castigated for the cost and the empty bravado and, quite possibly, the loss incurred. Politically, he was never going to win and, in the end, probably did the best job that he could under the circumstances.

> Few scholars still hold to the belief that Chamberlain's efforts to appease Nazi Germany were shaped by naiveté or negligence. Chamberlain's actions are now understood as hardheaded (rational) political calculations...appeasement was an understandable if imperfect strategy to cope with unforgiving international circumstances...Appeasement is not a singular response to multiple international threats; nor is it wholly attributable to domestic factors...appeasement is best understood as a strategy that cross-pressured leaders use to reconcile geopolitical and domestic imperatives.
>
> *When States Appease: British Appeasement in the 1930s* - Trubowitz, Peter and Harris, Peter (2015). Review of International Studies, 41 (02).

On the 3 September, 1939, Chamberlain had the onerous task of telling the nation that it was now, once again, at war.

It is impossible to know how he felt as he delivered the speech. He must have been exhausted, in just over a year he would be dead from colo-rectal cancer. Nowadays we might suppose that it had been brought on by stress; it must have been an enormous burden upon him. He must have felt saddened, dejected, isolated, as if he had failed.

On that Sunday morning, at 11.15, people gathered by their wirelesses in their thousands; mothers and daughters, fathers and sons, friends and neighbours, in silence and trepidation, and listened to his speech.

> This morning the British Ambassador in Berlin handed the German Government a final note stating that, unless we heard from them by 11 o'clock that they were prepared at once to withdraw their troops from Poland, a state of war would exist

between us.

I have to tell you now that no such undertaking has been received, and that consequently this country is at war with Germany.

You can imagine what a bitter blow it is to me that all my long struggle to win peace has failed. Yet I cannot believe that there is anything more or anything different that I could have done and that would have been more successful.

Up to the very last it would have been quite possible to have arranged a peaceful and honourable settlement between Germany and Poland, but Hitler would not have it. He had evidently made up his mind to attack Poland whatever happened, and although he now says he put forward reasonable proposals which were rejected by the Poles, that is not a true statement. The proposals were never shown to the Poles, nor to us, and, although they were announced in a German broadcast on Thursday night, Hitler did not wait to hear comments on them, but ordered his troops to cross the Polish frontier. His action shows convincingly that there is no chance of expecting that this man will ever give up his practice of using force to gain his will. He can only be stopped by force.

We and France are today, in fulfilment of our obligations, going to the aid of Poland, who is so bravely resisting this wicked and unprovoked attack on her people. We have a clear conscience. We have done all that any country could do to establish peace. The situation in which no word given by Germany's ruler could be trusted and no people or country could feel themselves safe has become intolerable. And now that we have resolved to finish it, I know that you will all play your part with calmness and courage.

At such a moment as this the assurances of support that we have received from the Empire are a source of profound encouragement to us.

The Government have made plans under which it will be possible to carry on the work of the nation in the days of stress and strain that may be ahead. But these plans need your help. You may be taking your part in the fighting services or as a volunteer in one of the branches of Civil Defence. If so you will report for duty in accordance with the instructions you have received. You may be engaged in work essential to the prosecution of war for the maintenance of the life of the people - in factories, in transport, in public utility concerns, or in the supply of other necessaries of life. If so, it is of vital importance that you should carry on with your jobs.

Now may God bless you all. May He defend the right. It is the evil things that we shall be fighting against - brute force, bad faith, injustice, oppression and persecution - and against them I am certain that the right will prevail.

Part Two
INTO SERVICE

The Phoney War?

There has always been a tremendous comfort to be found in being an island. It has, at the very least, given the illusion of security.

The reality, to be seen in the Roman invasions from 54 BC onwards, the Viking incursions of the 8th and 9th centuries, the determined usurpation of the throne by William the Conqueror in 1066, the return from exile and usurpation of Richard II's throne by Henry IV in 1399, the usurpation of Richard III by Henry VII in 1485, the destruction of British craft by the Dutch in the Thames in 1667 and the 'invasion' of William of Orange in 1688, all of which started beyond our coastline, is far from comfortable. If history proved anything, it was that, with a bit of planning, almost anyone, from almost anywhere, could land almost anywhere in the British Isles and hoist their flag. It was up to us to be prepared for it, to *expect* it.

It left Britain, England especially, in a mildly paranoid state, where we were constantly looking over our shoulder, towards the coast and out to sea, onwards to the far horizon in search of distant dark dots. We became rather xenophobic through our fears; some might say, isolationist. We patrolled our seas diligently and built our navy on the need to protect our shores. We are constantly reminded of the victories of our greatest sailors – Nelson at the Nile and Trafalgar, Drake against the Armada, the victory at Sluys – and we are reminded too of the great land battles of Waterloo, Rorke's Drift, Salamanca, Agincourt, Crécy, Poitiers and Plassey among many others.

The Great War of 1914-1918 did little to reduce our fear of 'outsiders'. The conflagration that set light to even the remotest parts of Europe and even managed to bring death directly to our island, merely made us even more grateful for the pond between us and the European continent and served to unite us. To get to us, the opposition had to have resources; transport, manpower, coal, wood and iron; they had to have money; they had to have the willpower, the drive, that was needed to send them overseas into an inhospitable land overlooked by high cliffs and ancient ramparts, that was almost unassailable even after the giant moat had been crossed. It gave us a certain confidence. We would see them before they saw us. We could finish our game of bowls and still have time for a leisurely pipe on the sun-soaked white cliffs before the navy growled and scudded across the white-topped waves and sent the enemy to the depths.

Yes, it was an illusion, to a certain degree but, at the very least, it provided a period of delay, a time to think, especially when considering the footprints and bones left in the long-dry mud of France.

Within half an hour of Chamberlain's reluctant declaration of war on that quiet September Sunday morning of 1939, at 11.28 am, the air raid sirens went off. It was a false alarm caused by an unidentified allied aircraft (and perhaps an, understandably, overly twitchy finger) but it still sent a chill of panic through the nation. Churches were suddenly vacated mid-service and people ran from the streets to find cover.

It was all indicative of an underlying tension that had been building since the mid-thirties and the onset of Nazism. Despite the well-intentioned Chamberlain's return from Munich in 1938 with a piece of paper in his hand and the veneer of relief in the newspapers and on people's faces, there was still a nagging sense that war was inevitable.

The country had already begun to take tentative steps towards a war-footing. Leaflets abounded, rumours abounded more, gas-marks were being carried around like lunchboxes, shelters were being prepared, windows taped, bumpers whitewashed and evacuations commenced.

And yet, for nearly a year after the declaration, nothing seemed to happen. It has been described as the nation holding its breath and, as time went on, the nation began to slowly exhale in the false hope that maybe, just maybe, the war wouldn't happen at all.

Such was the Phoney War, the *Drôle de Guerre*, the 'funny war', as the French called it or *Sitzkrieg*, the 'sitting war', as the Germans called it.

The name Phoney War possibly came from US Senator William Borah who, in September 1939, when faced by the apparent dormancy in Europe, said, 'There is something phoney about this war.' This period of uncertainty lasted from 3 September 1939 to May 1940 and ended almost as abruptly as it had begun.

As it turned out, there was really nothing phoney about it at all.

The State of Military Readiness in Britain in 1939

> ...in northwest Europe the Allied leaders invited their ground troops to fight the Wehrmacht with equipment inferior in every category save artillery and transport. German machine-guns, mortars, machine-pistols, antitank weapons and armoured personnel carriers were all superior to those of Britain and America. Above all, Germany possessed better tanks.
>
> *Their Wehrmacht Was Better Than Our Army* - Max Hastings: Washington Post. May 1985.

We have seen that there was an increase in military spending by the British in the run up to the war. It took a few years to catch up with the Germans' spending but, come the war, it overtook it. This however, was no indication of technical strength and the Germans had managed to get a head start in this arena by the initially secret build-up of the *Luftwaffe* - they had three times more single engine fighter planes than the British at the turn of war – and by the development of the Tiger and Panther tanks; the tanks had greater firepower and better armour but were more prone to breaking down. In the end, the American capacity for the production-line enabled them to build vastly more tanks than the Germans and support those tanks with air power. We didn't get our superb Centurion tanks until 1945 when the war was all but over. It is generally agreed that the tanks that the British army had at the beginning of the war were not fit for purpose. They were unreliable or rushed into service or perhaps unreliable *because* they were rushed into service. Indeed, from 1943, the British were equipped with the American Sherman Tank. It wasn't perfect by a long way and nowhere near as good as what the opposition had on offer, but the wonderous American production line ensured a regular and large supply of the vehicle.

So, cornered by the desire for peace, an out-of-date defensive system, financial worries, the teeth-baring aggression of European fascism and now conflict, the allies had some catching up to do – quickly.

The Army

However, it wasn't just about the hardware. It was also about the manpower, for without the required volume of the appropriately skilled people on the ground, all the machinery in the world meant nothing.

To start with, the British army was made up of the regular army and what was then called the Territorial Army (now called the Army Reserve). The reserve comprised 204,000 officers and men[39].

The regular army comprised 227,000 men[40], but much of the regular army was spread across the world. There were 56,000 troops in India and 14,000 other men in garrisons across the world, along with 21,000 in the Mediterranean and the Middle East. In the UK there were 107,000 regulars. By the end of September 1939, there were 160,000 troops in France and by the time of the Dunkirk rescue, 380,000.[41] The total number of men

---

[39] According to *The British Army Handbook 1939-1945* by George Forty, the TA field force numbered 325,000 with 96,000 Anti-Aircraft units.
[40] 224,000 in April 1939 according to *The British Army Handbook 1939-1945* by George Forty
[41] *The Making of the British Army* – Allan Mallinson

under arms was 645,000.

The difficulty though came from the fact that none of the leaders of this modern army had really seen combat. The leaders of the Great War had, as was the nature of the nineteenth century, seen some form of conflict. It had been twenty years since the end of the Great War, those who were supposed to become the guiding light of the new army generation had been killed. Despite modern beliefs, the officers in the Great War *had* led from the front and had died doing so, so when the time for battle came in World War Two, such as when the troops were sent abroad in the time leading up to Dunkirk, there was a lack of experienced, battle-hardened leaders.

> The First World War had taken the cream of our manhood. Those that had fallen were the born leaders of men, in command of companies or battalions. It was always the best that fell by taking the lead. Those that we had lost as subalterns, captains and majors in the First World War were the very ones we were short of as colonels, brigadiers and generals.
>
> Lieutenant-General Alan Brooke – Quoted from *The Making of the British Army* – Allan Mallinson

The army, a complicated device with many roots and branches, can be broken down, with wonderful simplicity, into what is called the 'teeth and tail', an American phrase intended to distinguish between the combat (the Arms) part of the force and the service part (the Services) of the force. Without the 'tail', it has to be said, the army would have had its 'teeth' pulled, so vital was the 'behind the scenes' contribution of the service end of the army.

The Combat Arms – The Teeth

The Combat Arms section consisted of the:

Household Cavalry

The Household Cavalry is today formed by the British Army's two most senior regiments: The Life Guards and The Blues & Royals. The Blues and Royals were themselves formed in 1969 from the merger of the Royal Horse Guards and the Royal Dragoons.

In September 1939, the Life Guards and Royal Horse Guards formed the Household Cavalry Composite Regiment and the Household Cavalry Training Regiment. The Household Cavalry Composite Regiment was a temporary, war-time only cavalry regiment. In 1940, these regiments were reorganised into the 1st and 2nd Household Cavalry Regiments; they were disbanded in 1945 and returned to their original regiments. The Second World War forced mechanisation upon the regiment – Hitler was up to date by comparison – to the point where the Secretary of State for War (1935-1937), Duff Cooper, felt obliged to apologise for the mechanisation of the cavalry, as if replacing horses with tanks was a pointless and deliberately offensive move. The fact of the matter was that, if Hitler was to be beaten, horses no longer cut the mustard.

It saw service in the Middle-East from February 1940 onwards and, as was (is) the chameleon-like way of the army, in November 1940 the Household Cavalry Composite Regiment changed to become the 1st Household Cavalry Motor Battalion.

Royal Armoured Corps

The RAC was founded on 4 April 1939 by Leslie Hore-Belisha, the Secretary of State for War. It combined regiments from the eighteen mechanised cavalry regiments and the Royal Tank Corps (later to be known at the Royal Tank Regiment). As the war progressed and other regular cavalry and Territorial Army Yeomanry units became mechanised, the corps expanded. In 1944, the Reconnaissance Corps became a part of the RAC.

Royal Regiment of Artillery

At the beginning of 1939 the Royal Artillery totalled about 105,000. By 1943 it had 700,000 men [42]. Artillery had always been an integral part of the British Army and has often been seen as the deciding factor in many of the great battles, including Bosworth in 1485 and Waterloo in 1815.

The importance and use of artillery became notorious in the Great War as the war of attrition set in and attempts were made by both sides to simply pound the enemy into submission or to clear the lines before an advance.

> The artillery increased enormously as the war went on...In 1914 Britain manufactured ninety-one guns or howitzers; in 1918 industry provided 10,680. In 1914 the Royal Artillery had 554 batteries in all theatres; by 1918 there were 1,796...It has been calculated that the Royal Artillery fired over 170 million rounds on the Western Front between 1914 and 1918.
>
> *Mud, Blood and Poppycock* – Gordon Corrigan

Their value, both in practical terms and in terms of sheer intimidation, was difficult to beat.

There is a wonderful diagram in Corrigan's book which shows the range of artillery in the Great War. It is a pertinent example of the ability to commit distant war and therefore lower the risk of losses due to close combat and a hint at the shape of things to come, where today we don't even have to be in the same country to pinpoint a target.

The range of the 12-inch Howitzer was 14,350 yards, the equivalent of Trafalgar Square to the outskirts of Croydon, about 8.5 miles. That is a phenomenal distance. It might be considered a

---

[42] *Unit History: Royal Artillery* - www.forces-war-records.co.uk

trifling distance today, but back then it was a laser point on the surface of the moon.

Corps of Royal engineers

The Sappers, as they were called, were possibly the renaissance men of the army. They were a highly skilled group of men who could turn their hand from work such as defensive construction work to mine-laying and clearing. Without the engineers there would have been no railways or roads or airfields and without those there would have been no supplies sent to the troops in the forward lines, no way for military vehicles to get into places that were previously inaccessible and no replacement troops.

Their role is neatly summed up by George Forty in *The British Army Handbook 1939-1945*:

> The Sappers...performed a wide variety of tasks in support of the field army...construction...of defences...mine-laying and clearing; bridge building...demolitions; the building, operating and maintenance of camps, roads, railways, airfields...including ports; specialised tasks including the purification of water – even the running of the military postal system...Mobile bath and laundry, salvage, bomb disposal and chemical warfare.

Such was the size of their remit that their personnel grew to over three times its original 1939 size by 1945; 90,000 to 280,000. During the Second World War they lost 25,000 personnel, among which were 750 from Bomb Disposal, more than half as many again as the tally of British aircrew who died during the Battle of Britain[43].

---

[43] *The men who ran towards the bombs: The Blitz heroes who saved countless lives defusing UXBs* - James Owen Daily Mail, 9 September 2010

Royal Corps of Signals

Where would any industry be without effective communications? Today, we have more ways to communicate than we have ever had, most of it wireless, small and extraordinarily portable.

The Royal Corps of Signals, which grew from the Royal Engineers Signal Service, had the responsibility of all the communications within the army, which included radio, wire, telegraph and teleprinter.

During the Second World War, the corps had over 150,000 members. It was, extraordinarily, the first British unit to see action during the Second World War when 12 Royal Signalmen had been sent to Poland just before the outbreak of war to see what could be done should an attack occur. By sheer coincidence, they arrived on the day war broke out and had the dubious honour of being the first British unit to see action in the Second World War.

The corps lost 4,362 members during World War Two. They were often first in and last out and were involved in some of the most secret, sensitive work of the war.

Infantry Regiments

It might be useful at this point to explain the structure of the army. It might equally not be as there seems to be a conspiracy of some sort to avoid giving a direct answer to the direct question, 'How many units are there in the army and how many people make up each unit?'

Of course, it's not a conspiracy, interesting though that would be, but the answer, quite simply, varies from country to country and from time to time; each unit can be enlarged or reduced to suit the needs, both financially and militarily, of a country at any given time.

The table below gives an indication of what were the generally accepted figures for the various units of the British army.

UNIT NAME	CONSISTS OF:	APPROX NUMBER OF MEN	COMMANDED BY
ARMY	2 or more Corps	100,000-150,000	Field Marshall Or General
CORPS	2 or more Divisions	25,000-50,000	General or Lt General
DIVISION	3 or more Brigades or Regiments	10,000-15,000	Lt General or Maj General
BRIGADE	3 or more Battalions	1500-3500	Maj Gen or Brig Colonel
REGIMENT	2 or more Battalions	1000-2000	Colonel
BATTALION	4 or more Companies	400-1000	Lt Colonel
COMPANY	2 or more Platoons	100-250	Captain or Major
PLATOON	2 or more Squads	16-50	1st Lt
SQUAD	2 or more Sections	8-24	Sergeant
SECTION		4-12	Sergeant

When the war began, the infantry consisted of five regiments of foot guards and sixty-four infantry regiments. To complicate the above table a little further, George Forty in *The British Army Handbook 1939-1945* says, 'most regiments consisted of two army battalions (one at home and one abroad) and from two to five TA battalions'. This could be further complicated by the specialisation within types of infantry battalions. Forty continues:

For instance, the basic infantry battalion was known as a 'rifle battalion', but when they were regularly carried in permanently allotted RASC transport (3 tonners) they became a 'motorised battalion'. It was these motorised battalions that formed the infantry brigade in the armoured division.

Later in the war, even more specialised units grew, such as the Parachute Regiments, Gliderborne Forces, the Special Forces and Commandos, such as the SAS and the Long Range Desert Group, and Intelligence, which was responsible for security among its own troops and the interrogation of any captured enemy.

Obviously, these six arms of the combat service were further broken down into smaller sections, each section meeting a particular need. This would be a book of its own and comprises a mind-bendingly complicated family tree far outside the remit of this book, which is intended to look at the effects of the events of the war upon the nation rather than the fascinating construction of the services. It is important to remember however that, for every member of every force going to the war, whether for training on home soil or abroad, there was one less person in the home or among the employed to keep industry rolling. It was all pebbles and ripples.

However, each of these sections had a role and it would have been a shame to mention them so briefly without having defined them.

The British Expeditionary Force and Dunkirk

It's difficult to talk about the early days of World War Two and the army without mentioning the British Expeditionary Force, its disastrous tour in France and celebrated return.

Once again, to go into the subject in any but the most

cursory detail would necessitate the felling of many trees and the creation of a thick tome of its own, which has been done very well by better than me, though I think it would though be remiss of me to bypass the matter entirely.

As already mentioned, the allies had amassed about 380,000 troops. There was no doubting their commitment but, when it came to the German offensive, the *Blitzkrieg*[44], we were found to be sorely lacking, both in preparedness and in hardware.

The lack of preparedness partly came as a hangover from the Great War. There was a belief that the advance across Europe would be a slow one and that there would be a 'digging in', similar to the Great War. The allies thinking was still dominated by the defensive role. The French army was sent to the Maginot Line, the heavily fortified border with Germany, to await a German attack. The BEF was sent to join the French troops defending the border with Belgium. It was simply a non-proactive approach.

This was the difference between the allies and their opponents. The Germans were willing and very able to take the initiative. What they had not had in the Great War was the mechanisation and there is a feeling that, had they had so, the outcome in 1914-18 would have been very different as they had a far more assertive approach than the allies.

The British quickly crossed the French/Belgian border and headed for the Dyle River as part of what was called the Dyle Plan.

> They were not there for long. The Belgian forts fell more quickly than in 1914, for the Germans did not tend to repeat obvious mistakes: they took Fort Eben Emael in a brilliant coup de main by parachute and glider troops...the Dutch...capitulated...leaving the Dyle's northern flank open.

---

[44] The first known use of the word blitzkrieg in an English publication occurred in an article in Time magazine on September 25, 1939.

The Making of the British Army – Allan Mallinson

The Germans, packed with over 800 tanks, surged through the Ardennes in the south and the allies were forced into a retreat.

The powerful components of the German army were described by Churchill in the House of Commons:

> However, the German eruption swept like a sharp scythe around the right and rear of the Armies of the north. Eight or nine armoured divisions, each of about 400 armoured vehicles of different kinds, but carefully assorted to be complementary and divisible into small self-contained units, cut off all communications between us and the main French Armies. It severed our own communications for food and ammunition, which ran first to Amiens and afterwards through Abbeville, and it shore its way up the coast to Boulogne and Calais, and almost to Dunkirk. Behind this armoured and mechanised onslaught came a number of German divisions in lorries, and behind them again there plodded comparatively slowly the dull brute mass of the ordinary German Army and German people, always so ready to be led to the trampling down in other lands of liberties and comforts which they have never known in their own. I have said this armoured scythe-stroke almost reached Dunkirk—almost but not quite. Boulogne and Calais were the scenes of desperate fighting. The Guards 788 defended Boulogne for a while and were then withdrawn by orders from this country. The Rifle Brigade, the 60th Rifles, and the Queen Victoria's Rifles, with a battalion of British tanks and 1,000 Frenchmen, in all about 4,000 strong, defended Calais to the last. The British Brigadier was given an hour to surrender. He spurned the offer, and

four days of intense street fighting passed before silence reigned over Calais, which marked the end of a memorable resistance. Only 30 unwounded survivors were brought off by the Navy and we do not know the fate of their comrades. Their sacrifice, however, was not in vain. At least two armoured divisions, which otherwise would have been turned against the British Expeditionary Force, had to be sent for to overcome them. They have added another page to the glories of the Light Division, and the time gained enabled the Graveline waterlines to be flooded and to be held by the French troops.

Winston Churchill to the House of Commons, 3.40 pm, 04 June 1940[45]

Nine German divisions stormed through the Netherlands and Belgium. 2,400 tanks in seven divisions cut through the right flank of the allies and carried on relentlessly towards the Channel.

We all know what happened next. 338,000 men were evacuated from Dunkirk by boats both big and small. It was the greatest rescue ever and possibly the greatest sense of victory ever seized from the maws of defeat. More than 700 private vessels were used as part of Operation Dynamo, the operation to evacuate the forces from Dunkirk.

It is estimated by the War Office that 66,980 men were killed, wounded or missing between 10th May 1940 and the last day of evacuation in June 1940. This equated to about 1 in 3 of the BEF. There are horror stories, of course. There was the 'massacre of Le Paradis', where 97 soldiers who had surrendered to the Germans were murdered on the orders of the SS. Two survivors, Privates William O'Callaghan and Albert Pooley, told their tale upon their return to Britain, but were not believed. Fritz

---

[45] War Situation. HC Deb 04 June 1940 vol 361 cc787-98 -www.api.parliament.uk/

Knöchlein, a SS commander, was convicted and executed in 1949 for this and other war crimes.

Over one thousand civilians around Dunkirk were killed, 126 merchant seamen died during the evacuation and about 40,000 British troops were taken prisoner. The allies left behind 2,472 guns, 63,879 vehicles, 20,548 motorcycles, 76,097 tons of ammunition, 416,940 tons of stores, all of which were utilised by the Germans. On 29 May the destroyer Wakeful was torpedoed with the loss of 600 lives.

However, it is the greatness of the achievement that is remembered; 98,780 men were lifted from the beach at Dunkirk and 239,446 from the mole, the wooden harbour that stretched out into the sea where the water had enough depth to take large boats.

It was a savage learning experience. The allies would have to change their mentality and their hardware. The speed and viciousness, the uncompromising determination of the Germans would have to be equalled and then exceeded.

Dunkirk marked the end of the 'Phoney War', if ever such a thing had existed. It was a wake-up call, both to the leaders and the people.

> The whole question of home defence against invasion is, of course, powerfully affected by the fact that we have for the time being in this island incomparably more powerful military forces than we have ever had at any moment in this war or the last. But this will not continue. We shall not be content with a defensive war. We have our duty to our Ally. We have to reconstitute and build up the British Expeditionary Force once again...All this is in train; but in the interval we must put our defences in this island into such a high state of organisation that the fewest possible numbers will be required to give effective security and that the largest possible potential of offensive effort may be realised...I have, myself, full confidence that if all

do their duty, if nothing is neglected, and if the best arrangements are made, as they are being made, we shall prove ourselves once again able to defend our island home, to ride out the storm of war, and to outlive the menace of tyranny, if necessary for years, if necessary alone...We shall go on to the end. We shall fight in France, we shall fight on the seas and oceans, we shall fight with growing confidence and growing strength in the air, we shall defend our island, whatever the cost may be. We shall fight on the beaches, we shall fight on the landing grounds, we shall fight in the fields and in the streets, we shall fight in the hills; we shall never surrender, and even if, which I do not for a moment believe, this island or a large part of it were subjugated and starving, then our Empire beyond the seas, armed and guarded by the British Fleet, would carry on the struggle, until, in God's good time, the new world, with all its power and might, steps forth to the rescue and the liberation of the old.

Winston Churchill to the House of Commons, 3.40 pm, 04 June 1940[46]

The Services – The Tail

Without some sort of back up, whether it was in the delivery of hardware, of food, of health and welfare (physical and spiritual), of discipline or of that most important of items, pay, the front lines could not have functioned. Part of the allies' plan to defeat the Germans was to disrupt and eventually cut off their supplies by bombing railways and fuel depots, and it worked. The Germans had tried to do it to the allies by the sinking of merchant vessels and had very nearly succeeded.

---

[46] War Situation. HC Deb 04 June 1940 vol 361 cc787-98 - www.api.parliament.uk/

These services, the 'tail' of the service arms, consisted of a whole host of services.

1. The Royal Army Chaplains Department
2. The Royal Army Service Corps
3. The Royal Army Medical Corps
4. The Royal Army Ordnance Corps
5. The Royal Mechanical and Electrical Engineers
6. The Royal Army Pay Corps
7. The Royal Army Veterinary Corps
8. The Army Educational Corps
9. The Army Dental Corps
10. The Pioneer Corps
11. The Intelligence Corps
12. The Army Catering Corps
13. The Army Physical Training Corps
14. The Corps of Military Police
15. The Military Provost Staff Corps
16. Queen Alexandra's Imperial Nursing Service
17. The Auxiliary Territorial Service
18. The Officers' Training Corps
19. The General Service Corps[47]

Many of them are self-explanatory, but it is the scale of the support that impresses. The Army Catering Corps, for example, in 1944-45, had to transport 14,363 tons of food from base to admin area to supply the 53rd (Welsh) Infantry Battalion in North West Europe in order to create over six million rations. This was just one area of an ongoing war. Multiply that by a worldwide need for sustenance (their motto is 'We Sustain'; not particularly full of gravitas, but accurate) and the organisation required from manufacture to mealtime must have been mindboggling.

The Army Dental Corps, surely one of the most shunned of corps until the pain became too much, was not simply there to

---

[47] *The British Army Handbook 1939-1945* – George Forty

pull the odd mouldy molar. At the extreme end of their role they were involved in maxillofacial surgery before the injured were shipped out. On top of this, the Dental Corps was required to visit all units to provide a dental service. This was the bread and butter of their role; poor teeth quite often led to poor diet and poor diet could affect performance. Even toothache which, if you have suffered it, manages to take over the entire body and every waking moment, can render a soldier inoperable. Many Army Dental Corps personnel were attached to field ambulances, casualty clearing stations or general hospitals. Many became prisoners-of-war as they remained with the sick and wounded.

The Royal Army Ordnance Corps was responsible for the procurement and issue of all ordnance stores. Until 1942 it was both a supply and repair corps. It had responsibility for weapons, armoured vehicles and other military equipment, ammunition and clothing and certain minor functions such as laundry, mobile baths and photography. The corps was also responsible for a major element of the repair of Army equipment, but this was later transferred to the Royal Electrical and Mechanical Engineers and the vehicle storage and spares responsibilities of the Royal Army Service Corps[48]. The Ordnance Department supplied 47 billion rounds of small-arms ammunition, 11 million tons of artillery ammunition, 12 million rifles and carbines, and 3.5 million military vehicles (it lost all of its own vehicles when they were abandoned in the run up to the Dunkirk evacuation). Once again, the organisation required to ship this around the world must have been incredible. By the end of the war, it was made up of 138,000 members and had lost over 5,000.

These three corps are highlighted for no more reason than they were randomly picked from the above list. Each of the above-mentioned required the same devotion to duty and the same brilliant organisational brains behind them in order to function and to send their services around the world. They are all equally deserving of mention and I would heartily recommend George Forty's *The British Army Handbook 1939-1945* as a starting

---

[48] www.lbmhs.co.uk/raoc_history

point.

The Royal Navy

> There was no 'phoney war' at sea...The hostilities commenced...within hours of war being declared...New technologies had changed naval warfare...Experiences from WW1 had been forgotten or were ignored - on both sides - while many of the new technologies were inadequately tested and tactics for their optimal use had not been developed. Above all, the aircraft had come of age and would play a role in both land and sea warfare beyond what most naval minds had been able to comprehend.
>
> *The Gathering Storm* – Geirr H Haarr

The 'Senior Service' (my father smoked that particular brand of cigarette), as it was known, was at the top of its form. It genuinely did rule the waves and was the most powerful navy in the world.

Britain had been fighting at sea since King Alfred's time, when it had fought against the invading Vikings. The navy had a towering history behind it; Trafalgar, Sluys, the Armada, the Nile and, not so far into the past, the battle of Jutland in 1916.

Jutland was controversial (it still is) because the British lost nearly twice the tonnage the Germans did, including three battlecruisers and three armoured cruisers and still won. The Allies also lost over twice as many men among the 9,823 deaths, 6,784 of them British and 3,039 German losses. Yet, the British still considered it a victory because, after the Germans had limped back to port minus eleven ships, the British remained upon that icy patch of sea and made it theirs. It was a typically defiant stance, characteristically stubborn and one that turned the horror of the worst kinds of death into a tight fist of victory.

In 1939, Britain had an impressive navy and possessed not

only the largest fleet of any of the war's protagonists, but also had the largest network of naval bases.

> In September 1939 the allies possessed a substantial superiority at sea over Germany. The combined British and French navies materially far exceeded the strength of the Kriegsmarine - as yet many of its warships remained uncompleted. Germany's unfavourable geostrategic position compounded its inferiority at sea...With allied command of the sea assured, the focus of naval operations was on the protection of maritime communications...
>
> *The War at Sea: A Naval Atlas – 1939-1945* – Marcus Faulkner

Personnel-wise, the navy was made up of three separate parts; the Royal Naval Volunteer Reserve (RNVR), the Royal Naval Reserve (RNR) and those in the regular navy.

The difference between the RNR and RNVR was that the RNR contained professional seamen from the merchant navy and fishing fleets or those with previous service; the RNVR comprised civilian volunteers who weren't professional seamen but were officers who had volunteered to join the service since the war began or joined the navy after conscription. The two were merged in 1958 to become the RNR.

Before the war started, the navy had 9,962 officers and 109,720 ratings to its numbers. There were 51,485 men in the Royal Fleet Reserve, 10,038 in the RNR (who were mostly in the Merchant Navy) and 2,049 in the RNVR.

Those ratings who had joined up voluntarily for the length of the war and not for the usual fixed term of service were known as 'hostility ratings' and usually went into the RNVR.

The Navy members were divided into branches:

    i.   The Seaman's Branch
    ii.   Engineering

iii. Medical
iv. Supply
v. Instructional
vi. Paymasters
vii. Chaplains[49].

The Board of the Admiralty was in control of the navy. The board was made up of both military and civilian members, the primary member being the First Lord, who was a cabinet minister. At the beginning of the war, this was Winston Churchill, who surrendered the role in 1940 when he became Prime Minister. As First Lord, he would have been assisted by the Naval Secretary and two junior politicians. The Naval Secretary was a junior flag officer[50] who had the specific role of helping the First Lord in the appointment and promotion of officers. The two politicians were the Parliamentary and Financial Secretary, responsible for overseeing the Admiralty's budget, and the Civil Lord, in charge of works and building and Admiralty contracts and dockyards. The chief civil servant was the permanent secretary, who looked after the Admiralty's bureaucratic side and its correspondence.

Day to day running of the Royal Navy was overseen by five Sea Lords who were all naval officers with a particular area of responsibility:

1. First Sea Lord and Chief of the Naval Staff: the First Sea Lord acted as the Chief of Naval Staff and was the professional head of the service.
2. Second Sea Lord and Chief of Naval Personnel
3. Third Sea Lord and Controller
4. Fourth Sea Lord and Chief of Supplies and Transport
5. Fifth Sea Lord and Chief of Naval Air Services

---

[49] *Encyclopedia of World War II, Volume 1* - Alan Axelrod, Jack A. Kingston
[50] A flag officer is a commissioned officer senior enough to be entitled to fly a flag to mark the position from which the officer exercises command.

There was also the Deputy Chief of the Naval Staff on the board, whose role was to assist the First Sea Lord and, along with the Director of Naval Intelligence, was responsible for plans[51].

Collectively, during the war this group was known as the Lords Commissioners of the Admiralty. At the commencement of the war on 3 September 1939, the members of the commission were:

- Winston Churchill, First Lord
- Sir Dudley Pound, First Sea Lord
- Sir Charles Little, Second Sea Lord
- Bruce Fraser, Third Sea Lord
- Geoffrey Arbuthnot, Fourth Sea Lord
- The Hon. Sir Alexander Ramsay, Fifth Sea Lord
- Tom Phillips, Deputy Chief of Naval Staff
- Harold Burrough, Assistant Chief of Naval Staff
- Geoffrey Hithersay Shakespeare, Parliamentary and Financial Secretary to the Admiralty
- Austin Uvedale Morgan Hudson, Civil Lord

Come May 1940, the one change was the First Lord – Winston Churchill, now Prime Minister, had been replaced by A. V. Alexander.

The remarkable thing about the Royal Navy is that pre-war and during the war (never mind the post-war traumas) it was required to go through tremendous changes in a very short space of time and proved itself very adaptable to altered circumstances. It was necessarily spread across the world - it had an empire to watch over - and was burdened by an incredibly complex organisation. The sheer volume of hardware and manpower involved in the service made its very existence an admirable achievement; to put it into the turmoil of war, to keep it manned, armed, fed and effective and able to react quickly to events was

---

[51] *The Royal Navy's Home Fleet in World War 2* - J. Levy

nothing short of miraculous. To adapt however, during 1939, forces were extracted from the more distant areas and deployed in smaller units to enable them to cover greater areas of ocean.

The navy had five main objectives:

1. The defence of trade routes and convoy organisation and escort, especially to and from Britain.
2. The detection and destruction of surface raiders and U-boats.
3. The maritime blockade of Germany and contraband control.
4. The defence of own coasts.
5. To escort troops to France and between Britain, the Dominions and other areas under Allied control[52].

To achieve these objectives, battleships from the Great War had been modernised and orders made for new ships. The navy had 1,400 vessels at its disposal including:

- 7 aircraft carriers:

   i. HMS Ark Royal - torpedoed 13 November and sunk 14 November 1941. 1 crew member lost.
   ii. HMS Courageous - struck by three torpedoes and sunk 17 September 1939. 518 crew lost.
   iii. HMS Glorious - sunk by gunfire 8 June 1940. Approx 1500 crew lost.
   iv. HMS Furious - placed in reserve 1944.
   v. HMS Eagle - hit by four torpedoes and sunk 11 August 1942. 260 crew lost.
   vi. HMS Hermes - hit by 40 bombs and sunk 9 April 1942. 300 crew lost.
   vii. HMS Argus - decommissioned 1942.

---

[52] www.naval-history.net

There were five more carriers under construction.

- 15 battleships and battlecruisers

i. 5 Elizabeth Class - HMS Queen Elizabeth, HMS Warspite, HMS Valiant, HMS Barham, HMS Malaya, HMS Agincourt – with 5 more under construction
ii. 5 Royal Sovereign (or Revenge) Class - HMS Revenge, HMS Resolution, HMA Royal Oak, HMS Royal Sovereign, HMS Ramillies
iii. 2 Renown Class – HMS Renown, HMS Repulse
iv. 1 Hood Class – HMS Hood
v. 2 Nelson Class – HMS Nelson, HMS Rodney

There were 5 more under construction.

- 66 cruisers – with 23 more under construction
- 184 destroyers – with 52 under construction
- 45 escort and patrol vessels – with 9 under construction and one on order
- 60 submarines – with 9 under construction
- 123 Miscellaneous - under miscellaneous are minesweepers, sloops, frigates, torpedo boats and various supply vessels or squadron motherships.

At this point, it might be useful to break down some definitions used at the beginning of the Second World War:

- A Fleet was a group of ships of more than one type led by a capital ship.
- A capital ship is one of the largest ships such as a battleship, battle cruiser, or aircraft carrier. These were run by captains.
- Squadrons were groups of between two and nine ships under a rear-admiral.

- A Flotilla was a group of the same type of ship. In charge of each ship was a commander, but there was one ship that was led by a captain, a rear admiral or a commodore depending upon the importance of the flotilla.
- A flotilla was divided into Divisions – a division was usually commanded by some of the rank of at least lieutenant.

The hierarchy of the Royal Navy goes something like this:

Officer/Commissioned Ranks
Admiral of the Fleet
Admiral
Vice-Admiral
Rear-Admiral
Commodore
Captain
Commander
Lieutenant-Commander
Lieutenant
Sub-Lieutenant
Midshipman

Enlisted Ranks/Non-Commissioned Ranks
Warrant Officer 1
Warrant Officer 2
Chief Petty Officer
Petty Officer
Leading Hand/Leading Rate[53]
Able Rate
Ordinary Rate/Rating/Junior

---

[53] There is, after researching many sources, a bit of difference among the names of the lower ranks. What you see from Leading Hand down is an amalgam of the titles by which those of these ranks are known. Apologies to any of those ranks who might be offended by the choice of title.

The Royal Navy was split into fleets which enabled it to cover the world and allocate resources effectively. Each fleet was run from a base such as Scapa Flow or Alexandria, though still under control of the admiralty, and from this base were run the various section of that particular fleet.

The two main fleets were the Home Fleet, which was based in the Orkneys at Scapa Flow, and the Mediterranean Fleet, based in Alexandria in Egypt. The Mediterranean fleet, which was created in June 1940 after the fall of France, was the principal force for the supply convoys to the strategically important island of Malta.

There were also the:

Eastern Fleet (previously the East Indies Station), formed in 1941, which was based in Singapore and became the basis for the British Pacific Fleet in 1944. On December 10 1941, three days after Pearl Harbour, Japanese planes attacked the Force Z section of the Eastern Fleet. The *Repulse* and the *Prince of Wale*s were both sunk with a total loss of 840 lives.

Winston Churchill expressed his horror at the event in his unique way:

> As I turned over and twisted in bed the full horror of the news sank in upon me. There were no British or American capital ships in the Indian Ocean or the Pacific except the American survivors of Pearl Harbour, who were hastening back to California. Over all this vast expanse of water Japan was supreme, and we everywhere were weak and naked.

The Second World War - Sir Winston S. Churchill

America and West Indies Command, 1939-1942 – this was renamed the Western Atlantic Station in 1942. In 1945 it became the America and West Indies Station.

Africa Command/South Atlantic Command, 1939-1942

– based in Simonstown, near Cape Town, South Africa, it became the South Atlantic Command in September 1939 with its headquarters in Freetown in Sierra Leone. The command became less significant after the creation of the West Africa Command and 1942, when South Atlantic Command was returned to Simonstown.

On home turf, there were also what were known as Traditional Shore Commands. These were recruiting and training commands and were responsible for naval operation in the local sea area. Each of the commands had at least one dockyard and was run by a commander-in-chief.

These commands were:

    i. Nore Command – based in Chatham, Nore Command (named after the sandbank at the mouth of the Thames Estuary) was responsible for naval operations from the straits of Dover northwards to Flamborough Head in Yorkshire. Responsibility for the straits of Dover was handed over to the reawakened Dover Command - which had been deactivated between 1919 and August 1939 - just after the outbreak of war and its area of responsibility therefore changed. Its southern boundary became North Foreland, on the Kent coast of southeast England. Its main role was to protect convoys off the eastern coast.

    ii. Portsmouth Command - based in Portsmouth, it was responsible for the middle part of the English Channel between Newhaven and Portland.

    iii. Plymouth Command – based in Plymouth, it was responsible for the western Channel, the South-West Approaches, Bristol Channel and the Irish Sea.

There were also other shore commands created, or reopened, for the war.

    iv. Rosyth Command - formerly the Coast of Scotland Command, Rosyth Command was divided in 1939 when an Orkney and Shetland Command (see below) was set up with responsibility for the north coast. Rosyth Command continued with minesweeping on the east coast and with protection of the northern part of the east coast convoy route. Its southern boundary was at Flamborough Head in Yorkshire, where Nore Command took over.

    v. Orkneys & Shetlands Command – took up the responsibility for the north coast when Rosyth was divided in 1939. Western Approaches Command (originally Plymouth Command), stretched at the beginning of the war from south-west England to the Firth of Clyde. In 1941, Western Approaches Command moved to Liverpool to play a part in the Battle of the Atlantic.

    vi. Dover Command - set up at the beginning war to protect the lines of communication with the army in France and to prevent enemy ships passing through the Strait of Dover. In June 1940 the command organised the evacuation of British and Allied troops from Dunkirk. After that it operated coastal forces and blocked the channel to the enemy[54].

There is also one aspect of the Royal Navy in World War Two that is worthy of mention, and that is the idea that it was the navy and not the RAF which prevented the execution of

---

[54] *Churchill's Navy: The Ships, People and Organisation, 1939-1945* - Brian Lavery

Operation Sealion, the planned German invasion of Britain.

Understandably, it still tends to stick in the craw of many navy men when credit for the cancellation of Sealion is given to a small number of aircraft and airmen, regardless of their indisputable bravery, when beneath them was a fleet of ships that had already in the war repeatedly proved themselves to be resourceful, brave and large enough to render the Germans wary of any intention to invade.

It is revisionist history, a point which seems to be made more loudly the further from the war we get, and I am not totally a fan of revisionist history; people have the habit of judging it by today's standards which borders on the irrelevant, the ignorant and often the disrespectful. However, in this case, we have facts and figures, paperwork, witnesses and, for once, a clarity of distance to allow us to look again at the role of the navy in the Battle of Britain.

In *Battle of Britain: The Naval Perspective* (2006. www.rusi.org), Dr Andrew Gordon lays down a convincing argument for the weight of numbers alone to be enough to discourage the Germans.

> At the beginning of September the Admiralty had disposed sixty-seven (destroyers) (plus six cruisers) for immediate response to an invasion alarm. The first warning of the invasion's sailing would come, it was hoped, from RAF reconnaissance over the assembly ports. But in case – as was likely – the Germans waited until after dark before commencing their 12-hour toil across to England, the Royal Navy had a pool of 700 armed patrol craft (requisitioned motor yachts and trawlers) of whom around 200 were on picket duty "off the north coast of France" every night. So, owing to either the air reconnaissance or the trip-wire patrols, there was a high likelihood that the German invasion armadas would have found British destroyers between them and their intended

landing-beaches when they approached on the morning of D-Day. As well as torpedoes and guns, each destroyer carried 40 depth-charges filled with 600-800lbs of Amatol...which could have demolished the tows of wallowing barges packed with soldiers and horses.

General Jodl, Chief of the Operations Staff of the Armed Forces High Command, felt that as long as the British Navy existed, 'an invasion would be to send my troops into a mincing machine'[55].

It would probably be unrealistic and a little unfair to exclude either service from taking credit for the cancellation of Sealion.

The Germans thought that if they could gain a victory in the skies, thereby rendering British industry inactive and the population vulnerable, then that would at least go some way to aiding an invasion by allowing their planes to attack the British fleet. But that probably would not have been enough. The British fleet was superior in almost every way and production of new resources outstripped the Germans.

In *Growth of Fighter Command, 1936-1940: Air Defence of Great Britain, Volume 1* By T.C.G. James, there is a letter by no less than Sir Hugh Dowding, Commander-in-Chief of Fighter Command, that acknowledges the role of the navy in the prevention of the invasion and that it was, importantly, a joint effort:

> I believe that, if an adequate fighter force is kept in this country, **if the fleet remains in being**, and if Home Forces are suitably organised to resist invasion, we should be able to carry on the war singlehanded for some time, if not indefinitely.

---

[55] *Battle of Britain was won at sea. Discuss* - Thomas Harding. Telegraph. August 2006.

The contribution of the navy in the Norwegian Campaign, Dunkirk and the Atlantic and the Pacific speaks volumes for its adaptability and ability.

From 1939 to 1945, out of a total of 885 Royal Navy ships, 278 were lost; that is 31% or just under 1 in 3 of all ships. Out of the 800,000 officers and men, there were 50,758 Royal Navy men killed in action (just over 6%), 820 missing in action and 14,663 wounded in action along with 30,248 Merchant Navy Deaths.

The Fleet Air Arm

On 24 May 1939, the Fleet Air Arm, which had previously been under the wing (sorry) of the RAF, became a part of the navy as a consequence of the Inskip Award. The Inskip Defence Review of 1937-38 was a review of the setting of strategic priorities, an attempt to marry the financial needs of defence and rearmament with the domestic needs of the nation. It was essential to maintain the economic balance of Britain, to keep up with the rapid increase of rearmament by Germany and maintain the country's own long-term economic stability.

Th report accepted the argument from the Treasury that money spent on defence should not be greater than the country's productive capacity, its ability to pay for imports or threaten confidence in the country's financial stability. Inskip placed great emphasis on the aspect of financial stability, to the extent that he called it 'a fourth arm of defence'. The psychological impact upon Germany of having to fight a country with no apparent financial problems, and therefore the possibility of an extended and expensive conflict, could not be dismissed, he said.

The FAA was formed in 1924, six years after the Royal Flying Corps and the Royal Naval Air Service had been combined to form the Royal Air Force. It was made up of those RAF units that were normally on aircraft carriers and fighting ships.

In 1939, the FAA consisted of 20 squadrons with only 232 aircraft, over half of which were Swordfish, while 191 more were employed on training work.

The Swordfish might well have been an old biplane on the verge of extinction, but it nonetheless managed to sink over 300,000 tons of Axis shipping and sink over 20 U-boats.

Among the other aircraft were the Skua, a two-seater, single-engine aircraft which combined the functions of a dive bomber and fighter, the Blackburn Roc, also used as a bomber and fighter, but less well-regarded than the Skua and the Sea Gladiator, a bi-plane fighter.

The FAA was intended to be used in the following roles:

I. Reconnaissance for the fleet to extend the vision of the surface ships and so enable the enemy to be first sighted by us and, after first sighting, to shadow and keep touch with the enemy.
II. Attack by striking forces on a faster enemy attempting to escape battle, thus reducing his speed to enable our surface ships to come into action.
III. To assist in protecting the fleet against submarine and air attacks and, in particular, to defend the carriers themselves.
IV. Spotting for the fleet's gunfire in surface actions or shore bombardments.

The FAA was forced to compete with other services for men, money and aircraft, along with demands for their services from other services.

The Royal Air Force

1. Creation

In 1911, some British army engineers formed a battalion of aircraft, airships and balloons. This could be considered as the moment that the Royal Air Force, as we know it, was conceived. This unit became known, in April 1912, as the Royal Flying Corps;

the RFC. At the beginning of the Great War, its main role was as an observation platform. In 1914 it deployed to France. Four Squadrons with 12 aircraft each were sent, which together with aircraft in depots, gave a total strength of 63 aircraft supported by 900 men. The RFC strength had increased by September 1915 to 12 Squadrons and 161 aircraft. By the time of the first major air actions at the first Battle of the Somme in July 1916, there were 27 Squadrons with 421 aircraft plus a further 216 in depots.

The problem with such rapid expansion, an expansion created by a need, was that the RFC had to be able to recruit and train quickly enough and to produce aircraft rapidly enough, to enable it to keep up with its needs. With deployment to the Middle East, the Balkans and Italy, the resources available were stretched further.

There also existed, from July 1914, the Royal Naval Air Service.

At this time, Britain somewhat lagged behind its German counterparts in the military air race. Britain had 113 aircraft in military service, the French had 160 and the Germans 246. With allied losses at around 4 to 1 when compared to the Germans, it was clear that there was some catching up to do.

Running parallel to the RFC, but fulfilling a quite different role, was the Royal Naval Air Service, the RNAS. This was formed in July 1914 and by August of that year had 93 aircraft, six airships, two balloons and 727 personnel.

The purpose of the RNAS was to patrol the British coastline and give forewarning of any approaching enemy ships and submarines and to defend London from bombers and Zeppelins. Balloons were also stationed at points along the coast to use as observation platforms, also to provide warning of any potential dangers. The RNAS were also used to attack German coastal positions in Belgium and were over time gradually pulled into the war abroad.

By the time it had joined with the RFC towards the end of the war, the service had 55,000 personnel, 3,000 aircraft and 103 airships.

Both the RFC and the RNAS served well, but it was

apparent that there was a competition for resources between the two areas which was affecting the success of the units (bearing in mind the high losses) and that to increase efficiency and reduce interdepartmental rivalry (and possibly save a few bob), something quite drastic needed to be done.

In 1917, Jan Christian Smuts, previously a South African Boer War enemy of the British who had decided post-war to work with his old enemy in order to maintain peace, was asked to produce a report which looked into the ways that the badly needed efficiencies could be achieved.

He was supported by Sir David Henderson, the first Commander of the RFC in France. Henderson had written to Smuts:

> It is difficult to indicate any method of overcoming the present illogical situation of divided responsibility in aeronautics, except by the formation of a complete united service dealing with all operations in the air, and with all the accessory services which that expression implies. A department would have to be formed on the general lines of the Admiralty and the War Office, with a full staff, and with a full responsibility for war in the air.
>
> www.rafmuseum.org.uk

The conclusion was almost inevitable; the two services had to be unified as an independent air force.

And so, it was done.

Led by an air ministry, the RAF, an amalgamation of the RFC and the RNAS, was created on 1 April 1918.

2. Formation

In the mid-thirties, the RAF was still in the process of being reorganised. There was on the one hand the rise to power of the fascists in Germany and the potential military threats that came with it, on the other the reluctance to spend money on the services during peace time and the ego scratching and political manoeuvring that goes on when any newish venture begins and people vie for money and power.

In 1937, the Fleet Air Arm went to the navy; rightly or wrongly, it was one less resource-hungry service for the RAF to worry about. It was also decided to reorganise the RAF on the basis of specialised commands. In 1936 four new commands were formed: Bomber, Fighter, Coastal and Training commands. In 1938 formed three new commands, Maintenance, Balloon and Reserve.

What the creation of these commands did was to remove the burden of the whole RAF from one man's shoulders and share the load. They could each have their own budgets, their own recruits, their own training and their own purpose. The hierarchical layout went something like this:

CABINET

AIR MINISTRY

AIR COUNCIL
Chief of the Air Staff

COMMAND
Commander in Chief

GROUPS

WING

SQUADRONS

FLIGHT

- Groups are the subdivisions of operational Commands responsible for certain types of operation or for operations in limited geographical areas
- Several Wings form a Group
- A Wing equals about three Squadrons.
- Each Squadron will contain around 12 to 24 aircraft planes.
- Squadrons were subdivided into two or more Flights

The hierarchy within the RAF is as follows:

Commissioned Ranks
Marshal of the Royal Air Force
Air Chief Marshal
Air Marshal
Air Vice-Marshal
Air Commodore
Group Captain
Wing Commander
Squadron Leader
Flight-Lieutenant
Flying Officer
Pilot Officer

Non-Commissioned Ranks
Warrant Officer
Flight-Sergeant
Chief Technician
Sergeant
Corporal
Junior Technician
Senior Aircraftman
Leading Aircraftman

Aircraftman[56]

> Air Ministry was relieved of detailed administration by delegation to the commands. This simplified the management of the air force and ensured the development of each arm. At command level the air officers commanding were able to devote themselves to the main task of strategic planning and direction by delegating as much of the administration as possible to senior air staff officers and air officers in charge of administration. While the Cabinet therefore decided general strategic policy, the Air Council was responsible for its execution through the Chief of the Air Staff. He issued directives for the guidance of commanders and preserved broad control over operational policy. It was then up to the air officer commanding the command to achieve results by using the forces at his disposal. Each command was divided into a number of subordinate groups. Each group was commanded by an air vice-marshal or an air commodore and consisted of a number of stations or wings under a group captain or a wing commander administering one or more squadrons.
>
> *The Narrow Margin* - Derek Dempster and Derek Wood

Fighter Command was under the command of Sir Hugh Dowding. It was broken down into a number of groups, each of which was responsible for specific areas of Britain. The groups were, rather unoriginally, numbered 10, 11, 12 and 13. 10 Group

---

[56] Once again, as with the Royal Navy, according to a wide range of sources, there is a bit of difference among the names of the lower ranks. Apologies again to any of those ranks who might be offended by the choice of title.

covered Wales and the south-west of England, 11 Group covered London and the south-east, 12 Group controlled the Midlands, East Anglia and northern England up to Yorkshire and Lancashire and 13 Group covered parts of northern England, southern Scotland and Northern Ireland.

These groups were themselves broken down into sectors each one of which had a main fighter base and a number of satellite bases attached to it. These divisions made it easier to maintain tactical control and a certain amount of autonomy under the umbrella of the service.

Bomber Command RAF played the central role in the strategic bombing of Germany in World War II. Controversially, it was involved in the area bombing over precision targeting, bombing targeted industrial sites and civilian manpower bases essential to German war production, therefore causing more collateral damage, under the command of Air Chief Marshal Sir Arthur 'Bomber' Harris.

> In total 364,514 operational sorties were flown and 8,325 aircraft lost in action. Bomber Command aircrews suffered a high casualty rate: of a total of 125,000 aircrew, 57,205 were killed (a 46 percent death rate), a further 8,403 were wounded in action and 9,838 became prisoners of war. Therefore, a total of 75,446 airmen (60 percent of operational airmen) were killed, wounded or taken prisoner.
>
> *Royal Air Force Bomber Command Losses, Volume 8: Heavy Conversion Units and Miscellaneous Units, 1939-1947: HCUs and Miscellaneous Units 1939 to 1947: v. 8* - W.R. Chorley

The intended role of Coastal Command was to protect convoys from U-boats and to protect allied shipping from the *Luftwaffe*. It was primarily a defensive role, a reconnaissance role in support of the Royal Navy, active not only around British waters but also in the Mediterranean, the Middle East and Africa. The defensive role often turned to attack in the Med and the Baltic Sea as it carried out attacks on German supply ships, but at the beginning of the war it was, as were all the services, stymied by the need for finances and therefore resources.

> 'Coastal Command was last in the 'food chain', so, in September 1939, it was a small and largely obsolescent force with aircraft that, in today's terms, would be viewed as 'not fit for service'.
>
> *Coastal Command's Air War against the German U-Boat* – Norman Franks

Despite this, with the use of the wonderful Short Sunderland and forty-nine other types of craft during the war years, the service still destroyed 212 U-boats, sunk 512,330 tons of German vessels and flew 240,000 operations. They lost 2,060 aircraft and 5,866 personnel.

Training Command was the RAF's command responsible for flying and ground training from 1936 to 1940. In 1940 it was split into Flying Training Command and Technical Training Command.

3. Action

> The Battle of France is over. I expect the Battle of Britain is about to begin.
>
> Winston Churchill, 18 June 1940

With the inevitable increase in the use of aircraft, the fall of France, the onset of the Blitz (see the separate section for the Blitz) at the same time as the Battle of Britain and the realistic fear of German invasion (planned under the name Operation Sealion - *Unternehmen Seelöwe*), reinforced by photographic intelligence, there was going to come a point in time when Britain would have to, once and for all, see off the German threat by taking the initiative; by taking to the air. On 10 July 1940, the make or break Battle of Britain began and it wouldn't be over until 31 October 1940.

The Germans, after the fall of Dunkirk, concentrated their attacks on British shipping, ports and industrial targets. They hoped that, with a diminution in supplies and an enforced isolation, with Britain weakened and vulnerable, the Germans could then, in much the same *Blitzkrieg*-style as in Poland and France, roll quickly into and over Britain with the joint efforts of land and air services – speed was always of the essence with Germany and had constantly proved successful. At the very least, Hitler could force a British surrender or a cessation of hostilities under his own stringent terms.

The allied air force had not done well during the fall of France:

> The force deployed (by the Allies) was completely inadequate: not only was it numerically inferior to the forces at the disposal of the *Luftwaffe*, but the aircraft were all hopelessly outclassed. Although highly manoeuvrable, the Hurricane lacked the speed of the Messerschmitt Bf 109, while the Gladiator was almost a museum piece. The design of the Battle stemmed from a belief that a single-engined bomber could have the manoeuvrability of a fighter and much of its speed - but it did not. Worse yet, it had still to be appreciated that bombing raids were best conducted by a concentration of as many aircraft as possible to force the defences to divide their fire...The *Luftwaffe* had 3,834 aircraft, including 1,482 bombers and dive-bombers, 42 ground attack aircraft, 248 fighter-destroyers...and 1,016 fighters...the RAF had 456 aircraft, of which 261 were fighters, 135 bombers and 60 reconnaissance aircraft...the French Armee de l'Air had 1,604 aircraft, many of them also obsolete or obsolescent...The Germans

scored in both quality and quantity, and through having combat-hardened aircrew... It took just two days for the RAF's bomber strength in France to be cut from 135 aircraft to 72, and of these another 40 were shot down by the third day.

The RAF Handbook 1939-1945 - David Wragg

The *Luftwaffe*'s aim was to gain air superiority over southern England before the end of August so as to enable a German invasion to be launched from the German-occupied Channel ports. Of the 900 raids mounted by the *Luftwaffe* in this period, some 300 were directed against RAF airfields and installations[57].

After Dunkirk, the RAF had a total of some 2,600 aircraft in the UK, facing the *Luftwaffe*, which had almost twice that number. On the Allies' side were the Spitfire and the Hurricane, the fighter planes needed to combat the German bombers *and* fighters, which consisted of the Messerschmitt Bf 109, the Messerschmitt Bf 110 as fighters and the Dornier Do 17, the Heinkel He 111, the Junkers Ju 88 and the Junkers Ju 87 (Stuka) as bombers.

Below is a comparison table for the three main fighters:

	SPITFIRE	**HURRICANE**[58]	**Bf 109**[59]
TYPE	Fighter[60]	Fighter	Fighter
ENGINE	Rolls Royce Merlin 1470	Rolls Royce Merlin XX	Daimler-Benz DB601A,

---

[57] *Through Adversity: The History of the Royal Air Force Regiment 1942-1992* - Kingsley M Oliver
[58] Mostly based on Hawker Hurricane IIC & I Specifications
[59] Based on the Messerschmitt Bf109E
[60] The Spitfire was used in multiple rolls – in photo-reconnaissance, as a low-level and high-altitude fighter and the F.XII as a fighter and bomber. The Mark V, in service between 1939 and 1941, of which 6,787 were made, is used to provide the majority of the statistics.

	hp	1,300hp	1,175 hp
UNLADEN WEIGHT	2,298 kg	2566 kg	1,190 kg
LADEN WEIGHT	2907 kg	3648 kg	2,665 kg
MAX SPEED	370 mph	327mph	348 mph
RANGE		460 miles	410 miles
SERVICE CEILING	37,500 feet	35,000 ft	36,500 feet
ARMAMENT	4x .303 Browning Mark II machine guns 2x 10mm Hispano cannon	four 20 mm Hispano cannons Ordnance: two 250-lb or two 500-lb bombs or eight 3-in rockets	2xMG FF Cannon 2x17.9mm MG Machine Guns
WINGSPAN	36 ft 10 in	40 ft 0 in	32ft 4½in
LENGTH	29 ft 11 in	32 ft 3 in	28ft 4½ in
HEIGHT	11 ft 5 in	13 ft 3 in	8ft 2½ in
CLIMB RATE	2,440 ft/min	2,750 ft/min	3,510 ft/min

The 109 climbed faster and dove quicker than both the Hurricane and the Spitfire. The Spitfire though, was better in the climb when they got to over 20,000 feet. The 109 was faster than the Hurricane, but it was probably on a par with the Spitfire. When it mattered, in the white-striped skies, scarred by the twisted contrails of acrobatic attack and counter-attack, both the Hurricane and the Spitfire, agile in the turn, were superior to their adversary. In the end, it pitted not only the skill and foresight of the planes' designers, but the skills of the individual pilots.

Despite its legendary reputation, it was not the Spitfire that did most of the work in the Battle of Britain; it worked *with* the Hurricane, each using its different abilities to its strengths. The durable and heavily armed Hurricane was used to fight off the bombers, whereas the faster and more agile Supermarine Spitfire was used against the bombers' fighter escorts, the Me 109. Due to the limitations of fuel range, the Me 109s could only supply brief cover, while the slow and heavy bombers were comparatively easy targets for the Hurricanes. By late August the *Luftwaffe* had lost more than 600 aircraft compared to the RAFs tally of 260 losses. However, the loss of pilots and machines had to be made up quickly if the Germans were not to gain the upper hand.

Thankfully, British industry was up to it. On the week ending 13 April 1940, 35 Hurricanes and 14 Spitfires were produced; on w/e 1 June, 87 Hurricanes and 22 Spitfires produced and on w/e 3 August, 68 Hurricanes and 41 Spitfires. In July alone, 1,110 fighter aircraft were produced. It was an astounding achievement[61]. The Germans produced 2,746 fighter aircraft during the whole year. Between June and October 1940, the British produced 5,185 and that was still 596 less than the target that was set[62]. The British also built 3,720 bombers in 1940[63] compared to the Germans' 2,852. The British set high standards.

Drawing from regular RAF forces, the Auxiliary Air Force and the Volunteer Reserve, the British were able to muster some 1,103 fighter pilots in July. About 20% of pilots who took part in the battle were from non-British countries. There were about 595 non-British pilots flying between 10 July and 31 October 1940.

It is estimated that between 10 July and the end of October 1940, the RAF lost around 1,023 aircraft whilst the *Luftwaffe* lost 1,887. As for the numbers of dead, 544 Fighter Command pilots and crew died, 700 from Bomber Command and 300 from Coastal Command. 2,500 *Luftwaffe* aircrew were killed[64].

Because of this hard-fought, 112-day battle, the German invasion plans were put on hold – forever.

There was one other piece of technology that contributed

---

[61] *The Spitfire* – Bob Carruthers
[62] As above
[63] *British Production of Aircraft by Year During The Second World War* - David Boyd
[64] *Battle of Britain 75th Anniversary: The Staggering Numbers Behind the Four-Month War Over UK's Skies* - Zachary Davies Boren. www.independent.co.uk. 10 July 2015

greatly to the victory of the Battle of Britain – radar (RAdio Detection And Ranging or RAdio Direction And Ranging).

Radar allowed the Allies to have warning of an impending *Luftwaffe* raid. It was part of a defence system called The Dowding System, named after Fighter Command's Commander-in-Chief Sir Hugh Dowding. The idea of the system was to bring together technology, ground forces and aircraft into a unified system of defence. As mentioned previously, groups were broken down into sectors, each one of which had a main fighter base (sector station) and a number of satellite bases attached to it. The Fighter Command Headquarters at Bentley received information about incoming raids and passed this information on to the sector station. Each of these main fighter bases had an operations room from which the fighters were directed into combat. Then the fighters were 'scrambled'. All the time, the situation was being updated as more information came in. Because the Dowding System was 'all-inclusive' i.e. made use of all RAF ground forces, it could also update other services such as anti-aircraft batteries, barrage balloon units and searchlight operators. This way, all resources could be used effectively and appropriately and, in theory, with good notice. By 1939, the 'Chain Home' network of radar stations stretched along the south and east coasts of England.

However, time was of the essence. The *Luftwaffe* could across the Channel in just six minutes and be over the first of Fighter Command's No. 11 Group airfields - 11 Group covered London and the south-east - in a quarter of an hour. It also took four minutes for information from the radar station to reach the airfields[65], and thirteen minutes for a Spitfire to reach 20,000ft. It was a very time-sensitive operation, hence the 'scramble' to get the planes off the ground.

A network of listening posts across the south of England allowed them to detect incoming German air raids. It meant pilots could scramble as the enemy approached, rather than wasting resources on air patrols or setting out too late.

---

[65] *The RAF Handbook 1939-1945* - David Wragg

Even though the Germans developed beam-based bomb targeting, which was a method of precision bombing developed in the 1930's as an aircraft blind landing aid, variously called *Knickebein*, *X-Gerät* and *Y-Gerät*, the Allies soon found ways to counter it and take away the German's advantage. Knickebein and Y-Gerät were successfully jammed by the Allies. The *X-Gerät* was the more successful and contributed to the demolition of Coventry in the Blitz.

Of course, Dunkirk and the skies over Britain were not the only places where the RAF saw combat, the defence of Malta in 1940-1942 being a good example. The RAF web stretched across the empire and took the service into the heart of enemy territory. During the Second World War, the RAF reached a total strength of 1,208,000 men and women, of whom 185,000 were aircrew. Over 70,000 RAF personnel were killed.

The *Luftwaffe*

At the beginning of the war, on paper at least, the *Luftwaffe* appeared to be a formidable force. It comprised:

> Thirty Bomber Wings—1,180 medium bombers.
> 18 equipped with Heinkel He 111F and He 111P aircraft;
> 11 equipped with Dornier Do 17M aircraft;
> 1 equipped with Junkers Ju 86G aircraft.
>
> Thirteen Day Fighter Wings—771 single-seater fighters.
> 12 equipped with Messerschmitt Bf 109E aircraft;
> 1 equipped with Arado Ar 68 aircraft.
>
> Nine Dive-Bomber Wings—336 dive-bombers.
> 9 equipped with Junkers Ju 87A and Ju 87B aircraft.
>
> Ten Attack Wings—408 escort fighters or "destroyers".
> 10 equipped with Messerschmitt Me 110C and a few Bf109D aircraft.

One Army Support Wing—40 dive-bombers.
1 equipped with Henschel Hs 123B aircraft.

Two Transport Wings—552 transport aircraft.
2 equipped with Junkers Ju 52 aircraft.

Twenty-three Reconnaissance Squadrons—379 reconnaissance aircraft.
23 equipped with Dornier Do 17 aircraft.

Thirty Army Reconnaissance Squadrons—342 scouting aircraft 25 equipped with Henschel Hs 126B aircraft;
5 equipped with Heinkel He 45 and He 46 aircraft.

Eighteen Naval Squadrons—240 aircraft.
14 equipped with Dornier Do 18, Heinkel Heii5, Blohm und Voss Bv 138 and Arado Ar 196 aircraft.
2 equipped with Arado Ar 196 aircraft only;
2 equipped with Heinkel He 59 and He 60 aircraft.

Sundry Units—55 aircraft[66].

Closer examination of the above list shows however that many of the above aircraft were not really appropriate to the needs and aims of the Germans at this time.

> Of the above machines, only the Junkers Ju 87, Dornier Do 17 and Messerschmitt Bf 109 types had to some extent fulfil the hopes of Hermann Goering and his staff. The Junkers Ju 86 was obsolete by September, 1939, and the Henschel Hs 123, Arado Ar 68 and Heinkel He 45 and 46 biplanes dated back: the earliest days of the *Luftwaffe*.

---

[66] *The Luftwaffe: A History* – John Killen

The Luftwaffe: A History – John Killen

The Bf 109 could only spend around ten minutes over London before it needed to be refuelled. The Bf 110 had a greater range due to a greater fuel capacity, but they were, quite simply, not as good as the Bf 109s and were comparatively easy prey for the Hurricanes and Spitfires. Indeed, the Bf 110 was found to be so vulnerable to the Hurricanes and Spitfires that they had to be escorted by the Bf 109s towards the end of the Battle of Britain, a fairly obvious waste of manpower and resources.

The British use of radar was also a massive hindrance to the *Luftwaffe*. The Germans lost the element of surprise and, even though the Home Chain was severely damaged in places, such as at Ventnor on the Isle of Wight, they were able to fill the gaps with mobile units.

Had the Germans persisted with their attacks on bases and the Home Chain, the outcome might have been very different. As was often his wont though, Hitler decided to change tactics. He was a very into micromanagement and didn't really trust anyone but himself to do anything. The outcome of D-Day might have been very different had the German army not had to wait for him to wake up in order to move their tanks from the north of France, where the attack had been expected, to the actual area of invasion. Nobody dared to wake the Führer at 4 am when it became clear that there were more than a couple of boats on the horizon.

Hitler's frustration at being unable to *blitzkrieg* Britain and Britain's audacity in bombing Berlin led to him to change tactics. Michael White in his article *Battle of Britain Was Won As Much By German Ineptitude As British Heroism*[67] says:

> The greatest strategic error arose from a chain of accidents. German fighters had been escorting the bombers, often at great cost in terms of lives and aircraft, but Hitler had told them not to bomb

---

[67] The Guardian. 31 August 2015.

London except on his express orders. Then, in late August, the British capital was accidentally bombed in mistake for military targets. The RAF duly bombed Berlin in retaliation on 25 August – something Germans had been assured would never happen... Hitler was furious... Berlin switched its full attention to daylight raids on British cities on 7 September, with 400 bombers and 600 fighters attacking key targets such as the London docks. The Blitz had begun. But the attacks on airfields ended and Fighter Command was spared to fight on, heavy losses rapidly forcing the *Luftwaffe* later to confine itself to night bombing raids. With both sides exaggerating their kill rate (easily done in the fog of war), the air battle's climax came on 15 September – now Battle of Britain day – when the Germans lost what is now said to be 60 planes to the RAF's 26. Two days later, Hitler postponed Operation Sealion until the following spring – i.e., indefinitely. He wasn't coming after all.

Who was the foolish pilot who 'accidentally' bombed London and set the world off on a different path? We shall probably never know, but I wouldn't like to have been in his shoes when he landed.

So, why did the *Luftwaffe* lose the Battle of Britain? They had been rebuilding their air force since the mid-thirties, despite the ban to prevent them doing so, and had initially superior numbers and pilots with far greater combat experience. After all, German pilots claimed roughly 70,000 aerial victories, which gives an indication of the scale of the arena in which they fought.

The *Luftwaffe*'s organisation was very different from the RAF. It was always envisaged that that the German air force would be a part of the *Blitzkrieg* mode, supporting the rapid advance of troops and hardware on the ground, whereas the RAF saw itself very much as an independent service where what happened 20,000 feet above the ground was its *raison d'être*, rather than what happened on the ground. That did not of course mean that it did not provide staunch and valuable support, Dunkirk and D-Day show this to be the case but, like the other services, they had their niche and valued their independence.

The *Luftwaffe* were differently organised to the RAF too. Unlike the RAF Commands, their air fleets – *Luftflotte* – were not based upon role but were 'self-contained formations with fighters, bombers and other elements'.

There was also the problem of supply. When planes were damaged, they had to go all the way back to Germany for repair and likewise new planes had to come from there. Even though they had taken Europe by storm, they had not established any areas to where they could return for repair and rapid turnaround. They had air bases, of course, but they were quickly established and simply did not yet have the facilities to cope with the aftermath of battle.

Dempster and Wood in *The Narrow Margin* summarise Germany's failure to win the Battle of Britain.

i. An inadequate production programme.
ii. No four-engined long-range bombers.
iii. Insufficient range for its standard day fighter, the Me 109, and a twin-engined long-range fighter, the Me 110, which was very vulnerable against modern single-engined interceptors.
iv. Very little radar equipment; no operational experience in its use, or in radar counter-measures, and a shortage of electronics specialists at all levels.
v. No adequate ground control for fighter aircraft.
vi. A shortage of good officers in the middle echelons such as at wing commander and group captain level.

vii. The actual strength of the *Luftwaffe* in the

> Munich crisis period and after was overestimated by other European countries and this belief was fostered by the German Propaganda Ministry. In fact, on August 1st, 1938, four months after the occupation of Austria, the total strength of the German Air Force was 2,929 aircraft, of which only 1,669 were serviceable. There were serviceable only 453 fighters, 582 bombers and 159 dive-bombers—hardly sufficient to embark upon a world war.

So, as ever with these things, it was a combination of events that saw the *Luftwaffe* lose this particular battle. One crucial point has to be Hitler's inability to maintain patience, even control, and to take more than a reactionary stance. The decision to bomb London simply because the RAF had bombed Berlin in retaliation for the previous 'accidental bombing' of London and push on to take out 11 Group was disastrous. Those British airmen and ground crew must have breathed a sigh of relief at his tantrum.

The *Luftwaffe* should not have lost. They had used the Spanish Civil War as a proving ground for their planes, had brought hell down upon Guernica.

> Questioned about the raid while on trial for his life at Nuremberg in 1946, he stated: "Guernica had been a testing ground for the *Luftwaffe*. It was a pity; but we could not do otherwise, as we had nowhere else to try out our machines." It was indeed a pity. The people of Guernica—not to mention the thousands who died in Hamburg and Dresden—would undoubtedly have agreed with him.

> *The Luftwaffe: A History* – John Killen

There was also one other deciding factor, possibly as important as Hitler's tantrum – Home Advantage.

If a plane needed repairing, it could be done so quickly and without fuss. If new planes were needed, they could be delivered the few miles across country, not across the continent of Europe as the Germans had to do. They could stay in the air longer because they didn't need their fuel to get across the channel. When a pilot was shot down, if he survived, he wasn't, unlike a *Luftwaffe* pilot, made a prisoner of war. He was treated and sent back into the fray. The British had radar and listening stations and dedicated civilian observers. They had the WAAF in the control rooms. They were better organised and they adapted when that organisation was found to be floored. It was by no means a democracy, war wasn't like that and Britain was forced for the duration of the war into an almost Totalitarian state of government, but Churchill bowed to the wiser words of others. The British pilots weren't conscripted either. They volunteered to fly. That makes a difference.

The RAF pilots, 20,000 feet up, could look out of their canopies and see what they were fighting for. They could see the patchwork quilt of fields, the distant conurbations where their families lived, where schools tried to press on and create a new future, where industry worked its fingers to the bone to keep them in the in the air and where there were millions watching those white plumes zig-zag across the blue summer skies sent them hope and prayers and would set them up as heroes for ever.

Yes, the *Luftwaffe* might well have won over 70,000 aerial victories during the war, but over 40,000 aircraft were lost. In the Battle of Britain 2,500 *Luftwaffe* members were killed. Hitler's 'tantrum' made a mockery of their sacrifice. Had Hitler had Churchill's (and Eisenhower's) ability to defer to others while taking ultimate responsibility and had a bigger appreciation of the situation, then who knows what the outcome might have been.

Women at War

Why, in this day and age of equality (mostly) would I decide to separate the women from the men in this book? It could come across as patronising to say the least; a pat on the head for a job well done.

That is most certainly not my intention.

My intention is to show that, despite the bigotry and occasional stupidity of men and the genuinely condescending attitude of men towards women in this era, that actually the world, in an extension to the new-found liberties (psychological if not always physical) of the Great War, was forced to acknowledge the vital role that women had to play in the war and, as a consequence, in society itself.

After the Great War, many men, on their return, had returned to their jobs and dislodged the women whom they had seen merely as placeholders for the duration. That war though, contributed greatly to the 'liberation' of women, to the Suffragettes' cause and to the eventual inclusion of women in having a say in about how the country was run.

The Representation of People Act became law in February 1918 and from that point on women **over 30, who were occupiers of property or married to occupiers of land or buildings with a rateable value greater than £5**, were entitled to vote.

> 4 (1) A woman shall be entitled to be registered as a parliamentary elector for a constituency (other than a university constituency) if she –
> (a) has attained the age of thirty years; and
> (b) is not subject to any legal incapacity; and
> (c) is entitled to be registered as a local government elector in respect of the occupation in that constituency of land or premises (not being a dwelling-house) of a yearly value of not less than five pounds or of a dwelling-house, or is the wife of a husband entitled to be so registered.
> (2) A woman shall be entitled to be registered as a parliamentary elector for a university constituency if she has attained the age of thirty years and either would be entitled to be so registered if she were a man, or has been admitted to and passed the final

examination, and kept under the conditions required of women by the university the period of residence, necessary for a man to obtain a degree at any university forming, or forming part of, a university constituency which did not at the time the examination was passed admit women to degrees.

(3) A woman shall be entitled to be registered as a local government elector for any local government electoral area-

(a) where she would be entitled to be so registered if she were a man; and

(b) where she is the wife of a man who is entitled to be so registered in respect of premises in which they both reside, and she has attained the age of thirty years and is not subject to any legal incapacity.

For the purpose of this provision, a naval or military voter who is registered in respect of a residence qualification which he would have had but for his service, shall be deemed to be resident in accordance with the qualification[68].

This still left many women disenfranchised. It could be seen not as *inclusive* law-making, but a law that further *excluded* women of a certain age and those who didn't meet the financial requirements. Women over 21 did not get the vote until 1928. By comparison, all men over 21 were able to vote from 1918 - which seems odd when you consider how many aged under 21 were returning from the Great War. Before this only 58% of the adult male population was eligible to vote. What the Representation of People Act did was to extended the number of voters by 5.6 million men and 8.4 million women. The Representation of the People (Equal Franchise) Act 1928 expanded upon the 1918 act by giving women electoral equality with men. It gave the vote to

---

[68] www.parliament.uk/documents/upload/1918-rep-people-act.pdf

all women over 21 years old, regardless of property ownership.

Suddenly, women needed to be taken into account. They had a voice.

When the Second World War came about, for good or bad, it was, as had the Great War, to further erode the fine societal balance of gender and class.

As far as the war was concerned however, women were at first utilised strictly on a voluntary basis. There still existed the mentality that the woman's place was in the home until, in 1941, the government was forced to admit, albeit reluctantly, that the country was short of about two million people in the services and munitions. This, combined with a growing need for hardware such as bombers and people to actually manufacture the hardware, urged them to accept that it was time for female conscription. The age for male conscription had already edged up to 41 and, with the advent of the second National Service Act of December 1941, it had crept up to 51. Up to 51, men were restricted to military service and, up to 60, to some form of national service such as civilian defence work, but even this had proved inadequate.

> It was always clear, however, that this time volunteering was not going to meet the demands of wartime production, and in 1940, a secret report by Sir William Beveridge demonstrated that the conscription of women, as well as of men, was unavoidable. From spring 1941, every woman in Britain aged 18-60 had to be registered, and their family occupations were recorded. Each was interviewed, and required to choose from a range of jobs, although it was emphasised that women would not be required to bear arms. Many women, however, were eventually to work - and die - under fire.
>
> *Women Under Fire in World War Two* - Carol Harris. www.bbc.co.uk

However, initially the Act applied only to unmarried women and childless widows between the ages of 20 and 30. They would be required to choose between the auxiliary services and jobs in a pertinent industry. Those who went into the auxiliary services would not be asked to enter combat; that was voluntary on their part. Women with children under 14 were exempt from service (social services would be apoplectic today if we left our 14-year-old and above babes alone while we hammered out a few shells!). A year later the age was brought down to 19.

Despite the media and gossip of the day describing this as the death-rattle of womanhood and the nation as a whole and questioning the moral standing of women in the services[69], most women actually were quite happy to contribute in some way. By the middle of 1943 almost 90 percent of single women and 80 percent of married women were employed in essential work for the war effort[70].

> Ninety-seven percent of women, so the Wartime Social Survey found, agreed 'emphatically' that women should undertake war work. Some men were...very glad of the extra money which women pushed into industry now brought into the home.

The People's War – Britain 1939-1945 – Angus Calder

At the peak of the war, there were over 7 million women employed in some form of war work. We will discover the individual services in which women took part, but the numbers in which they did take part certainly spoke of a significant contribution.

Special Operation executive (SOE)	3,200
Auxiliary Territorial Services (ATS)	212,500

---

[69] '...women's services, which had a reputation for impropriety' - *The People's War – Britain 1939-1945* – Angus Calder
[70] *The Home Front in World War Two* - Susie Hodge

Women's Land Army (WLA)	80,000
Women's Auxiliary Air Force (WAAF)	180,300
Industry	1,930,000
Women's Royal Naval Service (WRNS)	74,000
Women's Volunteer Service (WVS)	1,050,000[71]

The Auxiliary Territorial Service (ATS)

Formed in 1938, it was intended that the ATS take on 25,000 female volunteers for driving, clerical and general duties. Its roots lay in the Women's Army Auxiliary Corps which was formed in 1917 and disbanded in 1921.

> The ATS was made up from three organisations – the Emergency Services, First Aid Nursing Yeomanry and the Women's Legion[72]. All three were combined into one organisation known as the Women's Auxiliary Defence Service, which was itself, absorbed into the Territorial Army. A decision was made to change the name of the organisation to the Auxiliary Territorial Service as it was felt that the initials WADS would leave the unit open to derisory comments.

Auxiliary Territorial Service - C N Trueman

In the Great War, the women were used on the whole for clerical matters and as telephonists, cooks, waitresses and as instructors in the use of gas masks. In 1939, the role was extended to include translators, storekeepers and administrators. It was all rather unglamorous, despite the adventurous recruitment posters

---

[71] Data in each section indicates peak participation. Source: Dr Lucy Noakes, University of Brighton.

[72] They provided an officer cadre. Once established, further officers came from the ATS ranks.

which attempted to entice potential recruits into joining by using flattery and patriotism. One poster read:

> Women of ability are needed for the operating of delicate scientific instruments which are vital to the success of our Air Defences. The duties require mathematical and scientific ability, but for those whose talents lie elsewhere there is work of equal importance to be done. Age limits 17½ - 43 (applicants between 17½ - 18 need parents' consent). Those who served in the last war will be considered up to the age of 50. You can give no greater service to your country than this.

Standing at the anti-aircraft gun site would be as close to firing a gun as ATS members got. The use of weaponry was left strictly to the men (an order by Winston Churchill forbade ATS ladies from actually firing an AA gun as he felt that they would not be able to cope with the knowledge that they might have shot down and killed young German men); on the anti-aircraft guns, the women were expected to either use their 'scientific, mathematical' brains to calculate aim of fire via height and range-finders, to differentiate between friendly and enemy planes, to operate spotlights, predictors (a fully automated anti-aircraft fire-control system) and radar sets. At least 57,000 ATS women served with AA Command[73].

Despite the ban on combat duties, many women did get to go abroad, 9,000 serving in North-West Europe by 1945, and as the value of and need for the service grew, so did the role it played.

All women who joined the army went into the ATS, attached to the Territorial Army. After basic training, ATS members were sent to their units to take up their roles in the service.

---

[73] *The Second World War Through Soldiers' Eyes: British Army Life 1939-1945* - James Goulty

By September 1939, over 17,000 women had enlisted in the service; by September 1941, 65,000. During the war over 250,000 served in the ATS, in 'eighty different army trades, the largest contingents being office mess and telephone orderlies...cooks, cookhouse staff, drivers and postal workers...butchers, bakers, ammunition inspectors and military police'[74].

For some reason, as Angus Calder points out in *The People's War - Britain 1939-1945*, '...these girls...tended to come from the better off sections of society and had put travel or adventure higher on their agenda than the dubious pleasures of marriage in wartime'. This is slightly contradicted by James Goulty in *The Second World War Through Soldiers' Eyes: British Army Life 1939-1945*, but not completely.

> During the war women volunteered for the ATS for a variety of reasons. Ruth Aves...longed for a more active part in the war. She was spurred on by having a relative in the army, and hearing the catastrophic news that Singapore had fallen...Other women were motivated to join for patriotic reasons, or because they wanted revenge for a loved one killed during the war. Many women from less privileged backgrounds viewed the military as a means of escaping the drudgery of domestic service or factory work. The army appeared to offer a better future, especially if they were able to learn new skills and be trained in a trade. Consequently, those with comfortable middle-class upbringings could find themselves rubbing shoulders with working-class girls...Pam Hoare...remembered that in her unit were a variety of women, including shop girls, office workers, parlourmaids, a librarian and one or two...veterans of the First World War. With the passing of a second National Service Act in

---

[74] *The British Army Handbook 1939-1945* – George Forty

> December 1941...the social diversity of the ATS was increased further, although many officers still tended to have middle- or upper-class backgrounds.

Why would the better off, or any woman come to that, volunteer so readily?

Well, nowadays we might call it 'voluntourism', a chance to see the world, or at least a different part of it, at some other's expense, with a bit of adventure, possibly romance, thrown in. Maybe they did not yet want to settle down in front of the log fire with the King Charles spaniels and two terrible children, while hubby was out earning a crust. It could be that she did not want to end up like her parents, that plaint and fear of all young people. It could be that the slight scent of liberation released in the Great War had seeped through the years, the forbidden odour of rebellion and freedom, perhaps as the stuff of legend, and now came to the fore as women sensed a chance to make a break for it. It might have been a simple assertion of independence, a craving for identity in a samey, stale world. Perhaps they were trying to assuage their own guilt at being in such a fortunate position in society and wanted to give something back. Quite possibility it was a combination of all of these things, that frisson of excitement tinged with fear, the draw of independence and freedom, the sense of achievement and, ultimately, self.

> Before the war, nearly five million women in the United Kingdom had paid employment, but most would have expected to leave as soon as they married, or when they had their first child. With the onset of war, everything changed. Fathers perhaps joined the armed forces, or were sent away to do vital civilian work, so mothers often ran the home alone - and had to get used to going out to work, as well. Young single women, often away from home for the first time, might be billeted miles from their families. Flexible working hours, nurseries and

other arrangements soon became commonplace to accommodate the needs of working women with children. Before long, women made up one third of the total workforce in the metal and chemical industries, as well as in ship-building and vehicle manufacture. They worked on the railways, canals and on buses. Women built Waterloo Bridge in London.

Women Under Fire in World War Two - Carol Harris. www.bbc.co.uk

Despite the combat ban, there was not a ban on proximity to combat. 300 ATS went to France with the British Expeditionary Force. Communications being vital, many of those ATS who were engaged as telephonists were among the last to leave come the evacuation of Dunkirk.

As related in *Women in the Second World War* by Colette Drifte, Private Angela Cummins eventually ended up at the Battle of Monte Cassino as a clerk for Allied Intelligence.

> During the battle of Cassino, you could hear it from where we were – thump, thump, thump – which was actually the bombing of Cassino. It was a continual thudding and you wanted it to stop, just for a minute, to give you a rest.

The 'loan' of ATS members to other services became commonplace. They were to be found, among many other services, in the Royal Electrical and Mechanical Engineers and the Royal Signals Corps. Not only did this cause a need for greater recruitment to the ATS as, one by one, the services realised that with the help of the ATS personnel they could free up their own personnel to go to the front, but it also boosted the morale of those in the ATS by allowing them to take a more 'useful' role in the war and giving them the chance to expand their own repertoires, to learn skills that could be useful to them post-war.

With a separate income from their male counterparts and a skill by which to earn that money, women suddenly found themselves on a road to independence. Those operating searchlights in the all-female 93rd Searchlight Regiment were required to learn about electricity, electronics, mechanics, map reading, Morse code and first aid[75]. Many were attached to the Royal Army Ordnance Corps as clerks where they were accepted, as in many cases, such as the REME, to the point where they were able to wear the service badge and were promoted within that service. This promoted loyalty and a sense of belonging among the attached ATS members and gave a sense of value as their particular skills were put to good use.

The ATS also had its own military police, formed to maintain discipline within the ATS. Their duties would vary from guarding female prisoners of war to carrying out patrols and civilian checks. In the REME, the ATS members filled roles such as radio-mechanics, motor-mechanics, welders, turners, electricians, tinsmiths, draughtswomen and coach-trimmers, all previously dominated by men both in the military and in civilian life.

Even though they were not 'under the gun', there were still fatalities among the ATS. There was no doubt an inevitability to this; the wider their usefulness and therefore their remit became, the more likely they were to be closer to the danger.

> The first woman killed in action, Private J. Caveney (148th Regiment) was hit by a bomb splinter while working at the predictor...In another attack, Privates Clements and Dunsmore stuck to their posts despite suffering injuries, caused "by being blown over by a stick of bombs dropped across the troop position." The total ATS battle casualties

---

[75] *The Second World War Through Soldiers' Eyes: British Army Life 1939-1945* - James Goulty

were 38976 killed or wounded.

The World War Two Reader

Of course, there were times when women came closer to danger than any man could have conceived before the war; that was in the Special Operations Executive.

Special Operations Executive (SOE)

Set Europe ablaze!

Winston Churchill

The Special Operations Executive and the First Aid Nursing Yeomanry are so closely linked that I was almost tempted to put them under a single heading. In the end, there were three reasons I did not. One was that they were formed as separate services with separate agendas at different times. Another was that each deserved their own separate space. To have put them together might have been seen as the one diminishing the other. Thirdly, it helps the reader to keep the two distinct. They will become joined at the hip, as we shall see, but the journey of each service is as intriguing as the destination.

The beginnings of the SOE came about in 1940, the product of three sections involved in the darker side of war work.

Firstly, Section D of the Secret Intelligence Service, the SIS:

> Section D's aim was simple – 'to plan, prepare and when necessary carry out sabotage and other clandestine operations, as opposed to the gathering of intelligence.'

---

[76] According to *World War II: The Definitive Encyclopedia and Document Collection* (2016) by Spencer C. Tucker, there were 335 killed on duty, 302 wounded, 94 missing in action and 22 prisoners of war.

www.sis.gov.uk

Secondly, Military Intelligence (Research), MI(R), responsible for such inventions as the PIAT -Projector, Infantry, Anti-Tank, a portable anti-tank weapon, and the limpet mine - a type of naval mine attached to a target by magnets – and, thirdly, Department Electra House, a secret propaganda organisation in the Foreign Office.

The ideas behind the SOE were quite straightforward and direct.

OBJECTS AND METHODS OF IRREGULAR WARFARE

Sporadic risings are useless. Necessity to co-ordinate where possible has produced tabulation of United Nations' fundamental objectives in the waging of Irregular Warfare:

Politically.
To undermine enemy's morale and that of his collaborators.
To raise morale of Occupied Territories.

Economically.
To damage enemy's material.
To improve and augment our own material.
E.g. By infiltration of weapons, explosives, sabotage equipment.

Strategically.
To damage enemy's manpower and communications.
To improve our own manpower and communications.

E.g. By infiltration of organisers, radio sets and operators, etc.

www.nationalarchives.gov.uk

Hugh Dalton, the Minister of Economic Warfare[77], was placed in charge of SOE by Winston Churchill. SOE's first chief was Sir Frank Nelson, a former Conservative MP who had worked previously for SIS, so there was at least some understanding of covert affairs.

There was a chain of command which went thus:

Head of SOE
Hugh Dalton
|
Chief of SOE
Sir Frank Nelson
|
Deputy Chief SOE
Charles Hambro
|
Director of Operations SOE
Brigadier Colin Gubbins

Charles Hambro was a banker who had won the MC in 1917 for conspicuous bravery, while Gubbins was a multi-lingual

---

[77] The Ministry of Economic Warfare was created to wage economic warfare against the Axis Powers, in the belief that it could disrupt the German economy, and thereby aid the Allied war effort. This was expected to be accomplished either indirectly, through lowering German civilian morale, or directly, by interfering with German industrial production and food supply. Economic warfare was expected to reduce the magnitude of the challenge that the British military would face in fighting the German army. - *The Ministry of Economic Warfare And Britain's Conduct of Economic Warfare, 1939 – 1945*. Nechama Janet Cohen Cox, King's College London

officer who had worked for Military Intelligence (Research), who had also won the MC, in 1916, for conspicuous gallantry.

> Gubbins would soon be assigned to head up both the SOE's operations and the training areas. If there was a single personality that most characterized and shaped the SOE, it was Gubbins. He is the man who conceived the training structure of the organisation and primarily constructed its training syllabus—that is, the actual training given to recruits. It was Gubbins who was primarily responsible for conceiving the kinds of operations that would be used to undermine the enemy—he was a true expert and pioneer in the art of 'irregular warfare'.
>
> *Hidden Armies of the Second World War: World War II Resistance Movements* - Patrick G. Zander

In 1942, Nelson, who had retired due to ill-health, was replaced by Hambro as chief of SOE by the Minister of Economic Warfare, Lord Selborne, and in 1943 Gubbins replaced Hambro as chief. Hambro had resigned after a disagreement with Selborne.

The SOE initially had its headquarters at 64 Baker Street, in London. It built up a large network of secret establishments called Special Training Schools (STSs). It inherited facilities from two of its founding bodies: from MI(R) a group of large houses in remote countryside in Invernessshire in Scotland, and from Section D a school of sabotage and clandestine warfare at Brickendonbury Manor in Hertfordshire[78]. The SOE was originally made up of three similar parts to the above-mentioned sections: SO1, SO2 and SO3. SO1 dealt with propaganda and misinformation. SO2 dealt with operations and training, while SO3 dealt with research and planning. By 1941, SO3 had converged with SO2 and then the whole became a single

---

[78] *How to be a Spy – The World War II SOE Training Manual* – Denis Rigden

organisation known as SOE. Through reorganisation, the three-headed beast rose again and, by 1941,

> The new SOE was itself organized into three new sections. The first area consisted of the various 'country sections', each devoted to an occupied territory and responsible for developing the networks inside it and for conducting the operations in that territory. Secondly, there was the Intelligence and Planning Section, which had the dual function of conceiving and planning operations and strategies with the various country sections. It also sorted and organized all the intelligence gathered through operations and distributed it to the various government departments to whom it was meaningful (especially the SIS and the War Office). The third section was the Training Section, which was responsible for operating all the training facilities, and for delivering the instruction to all recruits.
>
> *Hidden Armies of the Second World War: World War II Resistance Movements* - Patrick G. Zander

There were interdepartmental problems which hindered the SOE. The SIS was concerned that SOE could compromise their own activities and interfere with the delicate formal diplomatic balance within Europe. Resistance work, such as the destruction of railway lines or direct attacks upon the German troops, could bring about the unwanted attention of the Gestapo or, at the very least, cause an influx of German troops to the affected area, with any concomitant local interference such as house searches and arrests, and this would lead to an impairment of operations while Allied agents were forced to lay low or even withdraw. There was also the concern that SOE was simply a waste of basic resources and indeed a competitor for what were already limited resources.

Governments-in-exile, such as the French and Czechoslovakian governments, urged caution because they were afraid of reprisals within their conquered countries from the Axis forces; the retaliatory excesses of the Germans were well known; they were not afraid to wipe out whole villages in their search for answers and revenge.

Another major headache for the SOE was where to get their resources. They had to travel over the water either by air or sea. The RAF did not want to divert its own resources in order to drop what were sometimes large payloads from their planes. It was not practical at all to use anything other than a bomber to meet the SOE's requirements, which took that plane out of the service for which it was intended: bombing.

It is understandable that other departments were precious about their networks and the resources, and SIS had taken great time and effort to place their people in so many countries at one time.

The training of the SOE members was rigorous and unsentimental. If you failed, you were out. If you showed any sign of weakness or fallibility, you were out. One favourite method of the instructors was to watch how much people drank in the social lives and whether it might lead to loose talk or betrayal.

The training itself was broken down into five parts.

1. Recruits went through the equivalent of basic training, where they trained in physical fitness, map reading, and the basic use of firearms. The separation of the wheat from the chaff started immediately.
2. The next part of the training included tutoring in mountaineering, small boat sailing, armed combat, unarmed combat, which included silent killing, and raiding techniques. Weapons training continued with the familiarisation of enemy weapons. The challenges set included a mission to blow up actual railroad tracks and trains

without detection[79]. Failure in this section accounted for as many as one third of the participants[80].

3. This stage involved parachute training at RAF Ringway. It was at this time that the real nature of the trainees' work was disclosed. If those involved were willing to travel to occupied Europe, the next stage beckoned.
4. Things became perhaps a little more 'real' from this point on as the recruits learned about tradecraft - the techniques, methods and technologies used in modern espionage - including cover stories, avoiding detection, use of codes, forgery of documents, safe-breaking and the use of enemy uniforms. These were all put to the test quite severely, involving such things a breaking into factories or planting explosives, to the point where the local constabulary were involved and the participants could end up in jail and only the use of a memorised telephone number would aid their release.
5. The final stage involved specific training aimed at specific operations such as a familiarisation with a particular type of factory work relevant to the mission.

In order to achieve its goals, SOE relied upon 470 agents in France, 117[81] of whom died in action.[82] Neither was the SOE

---

[79] *Hidden Armies of the Second World War: World War II Resistance Movements* - Patrick G. Zander

[80] *Rediscovering Irregular Warfare: Colin Gubbins and the Origins of Britain's Special Operations Executive (Campaigns and Commanders)* - A R B Linderman

[81] According to *SOE: An Outline History of the Special Operations Executive, 1940-46* by M. R. Foot, 118 died in action.

[82] *Encyclopaedia of Espionage, Intelligence and Security* - K. Lee Lerner and Brenda Wilmoth Lerner, Editors

too fussy sometimes about the calibre of recruit.

> ...the SOE would also comb police and prison records to find criminals with the kinds of specialized skills that were needed for such work. The criminal class was "a social stratum SOE neither neglected nor despised...indeed sometimes found most useful...SOE's forgery section would have got nowhere at all without help ... from some recently released professionals."
>
> *Hidden Armies of the Second World War: World War II Resistance Movements* - Patrick G. Zander

Among them was Eddie Chapman, a member of one of the Jelly Gangs, a bunch of London burglars and petty thieves, so called because they used gelignite to blow safes. He had been arrested in 1939 after the burglary of a nightclub, for which he was sentenced to two years, extended for one year after an attempted escape.

Chapman was from Jersey, one of a small group of British islands off the coast of France, which had been occupied by the Germans in June 1940. At this point, he was still serving time on the island and, when he was released in October 1941, he volunteered his services to the Germans as a spy. As an ex-soldier (he had gone AWOL after nine months and then spent two months in the stockade, after which he was dishonourably discharged from the army), the Germans must have felt he had some credibility, if only because of his apparent hostility towards his motherland; a failed ex-soldier turned bitter con must have seemed like a bit of a dream. He was also still wanted by the mainland police for a string of offences, but whether the Germans knew this is a moot point; it might well have stoked his bitterness, but might also have encouraged him to 'turn' if he was caught.

In December 1942, he was parachuted into Cambridgeshire, England, immediately turned himself in and became a very valuable double-agent known as Agent Zigzag.

For the SOE, it wasn't about who you were or where you came from. It was about what you could do for your country and to do that, they had to throw away convention and turn a blind eye to society's norms.

> SOE's agents were drawn from all social and professional backgrounds. They belonged to any non-Nazi and non-Fascist political party or to none. They were of any religion or none. They might he of any age...Even hardened criminals, especially those with useful skills such as burglary and safe-breaking, were not excluded. As Professor Mackenzie notes in his history, 'it is extremely difficult to say where SOE begins and where it ends'.
>
> *How to be a Spy – The World War II SOE Training Manual* – Denis Rigden

The independence and determination of SOE was apparent not only in their recruitment techniques and unflinching bravery. They were also rabidly inventive to the point where they were inventing gadgets, machinery and vehicles, such as one-man submarines, that were not needed by the service. The main problem was that there was a lack of actual field research and there was, to some degree, an assumption of what would be needed rather than providing equipment based on any experiential need.

This does not mean though that what they were doing was superfluous. More often than not, by learning as they went, they hit at the heart of the opposition by the sheer variety of inventions and by an understanding of covert war.

Most of their research was done by Dr Dudley Maurice Newitt, a chemical engineer, and his team, which was based at a requisitioned hotel in Welwyn, the Frythe, a 'Victorian red-brick mansion built in 1846'.

At the Frythe, Newitt and his team carried out four main strands of research: physical-chemical, engineering, operational and camouflage. It was a mixed bunch of specialities, especially for a group secretly stashed away in a hotel but, eventually, they were able to come up with, quite literally, an illustrated catalogue for the operative to browse and from which to order. Rigden continues:

> The 1944 edition of the catalogue contained descriptions, methods of use and other essential information about incendiaries, flares, fuses, grenades, limpet devices, time pencils, tyre-bursters, trip wires, percussion caps and much else related to causing explosions. Also listed were ordinary tools adapted for agents' use, such as wire-cutters, knives and jemmies. 'Sundries' included bags, balloons, luminous discs, Plasticine, magnets, adhesives, Alpine rope, rope ladders, nitrated paper, torches, and splinterproof windows that agents could build into their observation posts.

Add to this various surreptitious types of gun - sleeve guns, for example; guns designed to be hidden up the sleeve - underwater equipment, rations and even, wait for it, itching powder, then SOE could fairly be said to meeting of its operatives' every need.

Despite its inventiveness, determination and the undaunted and undoubted courage of its operatives, SOE didn't quite 'set Europe ablaze', as Churchill demanded, but it did contribute without doubt to the liberation of France and, along with the Maquis (the French resistance), managed to disrupt vital supplies to the enemy by its destruction of railways bridges and lines and other major installations along with the delay of opposition reinforcements reaching Normandy in 1944.

Its greatest achievement was, it is generally agreed, the prevention of Hitler's acquisition of atomic weapons through Operation Gunnerside, the destruction of the heavy-water plant in the Norsk Hydro complex in Norway. General, later President, Eisenhower, said that the various bodies of resistance had probably shortened the war in Europe by nine months.

By 1944, there were approximately 5000 SOE behind enemy lines with 10000 more support staff back home. They operated in places as far apart as France and Southeast Asia.

Of the 140 officially-recorded SOE casualties, only thirty-three have a recorded burial site. Their graves are located in twenty-one cemeteries around the world, of which fourteen are in France.

It is difficult to pinpoint the actual number of SOE deaths because of their attachment to other units and armed forces outside of the commonwealth. Others were recruited into the SOE abroad and did not undergo the usual training and assessment in the United Kingdom. As a consequence, no casualty report was submitted. There are also some members who were seconded to other special service organisations at the time they died. There were also considerable numbers of individuals who were involved in SOE but whose official connection with SOE cannot be verified[83].

> The SOE also was not averse to using women in its resistance operations...women played a vital role in resistance all over Europe. The SOE employed around 3,200 women within its administrative and operational personnel.
>
> *Hidden Armies of the Second World War: World War II Resistance Movements* - Patrick G. Zander

Of the 39 women who were sent into France by SOE, 15 were captured and only three of those captured survived. 12 were executed in concentration camps.

But how did they get there in the first place?

First Aid Nursing Yeomanry (FANY)

---

[83] *Unearthing Churchill's Secret Army: The Official List of SOE Casualties and Their Stories* - John Grehan and Martin Mace

> 'For God's sake, madam, go home and sit still! We want no petticoats here.'

> Lieutenant General Sir Arthur Sloggett to suffragette Dr. Elsie Inglis upon her suggestion of a female medical corps on the Western Front.

The above quotation is, though amusing in a Blackadder/General Melchett sort of way, quite probably inaccurate and might well be wrongly attributed.

It is a combination of two quotations, the first one, 'For God's sake, madam, go home and sit still!', said to Dr Elsie Inglis, has been attributed to both an unnamed MP and to the above Lt General Sloggett. It too has hung upon the page like a disowned ghost, with no attribution, no previous life. It has also been quoted as, 'My good lady, go home and sit still!'

The second part, 'We want no petticoats here', said to Vera Laughton Matthews when applying to the admiralty for a position, has been attributed to an anonymous reply by a representative of the admiralty, to the Lt General and to another wandering, unnamed spirit. Ironically, the lady and her petticoat became Director of the Women's Royal Naval Service.

None of that matters. The words were said in approximately that combination and they were uttered by some men in high positions in the services who should have known better, rather than just believing they knew better. The point is that, the words were representative of the attitude suffered by women from men at the turn of the 20th century.

That makes the story of the First Aid Nursing Yeomanry (FANY) all the more remarkable because, to become what it has, it had to overcome ambivalence, bias, prejudice, thickly layered social mores, backward attitudes, public ignorance, limited means, internal struggles and quite a lot of bad luck.

I could not possibly do the FANY justice, much like the SOE, in such a short time. I would heartily recommend *The FANY in Peace and War* by Hugh Popham if you really wish to go into any depth; it is dryly amusing, moving, wonderfully anecdotal and well-researched.

The context here, women in war and the effect that the war had upon them and theirs as individuals as part of the whole, needs some background to appreciate the difficulties of those who dragged the FANY up from nothing and became an essential part of the war effort, including SOE.

The first thing that struck me when I first heard about the corps was the name. The blending of 'first aid' and 'yeomanry' with what would have been considered 'ladies' in those days, seemed odd. But that is all part of the tale.

The corps was founded by Edward Baker, a warrant officer in the 21st Lancers who, way back on 2 September 1898, had been shot in the leg during the Battle of Omdurman, a major battle in the Sudan campaign. Quite naturally, when one has been shot mid-battle in the leg by a Mahdist Sudanese, his thoughts turned to the idea that it would have been rather nice to treated on the battlefield by a group of nurses specially trained for the task. If the appropriate care was given at the scene, then there was more chance that the victim would reach hospital alive and therefore have a greater chance of recovery.

Thus is the 'first aid' part of the name explained.

It wasn't until 1907 however that Baker brought the idea to fruition.

> Members of the Corps had to qualify 'in First Aid and Home Nursing, and in addition go through, and pass, a course of Horsemanship, Veterinary Work, Signalling, and Camp Cookery'. They also had to provide their own uniform and first aid outfit - 'which latter must always be carried when in uniform' - and pay for horse hire. They were to be between seventeen and thirty-five years of age, at least 5ft 3in in height, and had to join for at least one year. There was an enrolment fee of ten shillings, with six shillings a month subscription to the riding school and headquarters, and applicants were required to disclose whether they belonged to

any other organization.

The FANY in Peace and War - Hugh Popham

That might now explain the yeomanry part; the horsemanship was an essential attribute of the corps and, as it says on the FANY website, 'These early FANYs did indeed become proficient in the art of swooping down upon a wounded soldier at high speed, scooping him up behind the saddle and delivering him to the First Aid Post'.

There was also an attitude towards them as hobbyists. The corps required members to pay an enrolment fee, a monthly subscription to the riding school, to provide their own uniforms and first-aid outfits, to own their own horse or to be able to afford to rent one. The implication, by asking for women who could pass a veterinary course, also implied that the applicant had to be educated. This all gave out the impression that the people who applied came from 'money'. The constant refusal by branches of the forces to take the FANY seriously certainly emphasised the fact that women as a gender were not to be taken seriously.

Edward Baker, by recruitment drives, managed to gather together enough members, including his daughter, Katy, to kick-start the corps.

They were though, a long way from acceptance. Initial reaction to women taking on such a dangerous (and no doubt 'unladylike') role was dismissed out of hand by several of the services and even the public found time to openly mock them.

In 1910 though, Mabel St Clair Stobart, a member of the corps and supporter of women's suffrage, led a breakaway faction, apparently due to dissatisfaction with the FANY's financial arrangements[84]. She formed the Women's Sick and Wounded Convoy Corps and delivered sterling work in Serbia in the first Balkan war (October 1912 – May 1913).

After this, Edward Baker too gradually faded from the

---

[84] *Dorset's wartime heroine – Mabel St Clair Stobart* - Pete London. www.dorsetlife.co.uk - January 2015

scene. The circumstances under which his involvement diminished are not entirely clear. It has been suggested that he might have found the women in the corps a little too flighty for his tastes, but it is unclear. What is clear is that two very determined women, Lilian Franklin, 'always known as 'Boss'', and Grace Ashley-Smith, 'a feisty, no-nonsense Scottish woman', began to take the reins (again, sorry).

In fairness to the two women, especially Ashley-Smith, they worked like Trojans to get the corps recognised.

They were also, whether by stealth or accident, in the right place at the right time.

Roll back a couple of years and we find an example of this synchronicity in the form of Colonel Francis Cecil Ricardo (purportedly the template for Toad of Toad Hall in Kenneth Graham's *The Wind in the Willows*) a man who seemed to have many fingers in many pies.

In 1908 the corps were inspected by the Colonel, described as a British Army officer, police officer, and philanthropist, at their riding school. He had actually been in the Grenadier guards before he retired. He was so impressed after his inspection that he invited the FANY to attend the Royal Naval and Military Tournament. This was a true coup for Ashley-Smith as it aroused a great deal of public interest and 'applications from prospective recruits came pouring in from all parts of the country'.

Ricardo crops up again in 1909 at a charity matinée for the corps which was also attended by sixty patrons of the corps, of whom 'twenty had titles and twenty-five were of military rank'.

If success for any sort of independent voluntary group is to be found, it is achieved (and I confess to having my cynical hat on), not through what you know, but through who you know. Not only is the financial input from donors likely to be greater, especially in the sort of circles in which Ashley-Smith was now moving, but the right kind of contacts could be made; the military wasn't just about the military, it was about social standing and about the circles in which the upper echelons of the military moved. It was an absolute social rhizome. Ashley-Smith was not only determined, but she was astute and incredibly aware of the sort of creatures that moved in the sea in which she now swam.

By this time, there was a dissatisfaction in the corps with the way Baker was running things and the aforesaid Mrs Stobart at this point packed her bags with her group and went off to Serbia.

> The conclusion must be that poor Captain Baker had collected, on the one hand, a bunch of well-to-do, horsey girls who had been attracted to his corps by the lure of riding, the glamour of the uniform, and his romantic notions; and, on the other, a group of much tougher and more practical young women whose ideas were...rather less picturesque.
>
> *The FANY in Peace and War* - Hugh Popham

Whatever the reasons and the causes, Captain Baker's time was over. As so often happens in life, the cream of his dream had turned sour.

Now, with a substantial part of the Corps gone, that dream was all but dead. Then Ashley-Smith took charge and began, bit by bit and with the connections the corps had made, to bring the FANY back to life.

She continued to pursue her contacts and, despite being rejected time and time again, pushed on with numerous training camps where the corps was drilled and taught their craft.

Although still present in the background, Baker really played very little part in the running of the corps and, on 6 January 1912, Colonel Ricardo attended another inspection of the corps and formally took command of the FANY.

The coup was complete.

Ashley-Smith had by now disposed of the original uniform,

> ...a long dark blue skirt, a high collared scarlet tunic with white braid and a scarlet cap with a shiny black peak...completed by black patent riding boots,

white gloves, a riding crop and a first aid haversack. The Corps also had a 'mess uniform' of white muslin dress, worn with scarlet bolero and crimson sash... replaced in 1909 by a more practical, though less romantic, khaki uniform with a shorter skirt which could be buckled up to allow the wearer to ride astride, rather than side-saddle. The khaki uniform...had the symbolic advantage of visually linking the work, and potential sacrifice, of the Corps' members with that of the men in the armed forces...The move from Baker's romantic red and blue uniform to the more serviceable khaki, combined with riding astride, appears to have coincided with the rise through the ranks owl Grace Ashley-Smith and Lilian Franklin, both of whom had joined the Corps in 1909. Ashley-Smith and Franklin had less romantic notions about the identity and aims of the Corps.

Women in the British Army: War and the Gentle Sex, 1907–1948 - Lucy Noakes

They were aided by now by the Brigade of Guards who lent them 'tents and all the other gear they needed though they still had to hire a field (for fifteen shillings[85]) and a sanitary man (four shillings)'[86], while the 19th Hussars gave cavalry drill and equestrian instruction[87].

If the series of meetings with Colonel Ricardo didn't quite have the true smack of synchronicity about it, then the next twist of fate might well do.

The corps, regardless of their hard work, was still not

---

[85] The equivalent then of two days wages for a skilled labourer. Nowadays that 15 shillings would be worth about £250.
[86] *Women in the British Army: War and the Gentle Sex, 1907–1948* - Lucy Noakes
[87] *War Girls: The First Aid Nursing Yeomanry in the Great War* - Janet Lee

being taken seriously and, with the outbreak of the Great War, the FANY was desperate to become involved, yet still being regaled with condescending and dismissive tirades such as the one from the Director-General Medical Services, which went: My dear, you are overwrought and not seeing things in the right perspective. There are enough nurses to attend to the Army. Amateurs will be neither wanted nor welcomed, either as soldiers or nurses.

When war was declared, Ashley-Smith was on her way to see her sister in South Africa. On board ship she bumped into the Belgian Minister for the Colonies, Louis Franck, who suggested that the corps would be welcome in Belgium.

> By September 10th she was nursing the wounded at l'Hopital de Boulevard Leopold in Antwerp. In her memoirs, Ashley-Smith wrote:
> Whilst waiting, I registered at the Belgian Red Cross as ambulanciere and worked from morning to night with a motor ambulance, bringing wounded in from outposts and trenches near Lierre and Buchout. There were hundreds of wounded to be attended to and I worked in a ward of sixty-five beds for three weeks...I was offered first an empty house in Avenue Marie Therese for convalescents. A few days later they asked me to get the Corps over to staff a hospital of three hundred beds, fully equipped, in the rue de Retranchements...The FANYs quickly learned to cope and the hospital eventually had one hundred beds. More than four thousand patients were treated between 1914 and 1916.
>
> www.fany.org.uk

And so it began. There were, of course, many trials and tribulations for the corps to come, but through the determination of the remarkable Ashley-Smith and her colleagues, the corps found its place and, as it became more valued and its role wider, so members of the corps took their skills to other parts of the services.

By the end of the Great War, the corps had earned 17 Military Medals, 1 Legion d'Honneur and 27 Croix de Guerre. They had proven their courage and their worth in no uncertain terms.

While other female-led services such as the WRNS and the WAACS were put on ice after the Great War, the FANY, being an unaffiliated and independent institution, was able to carry on. They did consider the idea of affiliating themselves with other services, but there was a determination to retain that independence and their identity. They were undoubtedly elitist and proud of it. They believed all FANYs, by their very nature, to be officer material. 'We have the privilege of belonging to the educated classes with all the tradition of ruling behind us, and therefore rank as officers in everyday life', wrote one of them in the Gazette, their own journal.

It was a wonderfully preposterous, elitist, arrogant statement, but it oozed the confidence of an educated upper class which understood that they were *privileged*; they knew they were fortunate. They understood their position in society and appreciated the responsibility that they believed came with it. They were proud and had a right to be so.

Post-war, there was a gradual transition of the corps. It learned to adapt and continued to attract new members. In 1916, many members of the FANY were working as mechanics, while many continued to train, with less emphasis on the horsemanship and more focus upon the mechanics of transport. This re-emphasis of the role from a mounted corps to a motorised corps found the FANY's role change. Now, they became drivers for government and military officials. Along with vehicle maintenance, they also trained in communications, something that was to later prove devastatingly effective as well as dangerous during World War Two.

In 1936, the FANY's name changed to the Women's Transport Service (FANY).

> In September 1938 the driving section of the WTS transferred en masse to form the new ATS driver companies. The WTS remained in existence, providing drivers to the Polish Army in Britain, the British Red Cross and a number of overseas organizations.

The British Home Front 1939–45 - Martin Brayley

It was at this time that there was another sort of parting of the ways.

Many FANYs did not want to be incorporated, loaned or in any other way attached to the ATS. They had, quite reasonably, always been proud of their identity and independence. Their refusal to allow themselves to be in any way amalgamated with the ATS caused them to become known as 'Free FANYs'.

It was at this point that the SOE became interested.

> When the...SOE came looking for female agents to be parachuted into occupied Europe, FANY provided the largest numbers of recruits...Recruiting from FANY, an ostensibly civilian organisation, evaded armed service prohibition on women as combatants[88]. The SOE, along with the technology of the war, placed women in range of enemy bombing, blurring the distinction between combatant and noncombatant roles.

---

[88] Lifting the ban on women in combat roles will "drag our infantry to far below the required standard" and put people at greater risk of dying, according to a former SAS commander. "The infantry is no place for a woman, and to permit them to serve in close combat roles is a pure politically correct extravagance," Colonel Tim Collins has said, following David Cameron's announcement on Friday that women will be allowed to perform combat roles in the army. - Harriet Agerholm. The Guardian: Sunday 10 July 2016.

Women and War: A Historical Encyclopedia from Antiquity to the Present, Volume 2 - Bernard A. Cook

Colin Gubbins, the previously mentioned Director of Operations and Training, made contact with the commandant of the FANY. By now, this was commanded by Marian Gamwell, one of two Gamwell sisters, the other of whom had gone to the Polish Units, made up of Free Poles who had escaped the Nazis to England.

Now, here comes another one of those strange pieces of synchronicity.

Gubbins needed some female intelligence officers in the field and, as stated in the previous quotation, turned to the FANYs. When he telephoned, the woman who answered the phone was Phyllis Bingham, who was acting as Gamwell's temporary confidential secretary.

> The two recognised each other; they had been peacetime neighbours[89]. They met and Gubbins explained that he was going to need to recruit on a regular basis but because of the secret nature of the work SOE did he needed to do so discreetly. Bingham suggested that FANY act as his private recruitment agency. Suitable 'girls' would be recruited into FANY which would act as their cover employer though they would in fact be on SOE's roster. Thus the secretive 'Bingham's unit' was established in SOE headquarters from which a girl 'once posted, never returned'.

---

[89] According to *SOE's Mastermind: The Authorised Biography of Major General Sir Colin Gubbins KCMG, DSO* by Brian Lett, they were cousins. 'Through his cousin, Mrs Phyllis Bingham, he once again approached the ladies of the First Aid Nursing Yeomanry (FANY) and secured their services as drivers and administrators at SOE'. P169

Queen of Spies: Daphne Park, Britain's Cold War Spy Master - Paddy Hayes

From this call, Bingham set up 'Bingham's Unit, recruiting women to serve as signallers and coders. Eventually, the FANYs recruited by the SOE, worked worldwide.

There were many women who joined the SOE via FANY, all of whom are equally deserving of comment. I mention Violette Szabó as an example simply because she is well documented and because it was her very ordinariness as a wife and mother that made her so special.

Violette's husband, Étienne, a highly decorated French Legionnaire, died after sustaining wounds in battle in Egypt, in 1942. Five months previously, Violette had given birth to their daughter, Tania, who Étienne never saw. By the time Tania was aged four, both her parents were dead.

Violette, half English and half French, had been a member of the ATS since 1941. Not long after Tania's birth, she was contacted by a Mr Potter, who asked her to attend an interview in London. She duly attended and was told that her fluency in French and her knowledge of France would make her a prime candidate for 'special war work'. Despite having a baby, she agreed immediately, possibly with half a mind upon her husband and the chance offered to enact some small revenge for his death.

Her training was extensive and involved the use of weapons, escape and evasion, unarmed combat, night and daylight navigation, demolition explosives and communications and cryptography[90].

During her time in France, she was involved in the sabotage of roads and railways and the transmission of wireless reports to SOE.

She had two tours of duty and, on the second one, was arrested. Under interrogation she was tortured, sexually assaulted and beaten. Regardless of her pain, she gave nothing away. She was eventually executed in Ravensbrück concentration camp.

---

[90] *Women in the Second World War* – Collette Drifte

She was posthumously awarded the awarded the George Cross for bravery on 17th December 1946. In 1947 she was awarded the Croix de Guerre and La Medaille de la Resistance in 1973. In 1951, her daughter, Tania, emigrated with her grandparents to Australia. She went to college there and then spent some time as a psychiatric nurse. In 1963, she returned to England then, in 1976, moved to Jersey. She retired to a cottage in Wales.

Szabó was one of many. Women from all walks of life were filtered through the FANY to become a part of the secret war. They were chosen because it was thought that they would blend in better than men, who were watched closely by the Germans, the assumption being that men were more likely to be spies than women. Fifty female agents were parachuted into occupied Europe by the SOE, including twenty-four from FANY and fourteen from WAAF; fifteen of the fifty were captured by the Germans, all but three of whom were tortured and executed or died in concentration camps. Some agents disappeared after their drops and were never heard from again[91].

Gubbins himself summed it up perfectly:

> Women are excellent at keeping secrets - the ordinary women you see around you today in offices, stores, homes, [when they are] just given specialist training - of mind and body. [They were] despatched at a moment's notice, to India, Italy, Africa - to be maids of all work, twenty-four hours at a stretch.
>
> *SOE's Mastermind: The Authorised Biography of Major General Sir Colin Gubbins KCMG, DSO* - Brian Lett

The Women's Auxiliary Air Force (WAAF)

The WAAF came into existence in June 1939 and

---

[91] *Women and War: A Historical Encyclopedia from Antiquity to the Present, Volume 2* - Bernard A. Cook

mobilised in August of the same year, although RAF companies had existed within the ATS since 1938.

The purpose of the WAAF was initially the same as it seemed to be for all women in the other services; as clerks, kitchen orderlies, cooks and drivers, in order to release men for front-line duties. As also seems to be usual in these types of situations, the women excelled and, as the war continued and the needs of the service expanded, so did their roles, to include responsibilities such as mechanics, engineers, electricians, aeroplane fitters, reconnaissance operatives involved in the interpretation of aerial photographs, providing weather reports and as communications operatives, working with radio and telegraphy machines using codes and ciphers[92]. Many members of the WAAF worked in the radar control system as reporters and plotters[93] and, of course, some went to the SOE. At least eighteen trades were completely served by women, including dental hygienists and wireless telegraphy slip readers[94]. The WAAF came under the administration of the RAF and members, unlike in other services, did not serve in individual female units but as members of RAF Commands.

In command of the WAAF was a remarkable woman named Katherine Trefusis-Forbes, who had served in the ATS as Chief Instructor at the School of Instruction in 1938 and as Commander of No. 20 ATS RAF Company in 1939.

In 1936, Trefusis-Forbes, Helen Gwynne-Vaughan and Viscountess Kitty Trenchard launched the Emergency Service, an officers' training unit, to train women and organise them to be prepared in case of war.

> The Emergency Service members undertook to train at least one evening each week, attend summer camps and were sometimes referred to as a 'blouse and shorts army', for which they received an annual

---

[92] *Women in World War 2, The WAAF* - www.owlcation.com
[93] *Women's Auxiliary Air Force* - www.bbc.co.uk
[94] *The RAF Handbook 1939-1945* - David Wragg

fee of just 10s, government disapproval and social ostracism.

The RAF Handbook 1939-1945 – David Wragg

Helen Gwynne-Vaughan had been awarded the CBE in 1918 for her services to the Women's Auxiliary Army Corps, the first woman to be given the award. In the same year, she took charge of the WRAF after a critical report had led to her predecessor, Violet Douglas-Pennant, being dismissed. The WRAF however, was disbanded after the Great War and she was elevated to GBE for her services.

Trefusis-Forbes had been Chief Cadet in the Women's Emergency Service—the only organisation recognized by the War Office before the Second World War for the production and training of future women officers. Later she became the previously mentioned Chief Instructor of the A.T.S. School where officers destined for the R.A.F. companies of the A.T.S. were trained. At this school practically all the senior W.A.A.F. officers passed through her hands, and here, too, she worked under the direct influence of Helen Gwynne Vaughan[95].

On 28 June 1939, the forty-eight RAF ATS unit became the Women's Auxiliary Air Force with 1,734 members, commanded by Trefusis-Forbes. By 1943 there were over 180,000 in the WAAF, with 2,000 enlisting per week[96]. From September 1939 to December 1940, 14,546 were recruited and then from January 1941 to December 1941, a staggering 81, 928 were recruited. The voluntary levels fell in the following years, particularly due to the National Service Act. Recruitment overall fell up to 1945, but by the end of the war 183,317 had volunteered for the WAAF, while 33,932 had been conscripted, giving a total of 217,249[97], all based at six main training locations, West

---

[95] *The Work of The Women's Auxiliary Air Force in The War - Air Commandant K. J. Trefusis Forbes, C.B.E.* - tandfonline.com
[96] *Women in the Second World War* – Collette Drifte
[97] *The WAAF at War* – John Frayn Turner

Drayton, Harrogate, Innsworth, Bridgnorth, Morecombe and Winslow. By the end of 1940, women had replaced men in fifty-nine airmen's trades, with seventeen ancillary trades established solely for the WAAF and four specialist WAAF trades. One to one substitution had reached 43 per cent by 1945[98].

There was at first the idea that it would take three women to cover the job of two men; this, as ever, proved untrue and the ratio was very soon one to one (even though, as with all the services, women only received two-thirds of the male equivalent pay).

To start with, the organisation's focus was on training its members to become officers and NCOs. The idea behind this was that, when the war started, there would be a body of people in place which was ready to train the large numbers expected to join the WAAF.

> Training consisted of between two and three weeks, with the first day seeing the new recruits kitted out and given medical checks. They were marched everywhere in groups known as 'flights', including to and from meals, and slept in huts, with between twelve and twenty-three per room. They received lectures on the RAF, gas, fire, first aid and hygiene, and physical training, sports and drill, as well as tough discipline. At first many of the lectures and all of the drill were provided by male instructors. Trade training followed basic training, and was sometimes conducted in mixed-sex classes, often under high pressure, as the priority was to get the maximum number of trainees through the system and on to the bases as quickly as possible.

The RAF Handbook 1939-1945 - David Wragg

---

[98] *The Many Behind the Few: The Lives and Emotions of Erks and WAAFs of RAF Bomber Command 1939 -1945* - Dan Ellin from Air Ministry *Air Publication 3234*, pp. 132-133.

For the same reasons that women were not permitted to use weaponry such as anti-aircraft guns i.e. they had to remain non-combatants, neither were the WAAF members permitted to fly. The problem once again rose though, that they were wasting male pilots on non-combative duties such as ferrying aircraft between airfields or to and from factories for delivery or repairs.

To free up the flyers, the ATA, the Air Transport Auxiliary, a civilian unit, was formed, partly due to the Air Ministry demand that 'no work should be done by a man if a woman could do it or be trained to do it'. Women were therefore permitted to ferry aircraft between non-combat destinations. This was not a uniquely female (nicknamed 'Attagirls') unit however; what it did was also give the opportunity to fly to those men who were unable to participate in the war with the Royal Air Force or the Fleet Air Arm, by reason of age, fitness or gender. Physical handicaps were overlooked so long as the pilot could do the job; for this reason there were one-armed, one-legged, short-sighted and one-eyed pilots, fondly referred to as 'Ancient and Tattered Airmen'.

> ...they came from all walks of like. Some were accomplished athletes: a skiing instructor, an international ice-hockey player, and a ballet dancer. Several were mothers (and there was one grandmother!). They were wealthy socialites and working girls, whose pre-war occupations included stunt-pilot, mathematician, mapmaker, architect, typist, actress, and world famous record-setting endurance pilot (Amy Johnson, who was killed on a ferry trip in January, 1941).
>
> *British Air Transport Auxiliary* - E.M. Singer: www.airtransportaux.com

By 1943 they were ferrying all RAF and Fleet Air Arm aircraft. During the war the ATA, comprising 1,245 men and women from 25 countries, flew 415,000 hours and delivered more than 309,000 aircraft of 147 types[99].

Among the eclectic roles that the WAAF were asked to carry out, one of the more 'out there' ones must have been the crewing of barrage balloons. These were enormous 'blimps', which were 66 feet long and 30 feet high when inflated, filled with lighter than air gas (in the case of the British, hydrogen) and anchored to the ground by steel cables which were fixed to winches on lorries. They were originally thought to be too much for women to handle but, once again, the men were proved wrong; women eventually ran more than 1000 barrage balloon sites.

The balloons' purpose was to prevent low-level flying space being surrendered to enemy aircraft. If the enemy could be forced to fly high enough, then there was more chance that they would miss their primary targets, the drawback being of course that, if the bombs were dropped anyway, there was more risk of 'collateral' deaths. There was also the problem that barrage balloons were indiscriminate in who they took down.

Over three hundred allied aircraft hit balloon cables as opposed to just fifty-four enemy planes. About one third, ninety-one, of the allied aircraft that hit a cable came down, whereas only twenty-five enemy aircraft crashed with one aircraft being forced to land (technically not a crash then; perhaps more just a matter of timing). Twenty-one enemy aircraft hit cables, but were still able to carry on flying.

There was, naturally, an inevitably tragic side to the WAAF story. A total of 171,200 women served in the WAAF, 187 of whom were killed in service. Another 420 were wounded, and 4 went missing while on duty[100].

One example that is often stated, maybe to the point of unintentionally eclipsing others, is the story of Noor Inayat Khan, Aircraftwoman 2nd Class, who trained as a wireless operator and was recruited by the SOE.

Khan (codename Madeleine) came from royal, if distant,

---

[99] *Brief Glory: The Story of A.T.A.* - E. C. Cheesman
[100] *World War II: The Definitive Encyclopedia and Document Collection* - Spencer C. Tucker

blood. She was a direct descendant of Tipu Sultan, the 18th century Muslim ruler known as the Tiger of Mysore. Born in Moscow in 1914 to an Indian father and an Anglo-American mother, she was the eldest of four children. Her father was a musician and teacher, hence the reason they were in Moscow; he taught in the Kremlin.

The family came to live in England just before the Great War and then, in 1920, moved to Suresnes, near Paris, where Khan was educated and later worked writing children's stories and on children's stories for Radio Paris[101]. She went to the Sorbonne where she studied psychology and also studied music at the conservatoire. Along with this, she studied modern languages and was fluent in French.

When the Germans invaded France in 1940, Noor and her family fled to Bordeaux and sailed for Falmouth. Having worked for the French Red Cross in France, she enlisted in the WAAF on 19 November 1940 and was sent to Harrogate to train as a wireless operator.

> Now wearing the uniform of the FANY (...used to disguise the real work of SOE's women agents), she joined a batch of three other women...at Wanborough Manor near Guildford. Here they underwent a three week assessment course, testing...fitness and skills in armed and unarmed combat, wireless and cross-country navigation...Noor's training reports were less than encouraging...she was "pretty scared of weapons"...she progressed...to SOE's radio school at Thame Park, then to...Beaulieu, which taught how to operate in an occupied country. At every stage her kind-hearted, selfless nature was obvious to everyone, and prompted one instructor to describe her as "a person for whom I have the greatest admiration". But her deep moral

---

[101] *Unearthing Churchill's Secret Army* – John Grehan and Martin Mace

convictions were interpreted by others as a sign of a temperamental and difficult person. This was a potentially serious problem: SOE agents had to be capable of making expedient, sometimes ruthless, decisions...but for Noor work that involved "anything two-faced" or caused "mental conflict with her idealism" was simply unacceptable. Part of the course involved a mock interrogation...It terrified her, and raised yet another question mark about her suitability. The final report from Beaulieu characterised her as being "not over-burdened with brains" and concluded that it was "very doubtful whether she is really suited to work in the field". The response by the head of F Section, Maurice Buckmaster, was contemptuous. "We don't want them overburdened with brains..." For him the equation was simple. The demand for wireless operators was greater than ever; Noor wanted to go; and he needed a qualified "body" to send.

SOE Agent Profiles; Noor Inayat Khan – Nigel Perrin[102].

After being posted to a bomber training school, she found the work unfulfilling and applied for a commission.

Perhaps as a consequence of the interview, which she was convinced she had failed due to her strident pro-Indian independence stance and the, I'm sure, startling admission that she would willingly fight against the British in India after the war to achieve that independence should the need occur, she was called to attend for an interview by the Home Office, at which she was invited to become a wireless operator in France.

On 16/17 June 1943, with the codename 'Madeleine' and under the pseudonym of Jeanne-Marie Regnier, Khan was flown at night to into Northern France, the first female wireless operator

---

[102] www.nigelperrin.com

to be so.

It was not long after her arrival that her network fell into problems and Khan was almost caught. The organiser of her group, Francis Suttill[103], and many others had been arrested by the Gestapo. Khan, despite being warned by her chief in London, Colonel Maurice Buckmaster, head of the SOE's F Section[104], to get out, continued to transmit as she moved frequently from place to place and dyed her hair to avoid capture.

She was eventually betrayed to the Gestapo by Renée Garry, the sister of her network supervisor, Émile Henri Garry.

> Noor had always carried her notebook with her wherever she went. In it, she had kept a record of all the messages she had sent and received since her arrival in France, both in code and in plain text. This seems to have arisen from her misunderstanding the phrase in her operational orders, 'be extremely careful with the filing of your messages'. She seemed to be unaware that 'filing' meant 'sending', and she thought that she was

---

[103] Khan was a recruit for CINEMA, a sub-circuit of the PROSPER network. Major Francis Suttill was a British special agent who worked for the SOE in France. The network's correct name was *Physician*, but Suttill called it after his own codename, Prosper. He was captured and executed by the Nazis.

[104] The groups referred to are the networks, also known as circuits, established in France by F Section of the British Special Operations Executive during the Second World War. These groups were tasked with gathering information about the enemy and relaying said information to the SOE headquarters in London. At minimum, a circuit would be composed of three people: 1) Circuit leader: organize the group and recruit new members. 2) Wireless Radio Operator: know-how to work the wireless set, possessed an understanding of Morse code and as well the ability to encode and decode messages. 3) Courier or messenger: travel from circuit to circuit within the country acquiring intelligence about the enemy - *The Special Operations Executive (SOE) from 1940 to 1946* – www.home.earthlink.net

> supposed to keep them in a filing system...a breathtakingly dangerous breach of security precautions.

Women in the Second World War – Collette Drifte

From this, the Gestapo sent messages to London. There were inconsistencies in the messages which, had they been noted, would have given London some clue that she was compromised. Neither did they fail to heed a previously agreed eighteen-letter signal which she had sent which was intended to alert SOE of her arrest. Because of the inattentiveness of those in London, the Germans were aware of three more agents being dropped in France, all of whom were captured, at least one of whom was executed.

Despite escaping twice, Khan was recaptured and sent to Dachau concentration camp with fellow agents Yolande Beekman, Madeleine Damerment and Eliane Plewman and, on 13 September 1944, the four women were executed by a shot to the back of the head.

She was posthumously awarded the George Cross and a French Croix de Guerre with silver star (*avec etoile*).

Khan's is an oft-told story, but it is indicative of the dangers that so many women went through, aware of those dangers, and never made it home.

There are many other terribly sad stories that can be related to the WAAF, such as the plotter who heard her fiancé crash 'into the drink', never to be seen again, or those WAAFs who had to write the letters which informed the next-of-kin that someone was missing or killed.

These 'girls' were taken from their often closeted lives and required to live in less-than-homely conditions with a bunch of often very strange strangers.

> I found myself amongst a mixed bunch of recruits, debutantes and prostitutes, vicars' daughters and academics. We all lived together in Nissan huts,

heated by an antique boiler in the middle of the room, twenty odd girls, all equally as bemused as I was. I had lived a comparatively safe and sheltered life so imagine my surprise on the second day there to find a new recruit giving birth in the ablutions.

Not an Ordinary Life by Eileen Younghusband

The Women's Royal Naval Service (WRNS)

The WRNS was wound up at the end of the Great War but, as with the other services, there was a realisation that women would once again be needed, again for the same reasons, to 'free a man for the fleet' and to fill the roles vacated by those men.

The roles substituted started off, as ever, as the ones that seemed to be the first vacated; secretarial, clerical, accounting, shorthand typewriting duties, domestic duties as cooks, stewardesses, waitresses and messengers. As the need and the roles expanded, much as in the WAAF and the ATS, so women took on an abundance of tasks and were found to be as adept as their predecessors. The roles developed into driving, operating radar and communications equipment as wireless telegraphists, some became bomb range markers, radio mechanics, aircraft mechanics, torpedo servicers and provided weather forecasts. Some naval air stations had all-female anti-aircraft gun teams; WRNS motorbike dispatch riders were used by the Admiralty. Though not allowed to operate in open water, WRNS did provide service on small vessels in harbour, such as tugs and launches and a few Wrens did indeed serve on boats, as Stokers, Boats' Crew and coxswains.[105]

Those WRNS with an aptitude for language went to coastal stations to intercept and translate enemy signals and some even worked at the world-famous (now not then) Bletchley Park where they broke German and Japanese codes.

Some also worked with the Royal Marines while others

---

[105] *The Role of The Women's Royal Naval Service* - war-experience.org

worked with the Fleet Air Arm, maintaining the aircraft and the accompanying equipment.

There was a reluctance to send women abroad, a policy that the admiralty, who seemed rather befuddled by the sudden presence of women, was determined to pursue. However, they had to backtrack and in 1941 the first overseas draft of 20 Chief Wren special wireless telegraphy operators (GPO-trained) and a Second Officer went to Singapore. Once the curse had been broken, others followed and WRNS members were posted to places as far apart as America, Hong Kong, South Africa and area of Europe.

The person running the WRNS did not have an easy time of it. Vera Laughton Mathews became Director of the WRNS in 1939 with Ethel Goodenough as her deputy. She was second choice and had to follow in the shoes of the formidable Dame Katherine Furse, who had guided the WRNS through the Great War. The WRNS was so successful that it was used as a template for other organisations such as the Women's Army Auxiliary Corps and the Women's Royal Air Force.

Come World War Two though, she was disinclined to take the role on for a second time and had no hesitation in recommending Laughton Mathews.

There was however one singular and important difference between the WRNS of the Great War and the WRNS of the Second World War.

In the Great War, the WRNS had come under the auspices of the Admiralty – they were a part of the navy team. Now, in 1939, they came under the Civilian Establishment Branch and were administered through civilian channels. Laughton Mathews saw this as a regressive step.

> The Admiralty was split into a number of branches, including the Military Branch, Naval Branch, Legal and Civil Branch. The Military branch was responsible for the distribution of the fleet 'and in wartime acting as the channel of communication for operational orders'. The Naval Branch was responsible for deploying personnel and acted as

the main channel of communication for the Second Sea Lord. The Civil dealt with civilian establishments within the RN. This branch was a part of the Secretary of the Admiralty, Sir Archibald Carter's department. Headed by the Permanent Secretary, Le Maistre, the department was responsible for the general administration and coordination of the Admiralty.

The WRNS in Wartime: The Women's Royal Naval Service 1917-1955 - Hannah Roberts

In theory, it shouldn't have made any difference; there was a role to be carried out and it shouldn't have mattered under whose umbrella the task was fulfilled, so long as it was indeed achieved. The Civilian Establishment however took very little part in the WRNS and, because the WRNS was not under the direct control of the Admiralty, they were left in a sort of no-woman's-land without an identity of their own.

> ...the WRNS would be under the responsibility of the Second Sea Lord in name only. This was different from how it had been in World War I, and different from what Laughton Mathews... had expected...they had not realised the significance of the involvement of the CE branch. The new service would be regarded as civilian, not as part of the Navy...The assumption appears to be that this early duality did not affect the identity of the service. It is argued... that this was, in fact, extremely significant of the ability of the WRNS to shape its identity...numerous respects, the WRNS should never have been called 'civilian' unless the previous identity of the service had been overturned in the scheme of service...In numerous respects, the WRNS should never have been called 'civilian' unless the previous identity of the service had been

overturned in the scheme of service...

The WRNS in Wartime: The Women's Royal Naval Service 1917-1955 - Hannah Roberts

There seemed to be, throughout the services at the start of World War Two, a reluctance to surrender masculinity and the gender stereotypes of society of the time. Men's egos, however shadowed in regulation and a 'fear for women's safety', were proving to be fragile and there seemed to be an underlying awareness that once women's roles in the services were redefined, then so would their role in society and, more importantly, so would men's. There were underlying prejudices that were slowing down the implementation of female services because, quite frankly, even though the men knew that they needed the women, the men did not know what to do with the women and were afraid of what would happen once something was done. C.D. Le Maistre, the Permanent Secretary of the Admiralty who headed the CE, said in a letter that 'nobody can seriously maintain that there is a real connection between the "ranks" of the WRNS and those of the Navy' and 'the WRNS officers properly with ATS officers'. The WRNS saw itself as having a naval identity whereas 'the tone of Le Maistre's letter is sneering about this request, particularly shown by the term 'ranks' being in inverted commas'[106], along with the implication that WRNS officers were not on a par with ATS officer. There was a temptation to lump the WRNS in with the other female-led services such as the ATS, but Laughton Mathews was having none of that and stated clearly that she was 'not impressed with the arguments of the Head of CE. The object is to obtain for the WRNS the best working conditions possible vis-a-vis naval personnel and not be a comparison with the ATS'. The WRNS was not even deemed significant enough to have its own uniform, partly because of its civilian status. It wasn't until the Fourth Sea Lord, Vice Admiral Sir Geoffrey Arbuthnot, who was

---

[106] *The WRNS in Wartime: The Women's Royal Naval Service 1917-1955* - Hannah Roberts

also Chief of Naval Supplies, became aware of the situation that uniforms were provided for the WRNS, whether they were naval personnel or not.

We can laugh at this from seventy or eighty years away, yet even as I write we are still going through the same problems in Hollywood and within the British parliament. It's only since 1977 that WRNS were subject to the same discipline as men[107] and it wasn't until 1993 that the WRNS were accepted as a part of the Royal Navy proper and allowed to serve on board vessels as a part of the crew.

By September 1941, the WRNS ranks finally became comparable with naval officers' ranks.

It wasn't all simply about equality of rank and appearance, though these were significant cards to be played in the discussion; it was about the credibility of the WRNS and the contribution to be played through that credibility. How effectively women could work alongside their male naval counterparts if their ranks were not equivalent? There was a need for parity between the two services and with this parity would come a higher regard for the individual and the service that they represented. Laughton Mathews, unlike some of the men who surrounded her, took her role and the roles of those beneath her, seriously. To exist, the WRNS had to have purpose and to have that purpose, the male-dominated navy had to surrender something of itself in order for women to fulfil the role for which they were intended. The Admiralty could not have its cake and eat it; it could not say that it needed women to fill the roles vacated by men and then exclude the very people it had invited to take part.

The story of the WRNS in World War Two is not, of course, without its tragedies. On September 14, 1940, 10 WRNS were killed when their boarding house at Lee on Solent in Northern Ireland was hit by a German bomb. Then, on 19 August, 1941, the SS Aguila, a general cargo ship bound for Gibraltar with 22 WRNS, all volunteers, twelve of whom had served together in

---

[107] *Commandant Vonla McBride* - Dan van der Vat. The Guardian. Aug 2003

Scarborough, on board, was sunk by a U-boat. Twelve cipher officers, ten radio operators, and a nurse lost their lives. 58 crew members, the convoy's commodore and 89 passengers also died[108].

303 Wrens were killed during World War Two.

By the end of 1940, there were 10,000 WRNS; by 1942, there were 36,655 WRNS serving on the British islands and 952 serving overseas. At its peak in 1944, there were 74,635 WRNS serving in 50 branches with 90[109] job categories[110].

Vera Laughton Mathews had pulled the WRNS up by the boot straps and created a vital, almost indispensable service. At the same time, whether she realised it or not, she had contributed to the future of women, both in the services and in society, and had changed the role of women for ever.

The sentiments of the achievement might be best summed up by Jean Gadsden, who typed signals for distribution, who watched the last landing craft sail away towards the beaches of D-Day and thought: 'I'm watching history being made and I am part of it'.

We shouldn't forget either the non-military contribution of women.

> During the war the number of women in the Forces and Land Army rose to 550,000, there was an increase of 500,000 women in white-collar work, and over 1.5 million women worked in the essential industries (engineering, metals, chemicals, vehicles, transport, energy and shipbuilding).

You Weren't Taught That with The Welding: Lessons In

---

[108] *The Battle of the Atlantic: How the Allies Won the War* - Jonathan Dimbleby

[109] According to *Women's Royal Naval Service* on www.bbc.co.uk, there were over 200 different job types.

[110] *Women and War: A Historical Encyclopedia from Antiquity to the Present, Volume 2* - Bernard A. Cook

Sexuality In The Second World War - Penny Summerfield & Nicole Crockett (1992). Women's History Review

Women's employment increased by about 47% between 1939 and 1943, from about 5.1 million in 1939 to just over 7.25 million.

By 1943, 80,300 women had become members of the Women's Land Army, one third of them from towns and cities and most of them below twenty years of age. They earned one pound and eight shillings (one pound two and six as a minimum), (£55.08 by 2017 values) a week, less than their male counterparts, and lived in hostels on the land, working in what were often harsh, difficult conditions. They had taken on the men's work that initially they were deemed unable to do but, whether through conscription or voluntarily, they proved men wrong and kept Britain fed throughout those lean years.

They faced the same prejudices in factory work too, but still put in 60-hour weeks and were still paid less than the men. 100,000 worked on the railways and another 100,000 in the Post Office. There were already 265,000 members of the WVS when the war started and there was barely a nook or cranny in which they weren't involved helping the war effort.

Sadly, after all their contributions and achievements, women weren't quite able (or allowed) to grasp the nettle postwar. A return to 'hearth-and-home' was encouraged by government and (a male-dominated) society until, by 1951, the level of employed women had returned to its pre-war level. It was though still a time of subtle change, borne of thoughts and deeds conceived in the factories, behind the anti-aircraft guns and in the shade of the SOE, that gestated slowly through the following decades, and finally gave birth to the feminist movements of the sixties and seventies and the changes they wrought.

Britain's wartime women gained a new sense of power. There were women who could talk down aircrews, break codes, track battleships, drive 10-tonne trucks and save lives. No concession was made, however, for the fact that women had to go on running the home. After a 10-hour day in a factory making aircraft wings, a woman would still have to shop, clean, feed her family on rations and "make do and mend". After the war, the home was where they were expected to return...After the war, the divorce rate rocketed for many reasons, one being that many women had a new sense that they should be permitted a say in their own destiny. The old sexual contract was being exploded. Deep down, women knew they had exploded the inequality myth, but in practice, they were shattered and exhausted. Many wanted to be feminine again, to bring up their babies and rekindle the home fires.

The 1940s: 'Britain's Wartime Women Gained A New Sense of Power' - Virginia Nicholson - The Guardian. Feb 2018

Part 3
HOME

Conscription

Conscription began under the Emergency Powers (Defence Act) of August 1938, the Military Training Act of 27 April 1939 and then the National Service (Armed Forces) Act of September 1939. All British men aged 20 and 21 who were fit and able were required to take six months' military training[111]. Those men aged 20 to 23 were required to register on 21 October 1939, with later conscription of those of 40 years registering in 1941. More than 1.5 million men had been conscripted by the end of 1939. 1,100,000 went to the British Army and the rest went to the Royal Navy and the RAF.

There were of course, some areas of the population that were exempt from callup, the so-called protected occupations which were required to keep the country functioning. Someone quite literally had to keep the home fires burning and supply not only the country with food, iron, coal and all the daily resources that we take for granted, but also the services abroad.

Included in the list of these occupations were metal polishers, bedstead makers, bobbers, moppers, pony drivers, pony putters, galloway putters, safe makers, saw makers, rate fixers, spring makers and typecutters[112]. These appeared in the Schedule of Reserved Occupations (Provisional) where, in alphabetical order, all the protected occupations and the ages to which they applied, were meticulously listed. One can imagine the conflicting feelings of relief, guilt, disappointment and anger that welled inside someone who read this and found themselves either on or absent from the list. It was a challenge to masculinity, to conscience, to social standing, to the social status quo, to everything that made the individual in society a part of that society and every society an identifying part of the individual.

EXPLANATORY NOTES

---

[111] www.bbc.co.uk
[112] Schedule of Reserved Occupations (Provisional) - 1939

The occupations listed in this Schedule are those in respect of which in the general national interests restrictions will be placed in

peace time on the acceptance of volunteers for certain forms of enlistment or enrolment for service in time of war.

The restrictions apply to acceptance for service (otherwise than in the volunteer's trade capacity, or, in the case of women, in nursing or first aid services) which will be whole-time in war but not in peace.

If an age is printed opposite an occupation in the Schedule, this means that the restriction as regards that occupation applies only to volunteers of or above that age.

If no age is printed opposite an occupation in the Schedule, the restriction applies to volunteers in that occupation whatever their age.

Nothing in the Schedule restricts—

(a) acceptance for service which is whole-time in peace (e.g., service in the Regular Armed Forces, the Regular Police Forces or the Regular Fire Brigades);

(b) re-engagement for the same service of a person already engaged in a service;

(c) acceptance for whole-time service in war in the volunteer's trade or professional capacity;

(d) acceptance for A.R.P. service at the volunteer's place of employment;

(e) acceptance for service which will be only part-time in war, subject to the clear understanding that in the case of persons covered by the Schedule work in the occupation listed in the Schedule will have first claim on them in war-time;

(f) acceptance of women for nursing and first aid services.

The Schedule is subject to revision from time to time.

Schedule of Reserved Occupations (Provisional) Presented by the Minister of Labour to Parliament by Command of His Majesty January, 1939

The list of workers who were exempt included, usually for fairly obvious reasons:

Dock Workers
Miners
Farmers
Scientists
Merchant Seamen
Railway Workers
Utility Workers - Water, Gas, Electricity
teachers and university lecturers
Doctors (Unless in the Territorial Army)
Police officers
Certain Civil Servants
Students (Only for the duration of their studies. Undergraduates were deferred, but not fully exempted. They could be conscripted at the end of their studies, unless they had a criminal record or ill health)
Priests, monks, nuns and anyone in Holy orders
Journalists
Some artists involved in propaganda work
Other media workers (especially those involved in technical roles, such as lighting engineers, electricians, cameramen, photographers, sound engineers, etc)
Anyone running a small business, including government and local council contractors and their employees.

Local authority employees
Bank employees and employees of insurance companies
Company directors.

Within the above categories were sub-categories (hence the moppers and bobbers). The number next to the job was the age to which the exemption applied e.g. 25 and above. The list within the *Schedule of Reserved Occupations* highlighted how complex roles within society had become and how fine the line between staying and going had become. Agriculture was not just agriculture any more, it was now a multifaceted industry that had a major role to play, not just on a day to day basis, but in the defence of the realm.

AGRICULTURE AND HORTICULTURE

Farm Worker (other than Poultry and Fruit Farming) Working principal, e.g., farmer, crofter, small holder......25
Farm bailiff, steward, foreman, headman......25
General farm worker, general farm hand 25
Shepherd 25
Pigman 25
Cattleman, stockman, yardman...... 25
Carter, horseman, ploughman...... 25
Horse trainer, stud groom, stallion man 30
Agricultural machine attendant, tractor driver, threshing machine attendant 25
Ditcher, drainer, drowner, hedger 30
Hay-cutter, trusser, baler, straw binder (not seasonal worker) 30
Farm labourer, agricultural labourer (not seasonal worker) 25
Forester, Timber Feller Forester 25
Woodman, forest worker 25

Timber feller, tree feller ......25[113]

The Conscientious Objectors

Even God isn't a pacifist - he kills us all in the end.

Tribunal member to a Conscientious Objector

Alongside those excluded from service were those who faced daily criticism and intimidation from the population; the conscientious objectors.

There are a couple of pieces which stand out from a Guardian newspaper of 2009 which in themselves are worthy of comment. One of them will make you smile, the other will, I hope, not.

> The chairman...at the...conscientious objectors' tribunal...read a letter from WJ Hughes...stating that he wished his name to be struck off the list of conscientious objectors and asking the tribunal to send him a military certificate.
> The letter added: "You must not regard the statement I made as false, but I want you to understand that my wife has been doing nothing but nagging since I received my first objector's certificate. When I received the letter to appear before the tribunal she has been unbearable." He asked the tribunal to make it possible for him to hear no more about this objectors' business and arrange for him to be medically examined and called to the colours with the men of the 20-22 class in his district.
> He concluded his letter: "I am awfully sorry to cause this unnecessary trouble, but I would rather

---

[113] Schedule of Reserved Occupations (Provisional) - His Majesty's Stationary Office 1939

be in the armed forces for the rest of my life than stay at home with my wife for another month." His name was withdrawn from the register.

This says quite a lot about the pressure put upon people from within the family, never mind the pressures that were borne upon them from friends, neighbours and the press. It is easy to smile at the story, everyone loves a hen-pecked-husband-with-a-nagging-wife yarn, but the truth is that Mr Hughes was forced to put aside his objections to the war due to social pressure.

Who knows what pressure his wife was under to conform? Was she sneered at in the street because of her husband's stance? Was she short-changed when it came to rations because the butcher thought less of her and her husband? Did she genuinely disagree with his objections and now find him abhorrent?

Here is another, less amusing story from the same article:

> A 20-year-old coloured man named Frederick O'Cora, by trade a riveter, told the Lancashire conscientious objectors' tribunal in Manchester yesterday that he had had a hard struggle to gain the job he was now in owing to the colour bar. He did not wish to take any part in military service. He was not allowed to join in times of peace.
> "There is no freedom for the coloured man, whatever you say. We do not get treated as equals."...he said that, had he been treated as an equal, he would have fought. Judge Burgis said O'Cora had favourably impressed the tribunal by his frankness and honesty. He said that as in times of peace he was the victim of prejudice and had not an equal chance with the white man. The tribunal was satisfied that conscience did not prevent the applicant from joining the army, and his name would be removed from the register without

qualification[114].

This doesn't say much for the moral state of Britain at the time. We would happily fight for a bunch of strangers who we felt were being oppressed by something that we did not believe in, in some other, distant part of the world but, on our own doorstep, we had not the diligence or the courage to fight for the rights of an individual because of the colour of his skin. Did the fact that he had an Irish-sounding surname reinforce that prejudice? – 'No Irish, no dogs, no blacks'.

Neville Chamberlain himself believed that people should have the right to refuse service on grounds of conscience and he had served on the tribunals to hear the cases of conscientious objectors in the Great War.

Officially recognised support was given to the COs and in 1939 the Central Board for Conscientious Objectors was started, with government recognition, 'to consult on everything to do with' COs. They offered advice to COs, attended hearings with them and lobbied parliament.

There was also the Pacifist Service Bureau which helped to find employment for COs (many were fired or suspended from duty) and carried out voluntary activities such as youth clubs and helping those in air-raid shelters by organising food and drinks.

59,192[115] claimed CO status - there had been only 16,000 in the Great War – and 3,577 (only 6%) were given an unconditional exemption. 28,720 were registered as COs provided that they carried out approved work, such as agriculture or, if appropriate, carried on with their present job. 14,961[116] were registered for non-combatant duties in the forces, which could include such things as bomb disposal or medical units; it was a fine line between doing something for your country and yet not participating in the harmful aspects of war; to voluntarily go into bomb disposal showed a tremendous amount of courage in itself;

---

[114] Both originally from the Manchester Guardian
[115] *The People's War – Britain 1939-1945* – Angus Calder
[116] As above

465 took it on.

6,766 ended up in the Non-Combatant Corps (NCC). This was set up in August 1940. Many of them were among the first to go into France on D-Day as part of the Parachute Field Ambulances. They refused to carry revolvers or any other type of weaponry.

It was not a matter of courage, only of conscience.

The corps had its own badge and was recognised as a part of the army – members were still soldiers. Many members took this as a reasonable compromise, despite the fact that they were still sent to areas of combat to fulfil non-combatant roles. For some, this was simply too much and, after trying the NCC, surrendered themselves to a prison sentence rather than be a part of the combat support structure.

The roles that the NCC filled were various. 465 volunteered to specialise in bomb disposal. Others joined the medical corps while others carried out manual tasks such as road-building or worked in transport or army stores. Unfortunately, even within these 'pacifist units' they were still liable to condemnation as, quite often, they were joined by men who had been in some way deemed unfit for service and yet still wanted to play a part

Many COs carried out what was considered to be 'useful' civilian work; in forestry and agriculture or social services and in hospitals.

Out of those 59,192, 12,205 were turned down. They could still be called up.

Once turned down as an objector, any refusal to comply with the finding could lead to a prison sentence. About 5,000 men and 500 women were prosecuted and sentenced for their conscientious objection[117]; and most of them were sent to prison. About 1,000 were court-martialled and given prison sentences for refusing to obey military orders.

Many were members of the Peace Pledge Union. The

---

[117] Angus Calder says that about 3 in 100 ended up in prison, leaving the figure at somewhere between 3% and 9% of all COs.

concept was simple; if enough people refused to fight, then war, quite simply, could not happen. The immediate and obvious drawback to the idea was that it depended on the opposition to do the same. This was unlikely in the case of Germany, whose penalties for refusal were far more severe than the Allies and included being shot, forced into SS uniform and sent to the front or being sent to a concentration camp. On balance, I think the PPU might have had a problem finding their German equivalent.

It is easy to be flippant about the objectors, but these were real people who believed as strongly in peace as others believed in the war. They were supported by the church, but the church's official view was that 'when justice and decency were being obliterated by tyranny a Christian might conscientiously spill such blood as was necessary to overthrow the tyrant'[118].

Tribunals were set up with the task of deciding whether each individual's right to be an objector could or should be sustained. The chairman of the tribunal had to be a county court judge along with four others and, in theory, there had to be no bias in opinion, each case to be judged on its merits.

There were however, almost inevitably, clashes between those who were trying to pull the wool over the tribunal's eyes and those members of tribunals who were, shall we say, quite conservative in their opinions. It could lead to frustration for the panellists and humiliation for the objector. Sometimes, the conclusions were brutal:

> After being questioned...an objector...admitted: 'There is only one logical solution. A conscientious objector who does not want to help the war must commit suicide.' The chairman cordially agreed: 'I think so, or else leave the country.'

The Phoney War on the Home Front – ES Turner

'...Many private employers sacked pacifists...a

---

[118] *The Phoney War on the Home Front* – ES Turner

hundred and nineteen local authorities had decided to dismiss all COs from their service or to suspend them for the duration'.

The People's War – Britain 1939-1945 – Angus Calder

From this distance, eighty years away and generations apart, from the luxury of my war-free sofa and with the fresh light of a spring day pouring in through the window, it is quite easy for me to see it from both sides. I wonder how I might have been then. I confess, with some shame, that I have crossed a picket line and borne the brunt of my workmates anger; I had been a union member since the age of nineteen, proudly so, but my conscience compelled me to resign from the union under the circumstances. Multiply that feeling of social alienation, the pricking of my conscience and the intimidation of those who were once my friends and multiply that by a hundred and I might get somewhere near to the feelings of the two sides in the conscientious objector debate.

There also existed the power of the Ministry of Labour to compel the population into essential work where there was a shortage of staff.

The Emergency Powers Act of May 1940 gave the government the power to conscript people to work in the essential industries. Armed with the power, the government put that power to use and, in March 1941, the Essential Works Order introduced conscription. It was brought in reluctantly because there was a general consensus of opinion that people who worked willingly would work better, but the shortages in manpower had become so great that the government's hand was forced.

Women between ages 20 and 30 became liable for conscription. There were exemptions; women with children under the age if 14 were exempted. Many women volunteered anyway, able to go to work with the knowledge that their child would be safe in the day-care nurseries opened and funded by the Ministry of Health.

There was no doubt that the attitude to COs had changed

since the Great War, and having Neville Chamberlain give, at the very least, a reasonable understanding and sympathy towards their cause, made those less tolerant of COs less likely to display the overly and occasionally overtly aggressive stance of the Great War.

However, despite the veneer of government tolerance, COs were still attacked and verbally abused in the streets and sacked from their jobs. To a degree it is understandable; there was bound to be resentment among those who had lost husbands, sons and wives to the war and patriotism easily descends to baseness when whipped up by anger and vitriol and loss.

It is ironic that the fight to maintain freedom almost always, in some way, demands the instigation of oppression.

Rationing

Food

> I can't see the sense of defending our country if the troops are going to come back to find its inhabitants dead of starvation.
>
> Frederick Marquis, 1st Earl of Woolton, to shipping minister Ronald Cross.

Rationing was introduced on 8 January 1940. It was severe and affected every aspect and every level of society.

The reason it had to be introduced was that old double-edged sword of island status. It might well have made it difficult for the Germans to invade, but it also made us vulnerable in others ways. That strength of physical isolation was suddenly found to be a weakness.

The problem was that we relied immensely on imports. Ninety percent of fats and cereals, eighty percent of fruit, seventy percent of sugar and cheese and fifty percent of the country's meat were imported. This was 20 million tons of goods shipped in per year. A quarter of the country's butter and half of the country's cheese came from New Zealand, 11,617 miles away.

Less than one-third of the food available in Britain before 1939 was produced at home. It was a gift to the Axis forces.

At the beginning of the war, Britain had the largest merchant fleet in the world, more than Japan and the USA together. There wasn't a place that it did not go, but most of all it ran the seas between Britain and the USA but its size made it an easy target. 3,500 merchant ships were sunk by the Germans during the war, 1,006 in 1942 alone, along with 175 warships that were there to protect the convoys. By comparison, the Germans lost 780 U-boats. This became known as The Battle of the Atlantic. Across the other side of the world, Japan too prevented the trade of goods such as tea and sugar and rice, along with raw materials such as rubber and tin. By the middle of 1941 Britain was losing ships three times faster than they were being built. By the end of 1940, 728,000 tons of food making its way to Britain had been lost, sunk by German submarine activity.

There was nothing to do but tighten belts.

The food rations per adult per week went:

FOOD	ALLOWANCE
BACON and HAM	4ozs (100g)
BUTTER	2ozs (50g)
CHEESE	2ozs (50g)
MARGARINE	4ozs (100g)
COOKING FAT	4ozs (100g)
MILK	3 pints (1800ml)
SUGAR	8ozs (225g)
PRESERVES (every 2 months)	1lb (450g)
TEA	2ozs (50g)
EGGS	1 shell egg a week
SWEETS (every 4 weeks)	12 ozs (350g)

Needless to say, there are variables within these allocations. Cheese allocation sometimes (not often) rose to four or eight ounces. Cooking fat often fell to half the allocated amount, down to 2 ounces. Milk was sometimes capped at two pints and eggs were sometimes limited to one every two weeks. You could have one packet of dried eggs every four weeks. Yum. The shortage of eggs arose because, in 1940, millions of commercially-farmed hens had to be killed and sold off as food because there was a shortage of feed for them. This did however lead to an increase in the number of domestic chickens because the eggs they produced were unrationed. It wasn't as straightforward as all that, of course, hell no. If you had an egg-laying chicken, you lost your entitlement to rationed eggs. The silver lining to this negligible cloud was that you could get more grain to feed the chicken. Swings and roundabouts.

With regards to the tea; today's average tea bag has about 0.6 ounces of tea in it. With that, we would be permitted a little under four cups per week during the war. There would be anarchy, especially at my present workplace where they go through tea like a 1980s Range Rover goes through fuel.

Of course, the more vulnerable were allowed extra; babies, younger children and expectant and nursing mothers were permitted concentrated orange juice and cod liver oil (not as a cocktail I hope) from Welfare Clinics with a priority on the milk, which was also given to the disabled.

There was also some flexibility for those requiring special dietary needs. Vegetarians were issued with special ration books (today we have only just managed to get a green 'V' on most restaurant menus) and for those whose diet was restricted by religious obligations, those in hard manual labour, the poor and those with special health needs such as diabetes, hypoglycaemia, steatorrhoea and nephritis.

There was the usual amount of whining and scare-mongering from certain quarters, of course. This from the *Daily Mail*, always one to understate its feelings and put the people first:

> Your butter is going to be rationed next month. It would be scarcely possible-even if Dr. Goebbels were asked to help-to devise a more harmful piece

of propaganda for Great Britain. Our enemy's butter ration has just been increased from 3ozs to just under 4ozs. Perhaps because Goering's phrase, 'guns or butter' has given butter a symbolical significance. But mighty Britain, Mistress of the Seas, heart of a great Empire, proud of her wealth and resources? Her citizens are shortly to get just 4ozs of butter a week. There is no good reason to excuse Mr. Morrison, the Minister of Food, for this stupid decision.

However, it would seem that this middle-class bible was strangely out of step with the people at this time.

...the general public were not so hostile to the idea of rationing. A Liverpool housewife told Mass Observation, 'I wish to goodness they would introduce rationing. At last I would be able to go into a shop and get what I was allowed. As it is I've got to beg for certain commodities and make up large orders before asking for what I want...and then they turn around and say they haven't any, and if you go in the next day and ask, they're quite snooty, because you don't buy anything else. This constant scrounging is getting on my nerves.' Many believed that rationing would bring fair shares for all and stop profiteering. A Dorking cleaner thought that the 'Price of food at the local grocer is scandalously high. And I'm sure he's profiteering. He complains he'll be ruined by the war. I hope he will. I shan't register with a man who charges so high and has such poor supplies.'
Shopkeepers suspected of profiteering came in for a good deal of abuse, as one Mass Observer overheard: 'Profiteers! Money-grabbers! We know who reap the benefit in times like these. Blinking profiteers, that's what you are! Sucking money from

the poor!' And he concluded his report on 'Grocery in War': 'On one point grocer and customer are at accord. A hundred times a day the sentiment is expressed on both sides of the counter, I'll be glad when they start rationing. It'll put an end to all this.'"

Outbreak: 1939: The World Goes to War - Terry Charman

In a survey conducted by the British institute of Public opinion, shortly after rationing was introduced, it was shown that 60% of those questioned thought that rationing was necessary, while 28% were against and 12% did not know.[119]

As we all know, they did start rationing but, as with any form of prohibition or tightly maintained government control, this inevitably led to the leeches of society feeding off the suffering of others. In the same way that organised crime in the USA had benefitted enormously from Prohibition, so those so inclined in Britain benefitted from the scarcity of goods. This will be seen later in the section on crime in Britain in WW2.

There were essentially three ration plans:

1) Coupons: Coupons came in ration books. Issued by Ministry of Food offices, fifty million[120] were printed at the start of the war. Every person, adult or child, had their own ration book. Most adults had buff-coloured ration books. Pregnant women, nursing mothers and children under 5 had green ration books. Blue ration books went to children between the ages of 5 and 16.
Each book had to be registered with the nearest appropriate shop. When the customer bought

---

[119] *From Bread and Jam to Woolton Pie: Food Rationing and Improved Nutrition in WWII Great Britain* - Jennifer G. Joyner University of Washington
[120] *Life of a Teenager in Wartime London* – Duncan Leatherdale.

something from the shop, the appropriate coupon was removed. The ration for the allocated period had then been dispensed. You could not carry these over. If you missed your three pints of milk for one week, you could not get six pints the next week. Miss it, miss out – that was the rule. This did change later and there was a certain time limit on coupons for particular goods so, for example, you could save up four weeks' worth of coupons for something if you wanted to celebrate a birthday or other occasion.

If you lost your book, you had to pay a shilling for a new one and sign a declaration saying that it was lost. That way, if it turned up with the local leeches, it could be traced back to you and you could, if necessary, be prosecuted for trading in the black market.

2) There was also a points system introduced on 1 December 1941 via a separate pink ration book. Initially, the allocation was 16 points per month, which went up to 24 points and then back down to 20 after VE day. It ran in conjunction with regular coupon rationing, but was more flexible; it gave people more control over their shopping and you could pool your points or save them. A bonus to this system was that the buyer was not tied to any single point of purchase. A particular product was worth a certain number of points. The most common example of this is Spam. I choose Spam because I love Spam. Unfortunately, one tin of Spam used up your entire monthly point allocation. Personally, I think it would be worth it. You might not. If you preferred fish, 16 points got you a can or you could have 8lbs of split peas for the same amount of points. Here are some example of the cost of goods by points per pound or by per tin:

Sultanas..............................8
Skimmed Milk......................5
Currants............................16
Baked Beans........................2
Biscuits (dry)....2, (sweet)..........4
Herrings............................2
Sultanas..............................8
Stewed Steak......................20
Rolled Oats........................2
Sausage-Meat......................12
Best Red Salmon.................**32 per small tin**
Chopped Ham...................**3 per oz**[121]

As you can see, there were staples and there were luxuries and there was always a price to be paid. Don't forget, in this case points did not make prizes; on top of the restriction, you still had to pay for the goods.

> 3) The third method of distribution controlled goods such as milk and eggs. These were handed out when available with priority given to those in greater need such as pregnant women[122].

At this juncture, there is a remarkable man who needs a mention in despatches for the work that he put into rationing and into winning over the people to accept the concept in the first place - Frederick Marquis, 1st Earl of Woolton.

Occasionally in history, people and events collide as if they were meant to be together, as if their destiny had been preordained and they were to reach either a pinnacle or a nadir with that one particular moment in time. This was what happened to Frederick Marquis, 1st Earl of Woolton (he was apparently going to be made into a Marquis, but his real name, being Marquis, meant that he would have been Frederick Marquis Marquis etc.

---

[121] *Rationing and Shortages* - Ralph W. Hill. www.bbc.co.uk
[122] *Life of a Teenager in Wartime London* – Duncan Leatherdale.

Hence the earldom).

Frederick Marquis was born in 1883 to a saddler and his wife. He was educated at Manchester Grammar School (as was Ben Kingsley, the actor, Michael Wood, the historian, Chris Addison, actor and occasional comedian, Robert Powell, the actor, John Ogden, the pianist and a plethora of other famous and successful people) and then went to Manchester University where in 1906 he gained a degree in science. He then moved to Liverpool in 1908, where he took an interest in the social services while doing graduate work at the University of Liverpool.[123]

He was turned down seven times for service in the Great War due to a disability, but went to work at the British War office as secretary to the Leather Control Board. He resigned when his complaints about excessive red-tape went unheeded - *plus ça change*. He took up the post of warden of the David Lewis Hotel and Club Association, a social experiment established in the city's dockland slums by the successful and philanthropic Lewis's department store[124].

> It was during this time, while living in digs in Park Street, that Frederick underwent the formative experience of his life. His next-door-neighbour, a "woman of some refinement both of speech and appearance", was found dead, her body having lain undiscovered for some days.
>
> "Few things affected my life more surely," he later recalled. "We were young men … expounding economic history and theory … yet here we were, living in this sordid street, the surrounding houses of which were insanitary and verminous, where the sickening smell of overcrowded humanity was such that, as I write now, it still seems to nauseate me".
>
> Paddy Shennan - www.liverpoolecho.co.uk. April

---

[123] www.bodley.ox.ac.uk
[124] Paddy Shennan - www.liverpoolecho.co.uk. April 2016

2016

In 1920 he joined the firm of Lewis's and rose meteorically, to become chairman and senior managing director. At the beginning of the war, he was made Director-General of Equipment and Stores at the Ministry of Supply and then, in that collision with fate, became Minister of Food in April 1940 under Neville Chamberlain (taking over from Herbert Morrison). He remained apolitical, even under Churchill, but has been described as being on the fringe of liberalism.

It was probably down to this man that the country took so readily to rationing. He was a man of the people from humble roots, who had been lucky enough to have a good education and made use of that education to the benefit of others. He had a social conscience; he understood the value of money and of food and of personal dignity and was able to bring together the necessities of wartime austerity with the needs of the people.

> Woolton decided that it wasn't enough to just ration food or limit what people ate; he set the Ministry the goals of treating the British public as consumers, and explaining nutrition to them in simple terms so that they could get the most nutrition out of the available food despite the rations. Previously, before the war, the British government had been infiltrated by the thinking of Home Economists. Consequently, it was widely accepted by government in the UK that there was a strong link between diet, and a healthy population. Woolton's chief scientific advisor was Jack Drummond, who worked closely with Wilson Jameson, British Chief Medical Officer from 1940 to 1950. Their methods of communicating would prove to be effective: by the end of the war, housewives had become very educated in nutritional vocabulary. The Ministry issued many cooking leaflets, often dedicated to specific topics

such as the magic of carrots. The language used was practical, and realistic for the time...

British Wartime Food - www.cooksinfo.com

So fond were the people of him that he earned the affectionate nicknames of 'Uncle Fred', the 'Czar of the Kitchen Front' and 'Lord High Keeper of the National Larder'[125]. They even named the Woolton Pie after him, a recipe by housewives' favourite, Marguerite Patten:

WOOLTON PIE

Ingredients:

1 lb each of diced potatoes, cauliflower, swedes and carrots;
Three or four spring onions;
One teaspoonful of vegetable extract;
1 oz of oatmeal or rolled oats.
A little chopped parsley

Method:

Dice and cook the potatoes, cauliflower, swedes and carrots in boiling salted water.
Strain, but keep three-quarters of a pint of the vegetable water.
Arrange the vegetables in a large pie dish or casserole. Add the vegetable extract and the rolled oats or oatmeal to the vegetable liquid. Cook until thickened and pour over the vegetables.
Cook everything together with just enough water to cover, stirring often to prevent it sticking to the

---

[125] *Lord Woolton, 81, Food Minister In Early Years of War, Is Dead* - www.nytimes.com. Dec. 15, 1964

pan. Let the mixture cool. Spoon into a pie dish, sprinkle with chopped parsley.
Cover with a crust of potatoes or wholemeal pastry. Bake in a moderate oven until golden brown. Serve hot with gravy[126].

Here's another top-tip recipe from Marguerite:

CARROT SCONES

12 tbsp SR flour & 1 teaspoon baking powder – sifted together
2 tbsp softened butter or marg
4 tbsp sugar (caster works best)
8 tbsp grated carrot
A few drops of vanilla flavouring

Pre-heat oven to GM6/200°C. Grease a baking tray.
Leave the butter/marg out so that it becomes nice & soft to work with. This makes it easier to mix in the sugar. Beat these until they are light & creamed. Add in the grated carrot, a bit at a time. It will not look like the prettiest thing in the world – but stick with it.
Add in the vanilla.
Slowly add the sifted flour. The more you beat, the more moisture the carrots will release to bind the mixture together. I usually, after a minute or so, use my hands to combine. You will be left with a sticky carrot flecked dough.
Pinch and roll the desired amount between your hands. You should get 12 ample sized scones from this recipe.

---

[126] *WWII recipes from the Ministry of Food* - www.telegraph.co.uk 29 Mar 2008 and www.recipespastandpresent.org.uk

Place on baking tray and sprinkle with a little sugar if required.
Cook in the centre of the oven for about 20 mins.
Once firm on top & at the sides, they are done. Remove from oven & cool.
Serve with plain, with butter or with jam, cream (mock cream if you are going all out!) and a nice sunny day. Or a cold one with a nice cup of tea[127].

Due to the lack of egg to bind these, they can be a little crumbly. They last for about a week in a tin, longer in the fridge. However, only 2% of the population had a fridge at this time, so you would have to trust to that tin – big time.

My love of Spam is wholly counterbalanced by my loathing for carrots. I would rather have one tin of Spam a month that a thousand carrots a week. That's just me though. My wife is very pro-carrot and has little time for the delights of Spam.

The fact is that I and many like me could not afford to be fussy. Britain had to adjust and make do – and it did. Carrots replaced sweets for many children. There were recipes for everything; nettles, horse, hedgehogs, snails, squirrels, sparrows, rabbit, the inner bark of an elm tree, dandelions, pigeons, partridge, rooks and cardoon (artichoke thistle, apparently), among myriad others.

Incidentally, the claim that carrots could help you see in the dark also originated at this time. It was merely a crafty ploy to a) try and hide the fact from the Germans that we had radar and that it was actually carrots that helped us detect their aircraft and b) to make us eat more carrots. I have no idea if the Germans fell for that. Whatever their faults at the time, gullibility would have to have been pretty high on the list for them to fall for that.

To add to this, there was even the odd ditty in celebration

---

[127] www.queensofvintage.com from *The Victory Cookbook*

of our dirt-stained chums. Here's a catchy one about Mr Potato[128]:

> P is for Protection Potatoes afford
> O is for the Ounces of Energy stored.
> T is for Tasty and Vitamins rich in
> A is for the Art to be learnt in the kitchen.
> T is for Transport we need not demand
> O is for old England's Own Food from the land.
> E is for the Energy eaten by you
> S is for the spuds which will carry us through.

In October 1939, the Ministry of Food launched the 'Dig for Victory' campaign, where people were encouraged to grown their own produce. Not only was it intended to provide people with food, but it was also intended to free up valuable shipping space. It was astoundingly successful. The number of allotments jumped from 815,000 to 1,400,000 (with no 6 year wait like today's allotments). Meat was reared domestically in the form of pigs, chickens and rabbits. It was estimated that by 1943, two and a half million gardens were producing about £12 million pounds of product a year[129]. It seemed that every inch of spare ground was cultivated.

> Women's Institutes, working voluntarily, played an important part in food production, too. By the end of 1941 they were making 4,500 tonnes of jam and 120 tonnes of bottled fruit a year. They also rediscovered the value of natural medicines and tonics. In one year, for example, they picked 4 million wild rose hips that were made into a vitamin-rich syrup for children.
>
> *At Home in World War Two: Rationing* – Stewart Ross

---

[128] Characters called Potato Pete and Dr Carrot were both part of the propaganda drive to home-grow and eat veg during the war
[129] *At Home in World War Two: Rationing* – Stewart Ross

Even eating out had to bear the consequences of rationing. There was a feeling among the population that only the well-off could afford to eat out and that, because restaurant foods were unrationed, this gave those with cash to splash a distinct advantage. So, in 1941, the government limited the price of meals to five shillings (about a tenner today). Food was allocated to restaurant with dishes classed as either 'main' or 'subsidiary'. The 'main' comprised of foods such as meat or fish and only one of these was allowed and a total of only three courses permitted. This went some way to equalising the situation but, if you had enough money, you could go to as many restaurants as you wanted in one night. A 'grub' crawl instead of pub crawl, I suppose.

One other important thing that arose was the establishing of the British Restaurant. The main aim of these was to provide food at a reasonable, subsidised price to those who had lost their homes in bombings. However, they became popular places to eat of their own accord.

School meals also increased in popularity.

> Before the war, only about 250,000 school meals a day were served; by the end of the war, school meals happened just about everywhere, feeding about 1,850,000 children a day. The Ministry made it compulsory for any factory over a certain size to open a canteen to feed its workers. The number of factory canteens consequently went from 1,500 in 1939 to 18,500 in 1945.
>
> *British Wartime Food* - www.cooksinfo.com

In May 1941, approximately 79 million midday meals were being eaten in subsidised restaurants, canteens and school dining room. By the end of 1944, the number had reached 170 million[130].

---

[130] *Life of a Teenager in Wartime London* – Duncan Leatherdale

Once again, the war inveigled its way into everyday life. Food rationing became both an equaliser and a burden. It brought out the best in people and, as we shall see later, the worst in people, but to have survived upon the diet that Britain did, to have *adapted* the way Britain did and in a way that contributed not only to victory, but to the eventual victory of the Battle of the Atlantic, was to the nation's credit.

What Else Was Rationed?

Petrol

> Petrol ration books are available to-day on application at post offices or local taxation offices, but they cannot be used before Sept. 16 when the rationing system comes into force.
>
> After that date no petrol for any purpose will be obtainable except against ration coupons.
>
> Applicants who must produce the car registration book, will receive from the issuing clerk, two ration books one marked "first month" and one marked "second month" containing coupons for the quantity allowed them according to the rating of the car as shown in the registration book.
>
> Each coupon represents one unit, which for the present represents one gallon, but the unit may be changed later.
>
> Car owners should not that ration books are only valid during the period for which they are issued – the first between Sept. 16 and Oct. 15 and the second between Oct. 16 and Nov. 15. In other words, you cannot hoard your coupons.
>
> Article first published in the Daily Telegraph, Sept 8, 1939

Petrol was rationed from 16 September 1939. In an age when all had become motorised, when the world had shed the horse in favour of the combustion engine and people began to realise that they would not fall off the edge of the world should they venture outside Berkshire, it all came to a grinding halt.

Once again, the issue of petrol was governed by coupons, so not only was the driver restricted by finances, but they were now restricted by the government.

The petrol allowance depended upon the usage of your car, but generally each car was allowed between four and ten gallons per month. The cost of petrol then was 1/6 (equivalent to about £2.95 today). Now, my father had a lovely 1958 Rover 90. It was built like a tank and did 17 miles to the gallon. Most pre-war cars did about 15 miles or less to the gallon. If we are generous and take the Rover 90 as an example, a gallon would have got him from Bracknell (where we lived) to Windsor - about eight miles - and back with a mile or so to spare. Even on ten gallons a month and the 170 miles that it could have taken him, that would have been 10.5 journeys to Windsor and back. If he had worked there, it would have been a problem.

The trains, run by the 'big four' private companies - Great Western Railway (GWR), London, Midland and Scottish Railway (LMS), London and North Eastern Railway (LNER), Southern Railway (SR) - were taken under government control during the war, under the Railway Executive Committee and became a mainstay of public transport and they were geared towards war usage. Station names were blacked out to confuse the enemy in case of invasion and the public were encouraged to stay at home during holidays as the railways were used to move freight; extra food supplies, equipment, troops, raw materials and troops.

Because of the cutbacks in shipping and petrol rationing, the demand made upon the railways increased enormously, up to 500% in some cases. The use of the railways had to be prioritised, so preference was given to troop movements and to factory workers. Leisure travel could not be permitted to impede freight movement. Cheap fares were cancelled and public services cut or restricted to short-distance travel. Leisure travel was discouraged by the withdrawal of cheap day tickets and reduced or completely withdrawn bus services.

The basic civilian petrol ration was abolished on 1 July 1942 and fuel restricted to official use, such as the emergency services, bus companies and farmers. The fuel that was supplied to the approved users was dyed so that it could be easily identified should it be used inappropriately.

Clothes

Due to the difficulties with imports and a huge demand for war-related materials such as wool, (for the manufacture of uniforms), and silk (for making parachutes, maps, and gunpowder bags) there was an impact on the availability of clothes, soft furnishings and household linens. As is usually the case, because of the scarcity of fabrics, the prices went up and it became necessary, in June 1941, to introduce clothes rationing. This not only saved on materials and helped go some way to softening the impact of the shortages, but the reduced demand also released over a quarter of a million tons of shipping and helped free up almost four hundred thousand people to go into the services or war production.

What did clothes rationing mean to the ordinary person? Well, if you had money and could afford the best, then you could still afford the best; if you had very little money and could only afford the ordinary, that would not change either. The difference would now be that, rich or poor, you would still only be allowed to utilise a certain number of coupons per item of clothing over a year. It didn't matter what you paid, five bob or five pounds, that pair of pyjamas would still use up eight coupons out of the allocated yearly amount of sixty six coupons.

Initially, every adult was permitted sixty-six coupons, but as the war went on it dropped to forty-eight in 1942 and thirty-six in 1943. The allowances were slightly greater for children as they were still growing and they got an extra ten coupons if they were above average height or weight.

It is something that we take for granted nowadays.

Clothes are mass-produced, imported in bulk and made and sold cheaply. Production methods allow a very quick turnover of goods and the enormity of cargo ships and the advent of air distribution have produced a glut of cheap and ever-available goods.

Below are a couple of tables for men and women, adults and children, which show the item of clothing and the number of coupons required for each. Take a look. If you are single, you will have different priorities to someone married. If you are married, your priorities change again. If you are male or female (you should be one or the other), your priorities again will be different, especially in such a gender-biased society. Try and come up with a year's clothing.

CLOTHING FOR MEN AND BOYS	**ADULT**	**CHILD**
Unlined mackintosh or cape	9	7
Other mackintoshes, or raincoat, or overcoat	16	11
Coat, or jacket, or blazer or like garment	13	11
Waistcoat, or pull-over, or cardigan, or jersey	5	3
Trousers (other than fustian or corduroy)	8	6
Fustian or corduroy trousers	5	5
Shorts	5	3
Overalls, or dungarees or like garment	6	4
Dressing-gown or bathing gown	8	6
Night-shirt or pair of pyjamas	8	6
Shirt, or combinations—woollen	8	6
Shirt, or combinations—other material	5	4
Pants, or vest, or bathing costume, or child's blouse	4	2
Pair of socks or stockings	3	1
Collar, or tie, or pair of cuffs	1	1
Two handkerchiefs	1	1

Scarf, or pair of gloves or mittens	2	2
Pair of slippers or galoshes	4	2
Pair of boots or shoes	7	3
Pair of leggings, gaiters or spats	3	2

Aesthetically, it wasn't so bad for the men. They weren't exactly peacocks and clothes were more often than not simply a matter of functionality and an acceptable turnout for the office. It was difficult to mess up a shirt, tie, jacket and trousers.

For women though who, whether we like to admit it or not, are much more driven by their attire and their natural make-up, it was a difficult time.

CLOTHING FOR WOMEN AND GIRLS	ADULT	CHILD
Lined mackintoshes, or coats (over 28 in. long)	14	11
Jacket, or short coat (under 28 in. in length)	11	8
Dress, or gown, or frock - woollen	11	8
Dress, or gown, or frock - other material	7	5
Gym tunic, or girl's skirt with bodice	8	6
Blouse, or sports shirt, or cardigan, or jumper	5	3
Skirt, or divided skirt	7	5
Overalls, or dungarees or like garment	6	4
Apron, or pinafore	3	2
Pyjamas	8	6
Petticoat, or slip, or combination, or cami-knickers	4	3
Other undergarments, including corsets	3	2
Pair of stockings	2	1
Pair of socks (ankle length)	1	1
Collar, or tie, or pair of cuffs	1	1

Two handkerchiefs	1	1
Scarf, or pair of gloves or mittens, or muff	2	2
Pair of slippers, boots or shoes	5	3
2 ounces of wool knitting yarn	1	1
1 yard wool cloth 36" wide	3	3

Any luck? Have you done the kids' clothes? Have you ordered for your husband as he asked you to do, because this really isn't the sort of thing with which he should concern himself in this day and age. If you are a man on your own, how did you do? I used to work for a well-known bus company and we got a similar list every working year for uniforms. You have never seen such a bunch of perplexed men staring helplessly like dogs who had just had their food stolen, at a piece of paper, most of them not knowing what the difference is between one type of jacket and another.

If you are a single lady or girl, what matters most to you? Looking good for the men? Looking good to the other women at work? Looking smart and fetching for the boss? Do you want clothes for leisure or work? Don't forget, what you get now, has to last a year. Do you spend more than you can afford in the hope that it will last longer?

Those sixty-six points get munched up pretty quickly, don't they?

It's also an intriguing look into the fashions of a bygone era. Fustian, anyone? It is apparently 'thick, hard-wearing twilled cloth with a short nap'. And does anybody use handkerchiefs anymore? We are used now to stuffing our pockets with tissues and finding them in shreds in the washing machine, but these were material handkerchiefs designed to hold the sort of bodily debris that should most certainly not be stored in the pocket. Two a year? From a 21st century perspective, I would have to decline.

Clothes rationing merely emphasised the invasiveness of the war, how it managed to seep its way into every corner of the British daily life.

Partly because of the inequality that came with clothes

rationing, that is, the more money you had, the better the clothing you could afford, even within the restrictions of the coupon system, utility clothing was introduced.

In this context, 'utility' simply meant 'standard', but there was a fear that 'standard' meant 'awful'. In fairness, it probably did, but it was, importantly, price-regulated and quality-controlled.

> Utility clothing was also subject to price regulations. Profits were restricted for both manufactures and retailers which resulted in Utility clothing being significantly cheaper than non-utility clothing when first introduced. This together with the initial dislike by some retailers of reduced profits may have given utility clothing its bad name.
>
> *An Introduction to Utility Clothing* - Ian Baylay. www.1940.co.uk

And the government wasn't daft; it knew that people, under any circumstances, were still people, and people need to express their individuality, needed to feel special, to feel attractive, so it brought in fashion designers to design a range of utility clothing that was

> ...attractive, stylish and very varied. The Incorporated Society of London Fashion Designers (IncSoc) was founded in 1942 to represent the collective interests of the fashion industry in Britain, promote exports and develop standards of design. There were originally eight members: Peter Russell, Norman Hartnell, Bianca Mosca, Digby Morton, Victor Stiebel, Elspeth Champcommunal and Hardy Amies. Edward Molyneux and Charles Creed joined soon after. They were commissioned by the Board of Trade to produce designs for stylish yet economical outfits that could be produced under the Utility scheme.

As well as using Utility materials, the designers also had to work within the austerity regulations.

How Clothes Rationing Affected Fashion in The Second World War - Laura Clouting and Amanda Mason
www.iwm.org.uk

They went on sale in 1942 with a guarantee of quality and value for money, marked with a 'CC41' mark, which stood for Civilian Clothing 1941. It was actually a very cool logo and would do extraordinarily well today if some avant-garde had thought of it.

It's great, isn't it? It has been described as a couple of Pacmen (Pacmans?), but it was long before that tail-chasing piece of hypnotica and, for this writer at least, was futuristic and very cool.

There were rules that applied to utility clothing, clearly with the idea that money would be saved through the design and that no material would be wasted on excess. In *The Home Front in World War Two*, Susie Hodge gave us a list of the regulations to be applied:

- pleats, tucks, folds or gathers were restricted drastically
- no turn-ups on trousers
- no lace or embroidery trimmings
- similarly, no velvet, fin or leather trimmings
- ladies' skirts to be no longer than knee-length and straight
- no elastic waistbands or fancy belts on any ladies' clothes

- heels on ladies' shoes had to be less than two inches high
- no double-breasted men's jackets
- a maximum of three pockets were allowed on men's jackets
- a maximum of two pockets were allowed on men's trousers
- a maximum of three buttons were allowed on ladies' jackets

In Angus Calder's *The People's War: Britain 1939-1945*, the regulations are further revealed:

> ...notorious "Austerity Regulations" of the summer of 1942 did circumscribe design. Some forbade trimmings as embroidery and appliqué work; others limited use of scarce raw materials. Manufacturers were prohibited producing more than a set number of basic designs for the type of clothing - six shapes, in the case of female underwear - the object being to encourage long and economical runs in production. The number of pleats, seams and buttonholes in women's outerwear were fixed, and so were the widths of sleeves, hems and collars. For men, trouser turn-ups and double cuffs were prohibited, shirts were shorn of two inches of tail, pockets limited, and socks must not exceed nine and a half inches. These apparently petty expedients saved enormous saved enormous quantities of textiles.

The clothing was not overly popular, perhaps because of the stigma attached to it, perhaps because it simply did not have enough 'flair' or simply because it represented something, the war, that the people would just rather shy away from as much as possible. Things were adapted to try to suit the individual, but even those doing the adapting were limited by the materials with which they could adapt.

As with all these wartime gestures, clothes rationing too had to find a slogan. It came up with what was actually a very apt, almost fun idea: make do and mend.

As a 'movement', or a concept if you will, 'Make Do and Mend' was adopted by the government as a way to get the population to repair and reuse their old clothes. They even, in leaflet number eight, encouraged women to be their own 'Clothes Doctor'. It all worked too; aged wedding dresses were dragged form closets and turned into skirts or shirts, the frilly bits used as adornments. People darned until their fingers were raw, clothes were handed down from one generation to the next. Trousers were turned into skirts and vice versa.

In keeping with the anthropomorphic nature of the governments campaigns, along with Potato Pete and Dr Carrot came Mrs Sew and Sew. I hate to say this, but this monster creation was the stuff of nightmares; she had a cotton-reel body and clothes-peg legs and a couple of the widest staringest, creepiest eyes you could possibly imagine. She was the doll that stared from the dark corner of the room at night and forbade you sleep because, if you should fall into unconsciousness, your soul was hers. They got away with the veg folk, but this was Frankenstein Unbound.

That aside, the restrictions applied by war did have an effect on fashion and not just for the war. It wiped away the thirties fashions, the non-pleated skirt was fashionable during the remainder of the forties and into the very early fifties. Single-breasted men's suits became the norm.

More importantly, there was the need to rebel against the stern austerity of war-wear, which led to the bright colours and exuberance of the fifties. It was as if somebody had flicked a switch and released the rainbow and the imagination. Under with the influence of Christian Dior and others, femininity was back in fashion. Encouraged by the glamour of the film stars of the era, by the influence of America, first started by the island's influx of US soldiers, the ending of clothes rationing in 1949 and the need for the new, for a rediscovery of the self that had been hidden for so long in the dull, khaki colour of war, the population broke away, slowly at first, then bloomed wildly in the fifties and sixties.

> Governmental regulations dictated clothing styles for men and women, and though many believe that the war was a period of stagnation in style, it was actually an impetus leading to a post-war fashion revolution in America and Europe instigated by Christian Dior and his New Look in 1947... the majority of women embraced the New Look. For years, British women had endured shapeless, unfeminine-looking clothing...women were willing to give up their utilitarian, comfortable clothing for the New Look. Women ready to restore their femininity. Although the shape of the New Look was quite unnatural, it was undoubtedly alluring and glamorous. In addition, the New Look symbolized new hope and prosperity after years of scrimping and saving.
>
> *World War II and Fashion: The Birth of the New Look* - Lauren Olds. Illinois Wesleyan University. 2001

And us men? Give us a pair of trousers, a shirt, a tie and a jacket and we were happy – until the sixties anyway.

Water coal and soap were also rationed. Bath water was limited to five inches. Paper was rationed, so toilet paper was rationed, newspapers changed their size, reduced by fifty to sixty percent of their pre-war size. It even set the great George Orwell off on one of his lengthy whines (love him as I do, he was a bit of a whiner sometimes) because with less paper, fewer books were published, which affected the living of those who wrote for their bread.

> A particularly interesting detail is that out of the 100,000 tons allotted to the Stationery Office, the

War Office gets no less than 25,000 tons, or more than the whole of the book trade put together. ... At the same time paper for books is so short that even the most hackneyed "classic" is liable to be out of print, many schools are short of textbooks, new writers get no chance to start and even established writers have to expect a gap of a year or two years between finishing a book and seeing it published.

George Orwell, As I Please - Tribune, 20 October 1944

Whatever you think of the unhappy artist's opinion, he came up with a valid social point[131]. Not only did the rationing affect people's ability to make a living, but it impacted upon education. How many children did not reach their full potential for the want of a textbook? How did the lost potential affect Britain post-war?

Why was soap rationed? Surely, this was rationing *ad absurdum*. The answer was quite simple really - soap was rationed so that oils and fats could be saved for food. Glycerine could be used for explosives and fats to literally grease the wheels, were used by the military.

In the case of soap, four coupons were given each month. However, soap wasn't just soap. There was hard soap, toilet soap, liquid soap, soap flakes and soap powder and each different soap had a different coupon value.

Coal too was severely rationed. Almost all domestic heating was from coal fires; hot water was from coal fired boilers or coppers and many people were still using coal fired kitchen ranges. Industry, too, was powered by coal[132]. It had been put on

---

[131] Despite advanced tuberculosis, Orwell still managed to serve as a sergeant in the Home Guard. He also fought for the Marxists in the Spanish Civil War saying that, 'This fascism ... somebody's got to stop it'. He was a man of intellect, courage and conviction – and a bloody good writer.

[132] *Coal Rationing In and After 1940s Wartime Britain* - www.1900s.org.uk

ration in July 1941, domestic use restricted to fifty hundredweight (2540 kg) a year. This might seem a lot, but when its everyday usage, from heating to cooking to turning the wheels of industry, was taken into account, it had a great effect. The winters of the 1940s were also bitterly cold and people suffered accordingly. The obvious thing to do, for the Brits at least, would be to stick an extra layer on, but with clothes rationing, even that option was limited.

There was one infamous and final form of rationing that affected the nation in many ways, from health to home, and that was light.

The Blackout

> In the Autumn of 1939, during the slightly hysterical confusion that comes with the outbreak of war, Great Britain introduced stringent blackout regulations to thwart the murderous ambitions of the *Luftwaffe*. For three months it was essentially illegal to show any light at night, however faint. Rule breakers could be arrested for lighting a cigarette in a doorway or holding a match up to read a road sign...Not since the Middle Ages had Britain been so dark, and the consequences were noisy and profound. To avoid striking the kerb or anything parked along it, cars took to straddling the middle white lines, which was fine until they encountered another vehicle doing likewise in the opposite direction.
>
> *At Home* – Bill Bryson[133]

Okay, so the link to rationing might be slightly tenuous, but the very idea that such an abstract, the rationing of light, can

---

[133] I would normally say 'The Great Bill Bryson'. If you haven't yet read his works, put this book down and read his instead.

also be applied by a few grey men and yet be so invasive in its effects speaks buckets about the distant Führer's effect upon the nation.

British Summer Time had been instigated in 1916 as a result of war with the Summer Time Act 1916 (following Germany's example incidentally), due to a need to save coal.

Just to confuse matters further:

> In 1940 the clocks weren't put back at the end of summer, so we stayed an hour ahead of Greenwich Mean Time (GMT). In spring 1941 the clocks were still put forward an hour, meaning we were TWO hours ahead of GMT. It was the middle of World War Two, so all the extra evening daylight gave people longer to get home before the blackout. The government also hoped it would save fuel. Lighter evenings means darker mornings - something that can be problematic in the far northern parts of the UK. They were eventually put back in 1947.

The Time When the Clocks Changed By More Than An Hour - Jay Cockburn. www.bbc.co.uk

So, twenty-three years before the blackout started, the country was being manipulated into shifting daylight patterns for the war effort.

There was though a big difference between moving the hands of the clock around a couple of times a year and creating the necessary physical changes to the environment in order to comply with what were quite severe regulations.

It came about on 1 September 1939, before the war had even officially started. Between sunset and sunrise every available source of light had to be controlled so that the German bombers could not be guided by the mass lights of London or Sheffield or by the small rows of houses that sat on the Norfolk coast.

There was logic behind the idea. The light from a candle, assuming that the curvature of the earth could be overcome, could be seen from a distance of thirty miles. The light of a cigarette could be seen from three miles. These are if you are on the ground; from above, if a German bomber was at 17,000 feet (which is just over three miles) the pilot could in theory see the glow of a lit cigarette. One cigarette might not actually have any the devastating blow we might suppose, but a lot of people smoked in those days.

To combat light leakage, the lights that normally lit the streets and shopfronts were doused. Theatres sat sullenly in the dark. Buses were dimly lit and trains used blue-painted light bulbs and had blinds drawn down the carriage windows after dusk. Low-density street lighting was allowed in some parts of Britain, but no lighting at all was allowed within 12 miles of the south-east coast. Not only did the train-user travel in semi-darkness, when they got to their destination, the platform will have been in darkness and the name of the station removed, just in case you turned out to be the precursor to the German public transport invasion.

In the home, people blacked out their windows with material, the best suggestions being Holland, Lancaster or Italian cloth, which were all densely woven and prevented leakage. Cotton was not thick enough and had to be folded over several times in order to have the desired effect. Those without access to large amounts of cloth for financial or scarcity reasons, often resorted to painting their windows or creating shutters out of card. The efforts made might well have caused the planes to lose their bearings, but it made for a dark and drab life in the twilight hours.

The headlights on cars were subject to strict guidelines which involved the placement of a thick cardboard disc behind the glass with a semi-circular hole in the middle of it of not more than two inches, with the straight line at the top and not above the centre line of the lamp. I might be wrong to assume that the headlights in nineteen forty-whatever were not the vacuum-sealed, impenetrable lumps that we have today and that they could be dismantled to the extent where the required cardboard could be slipped into position. Even if I were able to take apart my headlights without the risk of having many parts left over with nowhere to go (come on, we've all done it), I'm not sure that I would get the cardboard in the right place. The instructions were very precise in an obscure sort of way and no doubt there were suitably punitive measures brought upon those who had a slip of the scissors.

There was a lot of confusion over the issue of headlights and many directives were issued from the beginning of the war. Eventually, after much toing and froing, a slatted mask system was settled upon, horizontal slits across the headlights, which only allowed the road a few yards ahead to be illuminated as the light was deflected downwards. The same was applied to traffic lights.

In 1940 it became illegal to drive a light-coloured car. A speed limit of 20 mph was set in built-up areas, but this was difficult to comply with sometimes as dashboard lights were not allowed. The first vehicle to be caught exceeding the speed limit was a hearse[134].

The regulations were tightly enforced. Failure to follow the blackout regulations could lead to imprisonment or a substantial fine.

It was the ARP (Air Raid Patrol) wardens who roamed the streets and reinforced the blackout regulations. We will always have the image of the arrogant and stubborn Mr Hodges from Dad's Army, shouting 'Put that light out!', to remind us of these much-maligned souls, but it was a thankless and unpopular task, the modern equivalent I suppose being the traffic warden. These people had the authority to report those that failed to comply with the rules and if they did, it could mean some time in court or a weighty fine.

If, in the back of your mind, you are wondering whether all this darkness was actually a recipe for disaster, I can confirm that it was. Death followed everywhere - on trains, in cars, on the pavements and in the home. Where an accident could happen, it invariably did.

Let me quickly turn to the Great Bill Bryson to put it in his own inimitable way in *At Home*.

During the first four months of the war...a total of

---

[134] *The People's War - Britain 1939-1945* – Angus Calder

> 4,133 people were killed on Britain's roads - a 100% increase over the year before. Nearly three quarters of the victims were pedestrians. Without dropping a single bomb, the *Luftwaffe* was already killing six hundred people a month...There were no lights on railway stations and although platform edges were painted white, there were many accidents and it became fairly common for passengers to get off at the wrong station - or even to get off the train where there was no station at all.

Those final few words are true – a man did indeed fall 80 feet down a viaduct after his train had stopped at some signals. He mistook it for his stop. He was badly injured, but apparently survived.

Deaths on the road reached ridiculous levels. In the second year of the war, the figures for road deaths were up by over 1,700 – 10,073 as compared to 8,358 the year before (6,500 in pre-war years)[135]. One person died for every two hundred vehicles on the road. Today the figure is one in every twenty thousand[136], and that is on far busier roads. The volume of traffic was only 10% of today's traffic volume. Traffic deaths in Birmingham rose by 81% and in Glasgow, they trebled. Children under ten suffered one thousand fatalities a year. In the second year of the war, child-involved accidents went up by 68%. In September 1939 alone, there were 1,130 deaths, 148 of whom were cyclists. There was even a court judgement which stated that if a cyclist was hit during a blackout, it was their own fault.

Accidents generally increased, from drownings where people fell into unlit canals, down unlit steps, from railway platforms or any other combination of events that you can think of when combining darkness with everyday tasks. The modern

---

[135] *Road-Deaths in War-Time* - H. M. Vernon

[136] *Look Out in the Blackout* - www.parliament.uk

world is now lit to the point where, in many places, we can no longer see the stars. Imagine if you will if all those lights were taken away and you were asked to carry out what, in the present climate, would be a mundane task.

We might have been safe from the Germans, but we just weren't safe from each other.

Which leads us nicely onto the next subject...

Crime During the War

A case could be put forward that, had the Volstead Act never been put into place in 1919, organised crime as we know it today would not have existed. Once you tell people that they can't have something, then they will want it more and will do almost anything to get it – even a drink.

Likewise, if you put temptation in people's way, then you create the market by which organised crime might thrive.

An equivalent today could be the illegal downloading of music and movies. People didn't know that they wanted this until they were offered it. It doesn't really occur to people that they are putting jobs at risk, that they are depriving artists of money through royalties, that they are supporting illegal websites, many of which are supported by criminals.

On a darker level, the most obvious example is the sale of drugs. Curiosity is piqued by the forbidden and from there comes demand and supply; a market and a provider. It's an oversimplification, but it is an example nonetheless.

Rationing provided similar grounds for offence. People became tempted by the idea of an extra cut of meat - where was the harm? – and, once in a while got a little extra from under the counter. This would be on a par, I suppose, with illegal downloading; a bit of a treat where the damage goes unseen and the reward is sufficient to negate any feelings of guilt.

Then it becomes a regular occurrence. If you have the money and the need, you could buy anything you wanted and, from this, comes the 'business' of demand and supply.

> In the spring of 1941, the chairman of the North Midland Region Food Price Investigation Committee, Sir Douglas McCraith, announced that cans of soup, sold by manufacturers at six shillings and sixpence a dozen, were reaching the public at fourteen shillings and sixpence a dozen, having passed through the hands of six middlemen, one of whom had bought the goods twice.
>
> *The People's War - Britain 1939-1945* - Angus Calder

On another level, people would do things that they would never have dreamed of before the war. They would never have stolen from their neighbours. They would never have picked the pockets of the dead or made a random grab for someone's property as it stood in the street next to the remains of what was once their home. But they did; the animal tore itself free of its human condition and did what it thought necessary to survive.

It is interesting to note that crime almost divided itself in two during the war. Non-indictable offences, those that can be dealt with at most by the magistrate's court fell while indictable offences, the more serious type of crime that came under the remit of the crown courts, rose. More serious crimes became more frequent. The only crimes to go up in the non-indictable areas was against children. This could have been because of evacuation and the placing of the wrong child with the wrong family or into the wrong environment – city kid to isolated countryside for example. It could be down to the basic frustrations of being an adult carrying the load at that time, an almost unimaginable burden today, or maybe the extraordinary circumstances just brought out the latent nastiness in people that the veneer of civilisation was able to control outside of the stresses of war. It could be that people were simply more willing to report each other, either through genuine concern or sheer vindictiveness.

The number of non-indictable offences fell from 709,019 in 1938 to 297, 438 in 1945. This does however include traffic offences, in which case the numbers were 233,895 to 149,019 respectively. Interesting, it is drunkenness and disorderedly behaviour that were most notably down. Non-indicatable assaults hovered around the ten to twelve thousand mark from 1938 to 1945.

2,677 people were imprisoned or fined for looting (roughly 50/50 split). 332 were imprisoned for blackout crimes against (wait for it) 898,330 being fined. 1,815 were imprisoned for black market offences with 101,729 being fined.

The trend downwards is only marred by the offences against children. Cruelty and neglect almost doubled, possibly for the reasons stated above, from 932 in 1938 to 1,634 in 1945. There was also an increase in prosecutions for failure to attend school from 4,620 in 1938 to 10,102 in 1945 – 18,778 at its peak in 1943. This is perhaps more easily accountable, that with the upheaval of evacuation and the bombing of schools.

In the area of indictable offences, there was generally a marked increase. Violence against the person increased from 1,538 in 1938 to 2,459 in 1945, up 59.8%. Sexual offences increased from 2,045 in 1938 to 2,400 in 1945. Bigamy (not a sexual offence) also increased, up three times in men, 195 to 595 between 1938 and 1945, a rise of 205%. Women bigamists actually leapt from 81 in 1938 to 233 in 1945, a 187% increase. I suspect that many hours could be wasted interpreting this figure alone.

The number of people found guilty of receiving stolen goods, fraud and false pretences went up by went from between 1938 and 1945 from 5,333 to 9,364, a 75% increase, while breaking and entering rose from 10,018 to 21,260, up a phenomenal 112%, for the same period. Larceny, crime by theft, rose from 56,092 in 1938 to 75,975, up 35%, in 1945.

Overall, the numbers of men found guilty of indictable offences rose from 68,679 in 1938 to 99,305 in 1945, a rise of 44.5%. Crimes among females went up by 73%, 9,784 in 1938 to 16,956 in 1945[137].

Why was there such an upsurge in serious crime? There were probably myriad reasons, but opportunities arose because of

---

[137] *Criminal statistics of England and Wales 1939-1945* – HMSO 1947

the blackouts, because of the bombings, because of shortages, because of poverty and because of wealth, because of the hyperbole of war, when everything seemed out of proportion and extreme situations demanded extreme responses.

There is one area that we haven't yet touched on, and that is murder. Actually, murder figures didn't really change too much. That's not to say that people didn't try to present new ways to commit murder. Husbands clubbed wives to death and then threw their bodies into the wreckage of bombed out buildings in the hope that the Nazis would be blamed for his crime.

Then there is a grey area, an interesting grey, but perhaps in only forty-nine shades – those crimes that the police knew that people had committed but were unable, for whatever reason, to pin on anyone.

> The number of crimes known to the police exceed the number of persons found guilty (a) because many crimes are committed of which the perpetrators remain undiscovered or, though discovered or strongly suspected, cannot for some reason be prosecuted, and (b) because a person convicted of one or two offences frequently admits numerous other offences and asks that they may be taken into account when the court passes sentence : in such a case, though there is only one person convicted the conviction covers many crimes. As has been pointed out in previous volumes, many occurrences come to the knowledge of the police which may or may not be crimes and the figures of crimes known to the police are liable to be affected by changes in the methods of recording suspected crimes and in the degree of emphasis which is laid on the inclusion or exclusion of doubtful cases[138].

The number of crimes known to the police

---

[138] As above

(excluding offences against defence regulations) is as follows:

	Violence Against the Person	Sexual Offences	Receiving Frauds and False Pretences	Breaking and Entering	Larceny	Other Crimes	Total
1939	2,899	5,015	17,561	52,295	219,478	6,523	303,771
1940	2,424	4,626	16,998	49,340	225,671	6,055	305,114
1941	2,727	5,608	21,392	52,876	268,738	7,314	358,655
1942	3,050	6,766	21,079	56,166	267,789	10,039	364,889
1943	30,430	7,784	20,964	58,543	272,186	9,851	372,760
1944	4,162	8,079	21,922	73,890	297,930	9,027	415,010
1945	4,743	8,546	23,254	108,266	323,310	10,275	478,394

If you look at sexual offences, in 1945 the number of offences known to have taken place was 8,546. Convictions were 2,400. That's 28% solved or, if you flip the coin, 72% unsolved. Breaking and entering convictions were at 21,260 in 1945, whereas, according to the table above, the police knew of 108,266. That's quite a disturbing difference, but it is indicative of the difficulties facing the police in such circumstances and for the reasons stated in the quotation above. That there was an increase in unsolved B&E from 52,295 in 1939 to 108,266 in 1945 – 81% unsolved - suggests that criminals took the opportunity offered by the blackout and the blitz, when homes were emptied as people went to the shelters, to pilfer. The total number of these indictable crimes rose, according to these figures, from 303,771 in 1939 to 478,394, a rise of 57%. That's pretty appalling whichever way you look at it and it must have been difficult to remain honest in a climate of acceptable dishonesty.

Lord Woolton, the man of the pie and the great architect of food rationing, claimed in 1941 that there had been 22,356 convictions[139] for rationing and price-control offences since the war had begun but at almost the same time denied the existence of a black-market in Britain. Yet there were 114,000 prosecutions during the war for black-market crimes. The Board of Trade, who employed people to check up on shops and shopkeepers,

---

[139] *Life of a Teenager in Wartime London* – Duncan Leatherdale.

calculated that millions of pounds worth of goods had come onto the black market. It was estimated that 700,000 ration books had been lost or stolen. It was known that some coupons were sold for cash and then sold on at a profit, so there was an unproven suspicion that the losses were quite often not losses at all. The black-market value for a book of coupons was £5 or 2 shillings per coupon[140]. When you are hard up, that's quite a temptation.

Some hard-hearted criminals 'dressed up as ARP wardens and stole items from the homes of those that they were supposed to be rescuing or took valuables from the dead or dying'.

Everybody was affected by war crime; even Ivor Novello, the songwriter, was sentenced to eight weeks' imprisonment - later reduced to four - for using extra petrol coupons given to him by a female fan.

Did the war, particularly rationing, give British organised crime a chance to flourish? Yes, it probably did; at the very least, it gave it a set of starting blocks from which to start itself.

One example is the story of Billy Hill, released from prison early, as were many others, because of the war. His story is told by Duncan Campbell in the *Guardian* in August 2010:

> Billy Hill, the dapper gangster from Seven Dials central London...would emerge from the war as the leading figure in the capital's underworld. He immediately appreciated what a fabulous opportunity the war presented. "I don't pretend to be a King and country man, but I must say I did put my name down to serve and until they came to get me I was making the most out of a situation," said Hill..."So that big, wide, handsome and, oh, so profitable black market walked into our ever open arms...It was the most fantastic side of civilian life in wartime. Make no mistake. It cost Britain millions of pounds. I didn't merely make use of the

---

[140] *The People's War – Britain 1939-1945* – Angus Calder

black market. I fed it." Hill also realised that the departure of so many young men to war would soon lead to a weakened police force...Early in the war his gang staged a series of jewellery robberies in the West End, including one in which they smashed their way with a car-jack into Carringtons in Regent Street and made off with £6,000 worth of goods. Within weeks of wartime rationing being introduced, Hill was selling everything from whisky to sausage skins at £500 a barrel. Despite spells back inside, he emerged from the war a wealthy man.

So, have the past few pages been a condemnation of Britain in wartime? A hearty cough of disapproval at the antics of those who thought that they were above the law and those who needed to circumvent the law, just to stay on an even keel? Far from it. I was not there and cannot possibly know what it must have like to have been there, no matter how much I read. I know that I would have been devastated to find my house turned to rubble after a night underground. I know that I would probably have taken anything from under the counter if it meant that my children could eat better than other people's children. Had I been rich, would I have abused my wealth and bought my wartime comforts? I would like to think not, but once again I have the benefit of distance.

I cannot agree with those who were willing to profit from the misery of others; I can understand it, the temptations must have been enormous, but to have run the risk of subtracting from the chance of victory, of depriving those who fought abroad for us at home, would probably have weighed too heavy upon me. But this is the great thing about the rear-view mirror – we don't all see the same thing, and that is what makes history interesting, because it constantly asks questions of us.

Above all, it is always wise to remember that events make headlines because they are different, not necessarily because they are the norm. The vast majority of the population were law-abiding, good people who sacrificed much with little grumbling to ensure a victory today for a safer world tomorrow.

In *The Phony War*, the dryly funny and superbly researched 1961 book by ES Turner, the author painted a dark and ironic picture of the effects of the laws passed during the period of the phoney war:

> One day sufficed to turn Britain into a totalitarian state. The necessary authority was contained in the Emergency Powers (Defence) Bill...under which the government was free to make regulations by means of Orders in Council. Five days later, the first hundred-odd regulations were published, and more followed almost every day...*Habeas Corpus*[141] (was) tossed into the nearest Whitehall *oubliette*.

Over several fairly restrained chapters (the reader can sense Turner biting his tongue) he relates how travel abroad was limited, which is understandable, and how photographers were now under all sorts of restrictions where it was made an offence to take pictures of anything that was vaguely military or photograph 'an assembly of persons for transport or evacuation,' 'any injured persons or person,' and any 'riotous or disorderly assembly or premises or other objects damaged in the course of such an assembly' (there was no mention of sticking a lens through a film star's bathroom window, so the majority of the paparazzi were still fine). Neither could they photograph three soldiers of the same regiment together, but you could take a shot of those soldiers if they were each from a different regiment. They weren't allowed to snap three soldiers approaching a vehicle either because, apparently, that constituted an assembly.

Free speech too came under attack. Regulation 39b made

---

[141] *Habeas Corpus* was the provision in law which protected the individual from detention without cause. No one could be kept in prison until their case had been heard in law and the law itself said that they may be detained.

it an offence 'orally or otherwise, to influence public opinion in a manner likely to be prejudicial to the defence of the realm or the efficient prosecution of the war.' This was probably aimed at stopping the newspapers leaking bits of juicy gossip about the failures of Whitehall and the inhabitants thereof. Just to add to the feeling of oppression, 'all letters overseas were subject to censorship. Envelopes had to bear the name and address of the sender and an indication of the language in which the contents were written'.

Today's papers really wouldn't have to worry about any paper rationing; their penchant for scandal and gossip would be gone in a sentence and we would be left with an unbiased account of Barnsley FC's rare away win, and nobody would believe that anyway.

Petrol rationing has already been mentioned, but the poor motorist was made to suffer in many other ways although, clearly, some people, songwriters included, were unaware that petrol coupons were neither 'to be sold nor given away'. Petrol could not be stored without a licence. If you were caught, the fine was £20 a day, £786.93 in at 2017 values[142], and even then, the petrol was confiscated.

It was now illegal to leave a car unattended without immobilising it. This wasn't another piece of modern-day insurance scamming, but a way to stop any passing German spy from using your vehicle as a means of escape. The law also applied to 'rowing boats, canoes, yachts and motor-boats'. Let's not forget that to immobilise a car in the 1940s did not simply involve removal of the ignition key, after which a series of magical episodes happened inside some wires which prevented theft, as happens today. Immobilisation, according to ES Turner,

> included removing part of the engine mechanism, and applying an adequate and substantial locking device to the steering wheels or road wheels. The usual part of the engine to be removed was the

---

[142] www.nationalarchives.gov.uk/currency-converter.

rotor arm of the distributor, and soon all drivers, whether their cars were open or closed, were carrying out this drill. Many women motorists, and not a few men, had first to be shown where the rotor arm was, and how to extract it.

Along with the Big Daddy pindown of Habeas Corpus came the Administration of Justice (Emergency Provisions) Act, which stated that 'a jury need no longer number twelve good men and true; it was permissible to reduce the number to seven'. This was apparently intended to reduce the number of people taken away from war-work or prevent people from joining the services. Somewhere out there is a mathematician who can work out your reduced probability of freedom when faced with a smaller jury who would make it clear, though pursed lips and narrowed eyes that, frankly, they would rather be outside on a day like this and want to get it over as quickly as possible.

Parliament even banned kites and church bells, icing on cakes and 'peeping over the edge of the prom'.

Along with food rationing came stern laws against food wastage. There were enormous fines too; three months in prison or a £100 fine - £3,934.64 by 2017 values - on summary conviction[143] (I'm assuming that this was not in any way related to summary execution) or two years in prison and a £500 fine - £19,673.20 by 2017 values[144]. It seemed to be unclear as to where the line was to be drawn. Was little Johnny likely to be fined if he pushed his greens to one side of the plate? Suppose he didn't want to finish that potato because he was full? Or was it aimed at restaurants and other large institutions who were more inclined to throw away large amounts at the end of the day, when that waste

---

[143] The conviction of a person, (usually for a minor misdemeanour,) as the result of his trial before a magistrate or court, without the intervention of a jury.

[144] In 1940, this was the equivalent to 352 days wages for a skilled tradesman. It could also have bought you a cow, should you have been so inclined, or 112 stones of wool.

could have been used for animal feed?

You would think that it was aimed at the latter, but it was also an offence to 'give excess meat to a dog' or 'to take steps to prevent it going bad' (the meat, not the dog) so, to this writer at least, there remains doubt as to where the line was drawn.

The final word on the subject shall stay with Mr Turner who, as ever, managed to find a lighter side to the burden of wartime crime.

> In July the Government decreed that henceforth no kites or balloons were to be flown, except by servants of His Majesty; this was a precaution against illicit signalling. The wise parent who at once put his children's kites out of reach in the attic had to take them down again less than three weeks later, when an order was made that all attics, unless reached by a fixed staircase, were to be emptied of movable, combustible material.

Turner was right; we did move into the realms of totalitarianism, the very thing against which we were fighting, but the government probably had little choice. This was the second war to end all wars of the 20th century and, to win it, the measures taken needed to be extreme.

The Blitz

Before Hitler threw his tantrum later in the month, in August 1940 he had sent out a directive making it very clear that he intended to bomb the United Kingdom and to intensify the air war. The bold is mine.

Directive No. 17
For the conduct of air and sea warfare against England

THE FÜHRER AND SUPREME COMMANDER OF THE ARMED FORCES.

FUHRER HEADQUARTERS.
1 AUGUST 1940.

10 COPIES.

In order to establish the necessary conditions for the final conquest of England I intend to intensify air and sea warfare against the English homeland. I therefore order as follows;

1. **The German Air Force is to overpower the English Air Force with all the forces at its command in the shortest possible time.** The attacks are to be directed primarily against flying units, their ground installations, and their supply organisations, but also against the aircraft industry, including that manufacturing anti-aircraft equipment.

2. After achieving temporary or local air superiority **the air war is to be continued against ports,** in particular against **stores of food**, and also against **stores of provisions in the interior of the country**.

Attacks on south coast ports will be made on the smallest possible scale, in view of our own forthcoming operations.

3. On the other hand, air attacks on enemy warships and merchant ships may be reduced except where some particularly favourable target happens to present itself, where such attacks would lend additional effectiveness to those mentioned in paragraph 2, or where such attacks are necessary for the training of aircrews for further operations.

4. The intensified air warfare will be carried out in such a way that the Air Force can at any time be called upon to give adequate support to naval operations against suitable targets. It must also be ready to take part in full force in 'Undertaking Sea Lion'.

5. I reserve to myself the right to decide on terror attacks as measures of reprisal.

6. The intensification of the air war may begin on or after 5 August. The exact time is to be decided by the Air Force after the completion of preparations and in the light of the weather.

The Navy is authorised to begin the proposed intensified naval war at the same time.

Signed: ADOLF HITLER

Hitler's Wartime Orders: The Complete Führer Directives 1939-1945 - Bob Carruthers

Now, it might seem cynical to suggest this, but just how sad was Hitler *really* when one of his bombers 'accidentally' dropped a bomb on London and the British retaliated by bombing Berlin? Was it perhaps the excuse he had been looking for to increase the bombings against the British? The Battle of Britain continued and would do so until October, but it hadn't been the smash and grab that he had expected. His omnipotent *Luftwaffe* had come up against a determined, skilful and now well-equipped RAF. Was he impatient for more? To get it over and done with? It is speculation, of course, but he wanted Operation Sealion, the invasion of England, to be carried out and in as much of a *blitzkrieg* fashion as had been done with the rest of Europe and supremacy in the air was an essential part of this. As victory in the Battle of Britain slowly slipped from his grasp, so did the potential for invasion.

On the night of the 24/25 August 1940, nine people were killed and fifty-eight hospitalised when those bombs were dropped on London, accidentally or otherwise, and this was really the beginning of the blitz. It's open to debate as to whether such bombings would have eventually taken place, but the chain of events was started and from that point there was no going back. The Blitz as a whole would not officially end until May 1941.

It is generally seen as broken down into three parts:

i. September 1940[145] to May 1941
  ii. A 'baby Blitz' between January and April 1944
  iii. The attacks by the V-1s and V-2s between June 1944 and March 1945.

What was possibly the most notorious and well-documented attack on London, when many people see the 'Blitz proper' as starting, was between 5pm and 6 pm on Saturday 7 September 1940, when over 300 bombers and 600 fighters blackened the skies over London and attacked in two waves. Such was the volume, there was little to be done to stop the bombing, despite the anti-aircraft guns and the fighters sent up to intercept the bombers. The attacks continued until about 4.30 am.

430 were killed and 1,600 injured. Over 1,000 fires were started, including the docks, the fires of which were a guiding light for a further 250 bombers to drop their load. 13,000 incendiary bombs, designed to start fires and cause maximum disruption and destruction, fell, along with 625 tons of high explosive bombs. Three train stations were destroyed. The Germans lost forty aircraft, while the RAF lost twenty-eight. After this night, there were 57[146] more consecutive nights of bombing in London.

On 10-11 May 1941, the biggest and most damaging attack on the capital was carried out. This from *The Blitz - The Hardest Night 10/11 May 1941, 11:02pm - 05:57am* at www.rafmuseum.org.uk:

> • The moon was full and the Thames had a very low ebb tide. These two combined

---

[145] Opinions differ; some say this is from June 1940.
[146] Various sources report anything from 56 to 76 consecutive nights/days of bombing. *The Luftwaffe: A History* by John Killen reports '59 endless nights', The Guardian of 7 Sep 2015 gives the number as 57 days, *Life as a Teenager in Wartime London* by Duncan Leatherdale reports 76 days. 'From 7 September to 2 November - 57 consecutive nights - London was bombed without respite' says www.westendatwar.org.uk

- with a maximum effort by the Germans...to produce one of the most devastating raids on the capital.
- 571 sorties flown by German bombers - some crews flying two and even three missions. Burning buildings in Queen Victoria Street, EC4, after the last and heaviest major raid mounted on the night of 10-11 May 1941.
- 711 tons of high explosive bombs (167 were recorded as unexploded the next day) and 86,173 incendiaries dropped.
- London Fire Brigade recorded at least 2136 fires, 9 of 'conflagration' level, 8 'major' outbreaks (rating over 30 pumps), 43 serious (up to 30 pumps), 280 medium (up to 10 pumps) and at least 1796 small.
- Approx 1436 people killed and 1800 seriously injured.
- The fires resulted in 700 acres of destruction - about double that of the Great Fire of London.
- Final costs of damage in 1941 values - £20,000,000[147] - about double that of Great Fire.
- Anti-aircraft guns expended 4510 rounds - 2 bombers claimed destroyed.
- Fighter Command in total dispatched 325 aircraft...One Hurricane was destroyed and another Hurricane and a Beaufighter were badly damaged...*Luftwaffe* actually lost twelve aircraft that night

All told, the *Luftwaffe* dropped 24,000 tons of high explosive on London in 85 major raids resulting in approximately

---

[147] £786,928,000 at 2017 values

20,000 deaths, almost half the blitz total of 43,000.

But it wasn't just London that took the hits. It took the most without doubt, but Hitler saw this as terror; not the ubiquitous word that gets used at the drop of a hat nowadays and is an addendum to news headlines, used much like cinema tag lines to draw in the viewers, but this was terror as a policy. He had said in Directive Number 17, 'I reserve to myself the right to decide on terror attacks as measures of reprisal' and was now putting that into effect.

The bombings were intended to kill and maim, to destroy and to disrupt, to work their way into the psyche of the nation, where sleep would be disrupted, morale weakened and people reminded of the effect of Hitler upon their lives by the broken

City	Tonnage of high explosives dropped.	Number of major air raids.
London	18,291	71
Liverpool/Merseyside	1,957	8
Birmingham	1,852	8
Glasgow/Clydeside	1,329	5
Plymouth	1,228	8
Bristol	919	6
Coventry	818	2
Portsmouth	687	3
Southampton	647	4
Hull	593	3
Manchester	578	3
Belfast	440	2
Sheffield	355	2
Newcastle	155	1
Nottingham	137	1
Cardiff	115	1

Major raids upon cities and the tonnage of explosives used[148]

---

[148] From *The Night Blitz* by John Ray, which shows the number of major raids upon cities and the tonnage of explosives used. A major raid is defined as one in which over 100 tons of bombs are dropped. Smaller raids are not included in the tonnage.

streets through which they walked, the lost industry and produce, the smoke and the fires and the deaths. He would, by attrition, gradually wear down the capital's and then the nation's will. Once London fell, the rest of the country would follow. Once the people broke, they would turn upon the government and the rot would set from within.

The most notorious bombing was probably that of Coventry, on 14/15 November 1940.

Coventry was bombed because it was an important engineering and armaments producer. The Germans dropped 30,000 incendiaries, 503 tons of bombs, among which were 50 parachute mines, which drifted down to ground level by and detonated either by contact or by a clockwork mechanism. The idea was that, because they exploded above roofs and there was no cushion-effect from the buildings around them, the damage would be greater.

568 people were killed and 1256 injured. 2,306 houses were destroyed and 624 or 35% of its shops. 61%, 111 out of 180, of its factories were damaged; 41%, 75, were destroyed[149]. The medieval cathedral was destroyed.

The Germans came up with a new word for the flattening of a city - Koventrieren or to 'Coventrate'.

Other cities too took their share of the terror. Birmingham was Britain's third most-bombed city. In total, 1,852 tons of bombs were dropped on the city, composed of 5,129 high explosive bombs and 48 parachute mines. 2,241 people were killed and over 6,000 injured. 12,391 houses were destroyed along with 302[150] factories and many other buildings. Bristol lost almost 1,300 people to the bombings. At the other end of the country, Sheffield, a steel centre of Britain, suffered 16 air raids between August 1940 and July 1942 in which 631 people died and 1,817

---

[149] This according to *Coventry's Blitz* - www.historiccoventry.co.uk. According to *The bombing of Coventry in 1940* at www.historylearningsite.co.uk, 33% of factories were destroyed and 50% 0f homes.

[150] Justine Halifax - www.birminghammail.co.uk. 2015.

were injured. Liverpool and the rest of Merseyside, as one of the famously targeted ports, had to live through eighty air raids. About 4,000 were killed in total. Manchester, Cardiff, Portsmouth and Plymouth, along with Glasgow, Hull and Belfast, were all put through the wringer.

The total deaths in the Blitz amounted to over 43,000. Total deaths from the different forms of air attack 1940-1945 were around 61,000. Of these approximately 8,800 were the result of attacks by V-Weapons[151]. Contrary to what most people think, over half the dead were men.

So, how did people get through every terrifying night and every exhausting day? We are drip-fed the horrors from Aleppo on an almost daily basis nowadays, but it is an echo of the devastation wrought upon many British and German cities during the Second World War.

Psychologically, the country was torn between determination and terror.

> In April 1941 Tom Harrisson, one of the founders of Mass-Observation, (suggested) to the BMJ...that doctors had missed an epidemic of hidden illness caused by the psychological effects of air raids. Traumatised civilians, he argued, simply went to bed and stayed there as stigma deterred them from going to see their family doctor... evidence suggested a significant increase in psychosomatic disorders. Felix Brown, a psychiatric registrar...observed an increase in cases characterised by medically unexplained symptoms in patients with no history of mental illness...In August 1940, after a series of raids on Bristol...a panel doctor...reported an increased incidence of indigestion cases, and estimated at least 15 per cent absenteeism from work after severe

---

[151] *Bombing, States and Peoples in Western Europe 1940-1945: The Bombing of Britain 1940 – 1945* – University of Exeter

> bombing...Edward Glover, a London psychoanalyst, argued that civilians suffering from the trauma of air raids tended to express their distress as bodily sensations and were either treated as cases of apparent organic illness or suffered without referral.
>
> *Air Raids and the Crowd - Citizens at War -* thepsychologist.bps.org.uk

There was no doubt a unity of fear that came with the Blitz. It was a comfort to be in the same position as others, to know that you were not the only one hiding, that there was temporary relief to be found in the company of others trapped in the same way - it all helped the people to endure, but there were also long-tern psychological effects that extended to long after the war was over; the psychosomatic illnesses as discussed in the paragraph above which were a presentation of psychological illness, the sudden awakening to mortality, a process akin to the grieving process, where people had to come to terms with their mortality, with what they had lost, what had been taken away and their powerlessness to control that. The loss of a home, off any or all possessions, was still a loss and a psychological process had to be seen through in the same way that the loss of a loved one had to be dealt with, just perhaps not to the same intensity; a country, a city or a town, is though made up of individuals and everybody reacts differently to every situation. Stress is unique to the individual.

There was an increase in peptic ulcers and other stomach disorders and in 'effort syndrome', something close to today's panic attacks, and PTSD, unrecognised then except in the extreme example of shell-shock, took its toll.

> The first large study of the long-lasting consequences of the conflict has found that living in a war-torn country increased the likelihood of physical and mental problems later in life. Food

shortages, displacement from homes and the loss of relatives all created a toxic legacy that was still being felt for decades after...1945. People who experienced the war were 3 per cent more likely to have diabetes as adults and nearly six per cent more likely to have depression...people exposed to the war had lower education levels as adults, took more years to acquire that education, were less likely to marry, and were less satisfied with their lives as older adults. Iris Kesternich of Munich University said: "War...takes a toll on the health and well-being of survivors over the course of their lives." Researchers...found that living in a war-torn country was consistently associated with having poorer health later in life. People who experienced heavy fighting also showed adverse long-term effects...poor mental and physical health later in life appears to be linked to lower education, changing gender ratios caused by high rates of deaths among men, wartime hunger and long-term stress leading to adult depression and lower marriage rates. The one notable exception is depression, which is significantly higher for those...who lived in regions with heavy combat action.

World War 2 Left Toxic Legacy of Ill Health and Depression - Sarah Knapton. Daily Telegraph - 2014.

Retrospectively, there has also been a re-examination of the 'myth of the blitz'. Heavy government propaganda pushed the idea that, as per the slogan 'we can take it', people were happy together in their shelters, that if they followed the air raid instructions they would be safe, that they shrugged off the rubble of their lives and simply carried on.

The truth was very different, with opportunistic thieves and looters thriving, the risk of disease from large numbers of people living in shelters for long periods of time, food shortages, lack of gas and water, no shops, no homes. The rich were able to flee to their country seats, while the ordinary and the poor were left to cower beneath a corrugated tin shed. It has been described as a time of class war. Churchill and the royal family were all booed.

In *Fighting Fit*, Laura Davies reinforces the fact that people were in fact unable to 'take it'. Social pressure and the need to just survive were motivating factors. In the devastation of either their properties or their personal lives (or both), people slipped into automatic and did what they had to do to get over the initial hump. A Mental Health Emergency Committee was set up in 1938 to look at the impact of the war upon the individual. There was a fear that the country would collapse into a bucket of neuroses. The effect was far more insidious. In 1938, people could cope. In 1939 and early 1940, during the Phoney war, people could cope. But when the tide started to turn, at Dunkirk, with the onset of the Battle of Britain and the cataclysmic onset of the Blitz, the patina of calm acceptance began to wear thin and the cracks started to show.

> The committee saw the truly tragic side of the war. The forty- seven-year-old East End fireman who had seen such horrors that he was unable to venture out from 'the deepest Tube station he could find'. Or the dog kennel owner who had been bombed and all her dogs killed or so badly hurt they had to be put down, leaving her 'unable to face life at all'. Or the thirteen-year-old girl who had been holding her neighbours baby when a bomb hit their shelter. The explosion had blown off the baby's head. After that, each time the air raid sirens went off, the girl would scream - and not stop.

The committee found that people did hold up well initially after a trauma such as a night of bombing. In the way of the automaton, they did what they had to do to put things right, but then, after that was done, a delayed reaction set in.

> Nearly a third of the residents of the bombed streets told the committee's investigators they had anxiety symptoms, including heart flutters and stomach problems, depression and loss of appetite. Some even had classic hysterical or shell shock symptoms...Most people, however, hadn't drawn a connection between their symptoms and the bombing raid. Those who had were often ashamed to go to see their doctor: it was well known that 'Britain can take it' and they didn't want to admit they were not 'taking it'. Instead, they would 'send for a tonic from the chemist and stay at home for some weeks in an apathetic state'.

It is fashionable to denigrate our past selves by using today's standards, to apologise for past successes or for making the most of necessary evils. We do it with all sections of our history, but it is easy and even a little bit lazy to do so.

Yes, all the above is true. There were resentments and the people, those that had little money or nowhere to go and were forced to remain beneath the bomb-heavy skies, did feel a certain amount of class resentment, but the truth is also that, as a nation, when forced, Britain did get on with it. People did help each other, people did get together and encourage a chin-up attitude and, because they were forced to, they did 'keep calm and carry on' (a slogan, incidentally, that was mooted but never used, despite recent popularity).

The horrendous, intense bombing of Germany, as a retaliatory process, as a psychological weapon and as a way to defeat the war-machine, was supported vociferously by the people when it started, but as time went on, it fell out of favour as people began to grasp the horror of what was being inflicted upon their innocent nemeses across the channel, along with the suggestion that, perhaps more importantly, it quite simply wasn't having the desired impact. The arguments over the rights and wrongs of the bombing of Germany, particularly in the light of the dreadful slaughter in Dresden in 1945, still go on and there are even calls for Bomber Harris's policies to be considered as war crimes.

However, what for some is a crime is for others a necessary evil. The Hiroshima and Nagasaki bombs undoubtedly saved the lives of thousands of allied servicemen and shortened the Second World War by some considerable time, but subjected Japan to devastation, horrendous injuries and years of bomb-related illnesses.

I still find it strange that war should have rules at all. The animal that hides in humanity will always out under extreme circumstances and to expect people to enter into such a state of opposition within a set of written rules borders on the absurd. War is there to be won, at any cost. That is its *raison d'être*. That anyone should be surprised when someone strays beyond the set boundaries is beyond me.

As a nation, though, what did we do to get through this inferno?

In a quite literal sense, we dug in.

The Anderson shelter was named after Sir John Anderson who was given the task in 1938 of preparing air raid precautions.

These shelters were 6 feet high by 4 feet wide, made of zinc-coated corrugated steel and buried 4 feet into the soil with at least 15 inches of dirt over the top - some even grew flowers on top of it.. In theory, it could hold up to six people, but with summer heat and the airlessness that comes with such cramped conditions, it must have felt awfully claustrophobic. Outwardly they appeared ramshackle and a little Heath-Robinson, but the corrugation and construction allowed for flexibility and was able to contain the concussive elements of nearby blasts.

> One month after war broke out, Anderson shelters went on sale. Any householder (with a garden) earning less than £250 a year (£9,836.60 at 2017 values) received theirs free, while those on higher incomes (more than £5 a week - £196.73 at 2017 values) could buy one for between £7 and £10 (£275.42 and £393.46 at 2017 values), depending

on the size. By the end of the war, there were 3.6 million Anderson shelters in Britain. But because they had to be partially submerged in the ground, they were susceptible to flooding and were usually damp, draughty, noisy and cramped.

The Home Front in World War Two - Susie Hodge

Neither would they survive a direct hit and the tense dread of remaining cowered in an airless shelter must have been close to torture for some.

The Anderson shelter was, from 1941, accompanied by the Morrison shelter, named after Herbert Morrison, the Minister for Home Security. This was an indoor shelter that could, when not required as a shelter, be used as a table. The shelter was 6½ feet by 4 feet, so it was just as cramped as the Anderson shelter, however, this was 6½ feet in *length* and 4 feet *high*. It was essentially a steel cage with wire on the sides and looked like something even the pet rabbit would decline. The cost was high, £7 12s 6d, which amounts to £300 today, but it was free to lower income families.

By the end of 1941 over half a million people were using Morrison shelters. In an examination of 44 bomb-damaged homes, three people had been killed and 13 seriously injured. This was out of total of 136 people using the shelters, which amounted to a fatality-rate of only 2.2% and a rate of 9.5% injured. That means that, in theory at least, you stood a 97.8% chance of survival and a 91.5% chance of remaining non-severely injured or uninjured. To be fair, the fatalities were in houses that suffered direct hits. It's not something that I would fancy putting to the test.

In *Air Raid Shelters of the Second World War* by Stephen Wade, one Londoner put his feelings about shelters quite succinctly, and I find his lack of faith rather understandable.

> Proper death traps they are in my opinion. A pal of mine over in Islington way has turned his upside down and used it as a duck pond – and that's about

> the best thing you can do with them – wouldn't get me in one of those things.

Despite Doubting Thomas, a further 100,000 of the Morrison shelters were added in 1943 to prepare for the V1s and V2s.

The government could not win no matter what it tried. No one from of shelter could survive a direct impact and the nature of the beast meant that someone had to take the blame. Many people simply decided to stay at home and risk it or to hide in the cupboard under the stairs. Many lived with the attitude that 'if your time's up, your time's up'.

Some local authorities built communal shelters that could hold up to 50 people, but they were not a success. Other alternatives were used such as the man-made tunnels covering some 22 miles in Chislehurst in south east London which had been mined over the centuries in a search for flint and chalk. Others chose to hide under railway arches, caves or large underground basements.

The Underground stations had never been intended for use as bomb shelters by the government. In fact, the use of the Underground as a shelter was positively discouraged by the government because of the lack of hygiene and the risk to health, the risk of people falling onto the lines and the worry that people just would not leave once the raid was over; quite whether they feared a new breed of subterranean dwellers is unclear. The idea of staying in the regurgitated, stale air of the Underground with only buckets to pee in cannot have been so appealing.

However, despite the government's objections, people flooded into the tube stations and the government was forced to relent and they fitted out

> ...79 stations with bunks for 22,000 people, first aid facilities and chemical toilets. Within a short time, 124 canteens had opened in various parts of the Underground system...Salvation Army officers, who helped with emergency services during the

war, also often handed out sweets to children sheltering in the Underground with their families...Air raid wardens were also appointed in the Underground stations, to supervise, to administer first aid and assist in the event of flooding.

The Home Front in World War Two - Susie Hodge

Stephen Wade's book goes on to conclude that, in the end, 'it was clear that there were four main categories of shelter...the Anderson...the Morrison...the communal one, including the tube and other subterranean ones'.

In 1940, the Ministry of Home Security published the comprehensive *Air Raids: What You Must Do, What You Must Know*. It's difficult to know whether the government was being brutally honest or trying to scare the bejesus out of people into following advice; it would have been a harsh and frightening read but, ultimately, with the shelters and the advice given, people were responsible for their own safety. All the government could do was inform and advise. The book had information on everything from Anderson shelters to haemorrhages, fractures and the use of respirators.

In the section on haemorrhages, it pulled no punches:

Treatment of External Hemorrhage (sic)
Blood escapes with less force if the patient is sitting and still less if he is lying...Except in the case of a fractured limb, the bleeding part should, where possible, be raised, to lessen the flow of blood to it...In the case of a severely lacerated limb, bleeding should be dealt with by bandaging over a splint even though no fracture has been definitely recognised.
Wounds in the Abdomen.
...If any organs protrude, no attempt should be

made to replace them, but they should be covered with lint, a soft towel, cotton wool, clean soft flannel, or similar material for protection, and the covering secured firmly, but not too tightly, with a broad bandage. It is desirable for the material used in contact with the wound to be wrung out of warm water to which, if it is readily available, table salt may be added in the proportion of one teaspoonful of table salt to a pint of clean hot water. On no account should a patient with an abdominal wound be given anything to drink.

Above ground too, the population was prepared to fight the consequences of the bombings.

There was a network of workers and volunteers such as the ARP wardens and firefighters who, while others were under shelter, ran towards the flames instead of away from them in an effort to save homes, businesses and lives. 23,000 auxiliary firemen joined the 2,700 regular members of the London Fire Brigade. In England and Wales, 700 firemen and 20 firewomen were killed in action and 6,000 seriously injured. During the war almost 7,000 Civil Defence workers (the name for ARPs after 1941) were killed.

The blitz was seen as a very Londoncentric event, but the figures say otherwise. The fact was that London was the seat of government, was an icon of the empire, was the epicentre of the pre-war British world and a magnet for the enemy. Saint Paul's cathedral was the towering emblem of Blitz survival. There are famous images of it emerging from the smoke unscathed, a beacon of hope, reinforcing the belief that God was on our side.

The Blitz remains a constantly revisited and controversial period in British history. Was it really due to the errant ways of a careless *Luftwaffe* pilot or part of a cynical long-term plan by Hitler? Would the war have been a year or two longer if it had not happened? Would we have ended up with the entrenched warfare of the Great War had there not been the Battle of Britain and the subsequent aerial apocalypse? It is, of course, impossible to say, but there is no doubt that the bombings changed forever lives in both Germany and England.

Evacuation

> If heavy bombing of the cities had begun in the first week of war, evacuation would have been hailed as a far-sighted triumph of planning...Because there was no bombing, human nature reacted in its familiar fashion. Grievances and inequalities received undue stress. Wives were reluctant to be parted from husbands who, at best, might be lonely and who, at worst, might be taking steps to relieve their loneliness. Husbands, left with the dirty dishes, found what it was that their wives used to do all day. They wondered whether it really was a good thing for wives to be thrust away in a distant community where the lanes were full of licentious soldiery; they hated to think of their children's personalities being remoulded by others, however well-intentioned.
>
> *The Phony War* - ES Turner

In 1937, the Committee of Imperial Defence assumed that the initial air attack on London would last sixty days and that 600,000 people, 10,000 a day, would be killed. And London wasn't alone; it was expected that every major city would suffer the same fate.

To keep the fallout to a minimum, the evacuation of the cities was planned by a committee over three months in 1938, in conjunction with railway officials, teachers and the police.

In ES Turner's caustic words: 'It therefore seemed both reasonable and humane to disperse a few million women and children, for an indefinite period, into the spare rooms of a few million strangers'.

His cynicism might well have been justified for, however well-intentioned the government's plans via Operation Pied Piper, as the evacuation was known, it led to both unpleasant surprise and chaos and not a few lives changed for ever.

The evacuation started before the war, if only by two days, on 1 September 1939. Within three days, one and a half million people left their homes to begin new, safer, albeit temporary lives, outside the cities.

Businesses too moved and about twenty-five thousand civil servants were moved to seaside towns or spa towns where the large hotels, whether they liked it or not, provided accommodation, so that the business of local and central government could continue with only a small pause.

Hospital beds were emptied in anticipation of the predicted casualties while over 3,500 prisoners and 'borstal boys' were released back into the community.

Altogether over three million women and children were expected to evacuate but only about 1.5 million did and 735,000 of those were children travelling alone[152]. After the first year, by March 1940, about 1.2 million had returned home, either homesick or confident now that the expected terror was never going to occur.

Then the bombing started in June 1940 and a second round of evacuations started. This time, 620,000 children left home. In 1944, due to the V1s and V2s, a third wave of evacuation took place, but this was aimed mainly at the south and south-east.

Each child was expected to take with them a gas mask in its case, two sets of underwear, spare shoes and socks or stockings and warm coat, a sweater and nightwear, along with soap, a towel, a toothbrush, toothpaste, hairbrush and comb. Each child had a label attached to them for the journey with their name on it.

Upon reaching their destination, there was the humiliation of the line-up at the marshalling centres, where they were either chosen or rejected by potential foster parents, who in best Crufts-style just them on cleanliness and looks, on speech and behaviour.

---

[152] *At Home in World War Two: Evacuation* – Stewart Ross

When children arrived in their reception areas, the solution to locating a billet for each child was to invite the potential foster carers to a communal selection viewing. This enabled fosterers to scrutinise, hand-pick and take home a child of their particular choice. It was certainly a critical moment...and everything depended on that first impression...An alternative method was this door-to-door approach where children, some of whom had been travelling all day, were taken around the village or town, knocking on doors in search of people who would take them in.

Children in the Second World War - Amanda Herbert - Davies

They might be split from their brother or sister or rejected because of their gender or because of a disability or because of their clothing. The homes to which they had been assigned and to which they were taken might reject them on the doorstep, because they were the wrong gender or because they were the wrong age or simply didn't look right. There were class barriers that barred the threshold and if a child was described as 'lively', then they might be rejected for that too, because not everyone wanted to inherit a child that needed too much looking after.

Many of the city children had lice and fleas and skin diseases such as impetigo, a very contagious bacterial infection which presented yellowish crusts on the face, arms, or legs, so some evacuees were welcomed with a chemical bath and a head-shave[153].

Some parents failed to keep in touch with their evacuated children while others squabbled with the foster-parents about money and clothing.

For couples who had never really wanted children,

---

[153] *A Day in the Life of a... World War II Evacuee* - Alan Childs

> the opportunity to shuffle them off on others was irresistible; and the children sensed that they were being sent away less for their safety than their parents' convenience.

The Phony War - ES Turner

Once settled, the evacuees could be moved again at a whim as child-swops, boys for girls, noisy for quiet, fit for less fit, were made to suit the home-owner.

The long-term effects were evident. Many children began bed-wetting, nightmares and long-term psychological problems.

> Findings indicated that former evacuees were more likely to have insecure attachment styles and lower levels of present psychological well-being...findings offer an indication that the experience of evacuation is associated with long-term psychological vulnerability through its relationship with insecure attachment.

The Evacuation Of British Children During World War II: A Preliminary Investigation Into The Long-Term Psychological Effects - D. Foster, S. Davies & H. Steele

For the three-year-old Bobby Harper, who had travelled far from the comfort and personal safety of 13, Thorpedale Road, Islington, London, the journey north had come to a sticky end. There had been no access to toilets and the evacuee had 'evacuated' in the most extreme manner, as well as somehow managing to fall on his face and arrive at his destination with blood pouring from his nose.

He was taken in a private car to his new home at 75, Wilthorpe Avenue, Barnsley, where Mr Jackson, who had been expecting a girl and whose wife was not at home, took the boy in and, at a bit of a loss as to what the correct procedure should be, showed him his vegetable patch and chickens, presumably until his wife came home and the boy could be given into the charge of someone who knew what they were doing.

Bobby was very lucky. He entered a home with two 'sisters', Kathleen and Joan, and a 'brother', Harry, who was at the time serving with the RAF in West Africa and India, all much older than him, and two adults, Edward and Sarah Jackson.

To Bobby, it was an adventure and, although there was a South Yorkshire, no-nonsense toughness about his surrogate mother, he felt loved.

He never went back to Islington.

In a very touching couple of letters, Bobby's fate was decided for him. Neither letter was dated.

31 Coleman Mans(ions)
Crouch Hill N8

Dear Mrs Jackson,
I am sorry I haven't written before, but it has been a very bad year for us down here, nothing has gone right, and each week we have just managed to exist. To stop all the worry I have arranged with the health people to stop payment to us on Bobby on the 15th October. I have had to put it forward like that because of the new book which start (sic) then. From that date Mr Jackson can claim allowance on Bobby on income tax. We have signed a statement here, that we have been sending what we can afford, but that you have asked us to stop sending anything as you wish to adopt Bobby, we think that taking all things to account, it would be best, if you still wish to, to adopt Bobby.
I am ashamed that we have not been able to send any money to you, and I hope that you won't think horribly of us on that account. If you wish to legally adopt Bobby, we shall sign any statements to that affect (sic), that you send down to us. We haven't the slightest doubt that he will be well looked after and cherished, by you and Mr Jackson. Give our love to Bobby and our very best wishes go to you and Mr Jackson and all at Barnsley.

I remain
Yours Sincerely
F Harper

31 Coleman Mans
Crouch Hill N8

Dear Mrs Jackson
I am sorry you are still being pestered by those people, we are not drawing any money for Bobby now, or since I last wrote to you. I have filled in a similar form to your one stating we last paid on 14 Sept 1951 and have not paid since. I hope this will be the last time they trouble you. I have had the family allowance taken off from that date so I don't see why they had to send these forms at all. Well Mrs Jackson I suppose you are all preparing for Christmas. I bet you find plenty to do, although the children love the preparations.
I would like to send my best wishes to you and Mr Jackson and all at Barnsley and wish you all a merry Christmas. Give our love to Bobby. We shall be writing to him before Christmas. Well I think this is all for now. We are all quite well at present.
I remain
Yours Sincerely
F Harper

That's all that exists of the correspondence between the adults involved in Bobby Harper's life. I'm sure there was more.

It's evident that his biological parents were strapped for cash and that they believed that Bobby had found somewhere safe to be. It's impossible to say whether the decision was made with cold common-sense or with the knowledge that some money could be saved if Bobby was not back at home or if it was the heart-breaking wrench that most of us would feel. Whatever the reason, Bobby stayed in Barnsley.

Bobby by was finally adopted and became Robert John Jackson on 25 November, 1952, over eight years after his journey began in that sunlit London station.

He turned out well and made friends for life; one in particular, Roger Fieldhouse, has been his friend for over sixty years. They still go out for a pint together each Tuesday night and with their wives as a group each Thursday night. Every Saturday they play snooker for a small cup. They frequently swear at each other by text. He is about as Yorkshire as Yorkshire can be.

Bob married Norma Valentine (guess when her birthday is) Holdsworth on 21 August 1965 and had one daughter, Sally, who married me, a southerner. They have three grandchildren, Georgina, Eleanor and Francesca.

Without Adolf...? Who knows?

Bobby Harper

In Search of the Phoenix

This was of course a *world* war. Japan was our enemy and, for some time, so was Italy. It could be said that Japan's vicious incursion into China in 1931 and Italy's barbarous takeover of Abyssinia (Ethiopia) in 1936 contributed to the evolution of the war. The League of Nations did nothing to stop either intervention other than whimper disapproval and, in the eyes of those countries' leaders, it was almost a permission slip to wander where they wanted. Neither did the League of Nations do anything to stop Germany's involvement in Spain, where it tried out its troops and its hardware. The Russians were in the mix too and no one said a thing. The League of Nations was proven time and again to be a toothless tiger.

The rise of fascism in Italy under the bullying Mussolini presented a template for the rise of fascism in Europe and in particular Franco in Spain and Hitler in Germany. Neither was England free of fascism, from Oswald Mosely to Edward, Duke of Windsor and Wallis Simpson. There was indeed little royal shyness about Nazism in the thirties. Edward VIII was known to have some Nazi sympathies and even met the dictator in October 1937.

For the wealthy, who were starting to feel vulnerable with the slow carpet of red spreading from the east, it was easier to turn towards the antithesis of communism and adopt a right-wing stance. There was also a certain confidence given by the fake stability of Germany (and Italy) at the beginning of Hitler's reign. It wasn't long ago that one national newspaper showed pictures of Princess Elizabeth in the garden with her mother and siblings giving the Nazi salute and having a good laugh about it. Had they known that Dachau had been in full swing since 1933, they might well have behaved a little differently.

So, even though this book focuses strongly upon the wartime relationship between Germany and Britain, it is clear that it was a *world* war, not an isolated spat between two major European powers.

For the purposes of this book though, I wanted to show the more immediate effect of the war upon the individual in Britain, up to just after the Battle of Britain, something that has been in my mind ever since I first heard my father-in-law's story.

History in some way affects every single one of us, but the Second World War, particularly that part of it between the Germans and the British, infected every aspect of our daily lives like a cancer. It nearly did for us and the cure, as is so often the case, was often worse than the illness, and the side-effects devastating. I often wonder how we would deal with it nowadays.

So, who was the phoenix that emerged from the smoke and ashes of World War Two? Was it Germany? Once out of the embers of the Great War, Germany foolishly threw itself back onto the fire, but it became a powerful driving force behind the European economy and contributed greatly to the tenuous post-war peace which we hang on to today.

What about Europe itself? Well, it too was dragged back into the conflagration by Germany but has sought to work as one since the end of the Second World War. Now, with Brexit (what an awful word), the rise of the far right and the shouts of the far left, it appears to be dismantling again.

And what about Britain, divided by Scottish and Welsh devolution, wracked for so long by the troubles in Northern Ireland and now with barely an industry to its name. Yet we are still regarded as the flag-bearers of Europe, the place that people want to come, a Titan of democracy in an ever-changing, security-driven world, a safe-haven for the war-torn and homeless and a society where free speech and elections are guaranteed.

For me though, there is only one phoenix and that is little Bobby Harper. He emerged from the smoke of his London life to become Robert Jackson, Barnsley man - a good, honest, kind-hearted, hard-working man; a husband, a father, a grandfather, a father-in-law and a friend.

Bob and Norma Jackson 2017

Sources

Books

1918: The Last Act – Barrie Pitt
Adolf Hitler: A Biography - Ileen Bear
Adolf Hitler's Family Tree – The Untold Story of the Hitler Family – Alfred Konder
Air Raid Shelters of the Second World War - Stephen Wade
At Home – Bill Bryson
At Home in World War Two: Rationing – Stewart Ross
At Home in World War Two: Rationing – Stewart Ross
Fighting Fit - Laura Davies
Hitler: 1889-1933 - Donna Faulkner
Hitler's Nibelungen - Anna Rosmus
Hitler's Wartime Orders: The Complete Führer Directives 1939-1945 - Bob Carruthers
Life of a Teenager in Wartime London – Duncan Leatherdale
Mein Kampf – Adolf Hitler
Mud, Blood and Poppycock – Gordon Corrigan
Outbreak: 1939: The World Goes to War - Terry Charman
Private Hitler's War - Bob Carruthers
Queen of Spies: Daphne Park, Britain's Cold War Spy Master - Paddy Hayes
SOE's Mastermind: The Authorised Biography of Major General Sir Colin Gubbins KCMG, DSO - Brian Lett
The British Army Handbook 1939-1945 - George Forty
The British Home Front 1939–45 - Martin Brayley
The Economics of the War with Nazi Germany - Adam Tooze and James R. Martin
The FANY in Peace and War - Hugh Popham
The First World War 1914-1918 - G. Hardach
The First World War: A Very Short Introduction – Michael Howard
The Gathering Storm – Geirr H Haarr
The Home Front in World War Two - Susie Hodge

The Luftwaffe: A History – John Killen
The Making of the British Army – Alan Mallinson
The Narrow Margin - Derek Dempster and Derek Wood
The Origins of The Second World War - A.J.P. Taylor
The People's War: Britain 1939-1945 – Angus Calder
The Phoney War on the Home Front – ES Turner
The RAF Handbook 1939-1945 - David Wragg
The Second World War Through A Soldiers' Eyes: British Army Life 1939-1945 - James Goulty
The Spitfire – Bob Carruthers
Why the Germans Lose at War: The Myth of German Military Superiority – Kenneth Macksey
Women in the Second World War by Colette Drifte

Index

Anderson, shelter, 284
Appeasement, 107, 108, 109, 111
Army, 120
Article 48, 83, 85, 87
Ashley-Smith, Grace, 192, 193, 194, 195
ATA, Air Transport Auxiliary, 204
ATS, Auxiliary Territorial Service, 171, 172, 173, 174, 175, 176, 177, 197, 199, 201, 202, 210, 213
Autarky, 100, 101, 102
Baker, Edward, 181, 190, 191, 193, 194
Battle of Britain, 124, 145, 146, 155, 158, 159, 160, 163, 164, 165, 167, 274, 282, 288, 297
Beer Hall Putsch, 74, 89
BEF, 128, 130
Bf 109, 156, 157, 162, 163
Bingham, Phyllis, 198, 199
Blackout, 257
Blitz, 272
Blitzkrieg, 128, 156, 164
Brest-Litovsk, 32
Bruening, Heinrich, 85
Chamberlain, Neville, 13, 107, 108, 109, 110, 111, 118, 227, 231, 239
Chapman, Eddie, 185
Churchill, Winston, 21, 129, 130, 132, 137, 138, 142, 144, 155, 167, 173, 178, 180, 187, 188, 206, 239, 282
Clemenceau, Georges, 34, 35
Clothes, rationing, 247
Communism, 30, 32, 65, 79
Conscientious Objectors, 225

Conscription, 106, 221
Coolidge, Calvin, 55
Corps of Royal engineers, 124
Crime, 262
Dachau, 89, 90, 91, 209
Dalton, Hugh, 180
Dawes Plan, 54, 55, 58, 59, 78
Dig for Victory, 243
Dowding, Sir Hugh, 146, 153, 160
Drexler, 66
Dunkirk, 120, 121, 127, 129, 130, 131, 134, 144, 147, 156, 157, 161, 165, 176, 282
Dyle Plan, 128
Ebert, Friedrich, 51
Enabling Act, 85, 87
Evacuation, 289
FANY, First Aid Nursing Yeomanry, 188, 189, 190, 191, 192, 193, 195, 196, 197, 198, 199, 200, 206, 299
fascism, 120, 256, 296
Fascism, 30, 65
Fleet Air Arm, 147
Fordney - McCumber Tariff, 60
Four Year Plan, 102
Frythe, 186
Führer, 67, 74, 98, 163, 258, 274, 299
German Workers' Party, 65, 67
Germany, 27, 31, 33, 34, 35, 37, 38, 40, 41, 42, 43, 44, 45, 46, 47, 48, 50, 52, 53, 54, 55, 56, 57, 58, 64, 66, 67, 68, 70, 72, 74, 77, 78, 79, 81, 85, 86, 88, 89, 90, 91, 92, 97, 98, 99, 100, 101, 102, 103, 105, 106, 107, 109, 110, 111, 112, 119, 128, 136, 139, 147, 151, 154, 156, 165, 229, 258, 283, 289, 296, 297
Gestapo, 89, 182, 208, 209
Glasl-Hörer, Anna, 16, 17

Goebbels, Joseph, 79, 80, 81, 89, 233
Groener, William, 85
Gubbins, Colin, 180, 181, 184, 198, 200, 299
Guilt Clause, 37
Gwynne-Vaughan, Helen, 201, 202
Hambro, Charles, 180, 181
Harper, Bobby, 3, 9, 10, 20, 91, 292, 294, 297
Harris, Air Chief Marshall Sir Arthur, 107, 111, 154, 170, 176, 284
Heidler, Johan Georg, 14, 17
Heidler, Johann Nepomuk, 14
Hess, Rudolf, 91
Hitler, Adolf, 16, 17, 18, 19, 20, 31, 43, 51, 63, 65, 66, 67, 73, 74, 75, 76, 78, 79, 80, 81, 82, 83, 85, 86, 87, 88, 89, 90, 91, 92, 93, 94, 99, 100, 101, 104, 105, 106, 112, 122, 156, 163, 164, 166, 167, 187, 272, 274, 277, 288, 296, 299
Holocaust, 92, 94, 99
Household Cavalry, 122
Hurricane, 157
Infantry Regiments, 125
inflation, 47, 53, 103
Inskip, 147
Italy, 24, 29, 35, 38, 42, 43, 49, 55, 149, 200, 296
Jackson, Robert John, 294
Jews, 64, 65, 72, 73, 74, 76, 79, 92, 93, 94, 95, 96, 97, 98, 99, 101
Kellogg-Briand Pact, 42
Khan, Noor Inayat, 205, 206, 207, 208, 209
Kristallnacht, 92, 98, 99
Labour Service Act, 101
Laughton Mathews, Vera, 211, 212, 213, 214, 215
Lausanne Conference, 58
Le Paradis, Massacre of, 130

League of Nations, 21, 34, 37, 39, 40, 41, 42, 49, 52, 89, 90, 105, 107, 296
Lebensraum, 31, 65, 72, 73, 81, 99, 100, 103, 107
Liebknecht, Karl, 50, 51, 52
Lloyd George, David, 35, 37
Ludendorff, Erich, 74, 75, 76
Luftwaffe, 119, 154, 156, 157, 159, 160, 161, 162, 163, 164, 165, 166, 167, 257, 261, 274, 275, 276, 288, 300
Luxemburg, Rosa, 50, 51, 52
Matzelsberger, Franziska Fanni, 16
Morrison, shelter, 285
Munich Conference, 107
Nazi, 65, 72, 74, 75, 76, 78, 79, 80, 81, 83, 85, 86, 89, 90, 92, 93, 94, 95, 98, 100, 101, 102, 103, 104, 105, 110, 111, 186
Nelson, Sir Frank, 117, 140, 180, 181
Newitt, Dr Dudley Maurice, 186
Night of the Long Knives, 89, 90, 92
NSDAP, 67, 100
Operation Dynamo, 130
Operation Sealion, 145, 155, 164, 274
Patten, Marguerite, 240
Penz, Thekla, 15
Petrol, rationing, 245
Phoney War, 117, 118, 119, 131, 229, 300
Poland, 21, 38, 42, 48, 106, 107, 110, 111, 112, 156
Polzl, Klara, 17, 18
putsch, beer hall, 78
radar, 160, 163, 165, 167, 173, 201, 210, 242
RAF, 144, 145, 147, 150, 151, 154, 155, 156, 157, 159, 160, 161, 164, 165, 166, 167, 183, 184, 201, 202, 203, 204, 221, 274, 275, 293, 300
Rationing, 231
Rearmament, 100, 104, 105
Reichstag, 84, 87

Reparations, 39, 46, 47, 48, 49, 55, 74
Ricardo, Colonel Francis Cecil, 192, 193, 194
Röhm, Ernst, 83, 89, 90, 91
Royal Air Force, 148
Royal Armoured Corps, 122
Royal Corps of Signals, 125
Royal Flying Corps, 147, 148
Royal Naval Air Service, 147, 149
Royal Navy, 123, 135, 137, 138, 142, 144, 145, 147, 221
Royal Regiment of Artillery, 123
Ruhr, 41, 52, 56, 74
Russia, 21, 23, 31, 33, 35, 110
Schicklgruber, Alois, 13, 14, 15, 16, 17, 18, 19, 20
Schicklgruber, Maria, 13, 14, 18
Smuts, Jan Christian, 150
Social Democratic Party, 50
SOE, Special Operations Executive, 171, 178, 179, 180, 181, 182, 183, 184, 185, 186, 187, 188, 189, 190, 197, 198, 199, 200, 201, 205, 206, 207, 208, 209, 216, 299
Spartacists, 50
Special Operations Executive, see SOE
Spitfire, 157
stock market, 58
Stormtroopers, 76, 83
Sturmabteilung, 75, 83
Szabó, Violette, 199
Treaty of Neuilly, 49
Treaty of Sèvres, 49
Treaty of Trianon, 48
Treaty of Versailles, 21, 32, 34, 35, 39, 42, 43, 46, 50, 54, 58, 63, 64, 104, 105, 106, 107, 109
Trefusis-Forbes, Katherine, 201, 202
von Papen, Franz, 85, 86
von Schleicher, Kurt, 85, 89, 90, 91

WAAF, Women's Auxiliary Air Force, 167, 172, 200, 201, 202, 203, 204, 205, 206, 209, 210
Weimar Republic, 50, 74, 75, 85, 89
Wilson, Woodrow, 21, 22, 26, 27, 28, 29, 31, 32, 33, 34, 239
Woolton, Frederick Marquis, 1st Earl of, 231, 235, 237, 239, 240, 266
WRNS, Women's Royal Naval Service, 172, 196, 210, 211, 212, 213, 214, 215
Young Plan, 58

ABOUT THE AUTHOR

Chris Bradbury was born in 1962. He attended schools in Bracknell, Windsor, Mauritius and Bloxham and, despite all these, failed to learn a thing. He spent his formative years in a cocoon and failed to see the time go by. When he woke up, he realised that it was too late.

He has been a shop worker, a hospital porter, worked in medical records, in the CSSD department of a hospital, as an estate agent, as a nurse, as a delivery driver, a bus driver and as a teaching assistant. At the moment he works in a warehouse.

He lives in Yorkshire.

He is married to a lady and has some lady children.

He loves them.

He has always wanted to write or act or do something that brings him praise and attention.

He is also the author of:

The High Commissioner's Wife
The Devil Inside
Catfish
Eidolon
The Stilling of the Heart
Shorts – A collection of novellas
Condition of Life - The Poetic Confessions of a Grumpy Old Man
The Ghost of Dormy Place and Other Tales
The Ashes of an Oak
A Kind and Gentle Man
Praxis (Sci-Fi Fantasy - with Ian Makinson)
Praxis – Part Two: Regeneration Paradox (Sci-Fi Fantasy - with Ian Makinson)
Praxis - Part 3 The Liar's truth - (Sci-Fi Fantasy - with Ian Makinson)
Earthbound
Earthbound Part Two - Hellbound

Chine (Horror)
Uncomfortably Numb (Play)
The Scarlet Darter (fiction for children)
Unton's Teeth and Other Tales of Wordful Mystification (poems for children)
A Beginner's Guide to the Wars of the Roses
A Beginner's Guide to Creative Writing
A Beginner's Guide to Death

Made in the USA
Columbia, SC
21 June 2018